PRAISE FOR BRODEUR:
BEYOND THE CREASE

"...an entertaining and insightful read from a certifiable hockey achiever."

Stephen Smith, *The Globe and Mail*

"What sets this book apart from the typically dull athlete's biography is Brodeur's honest, blunt and ever-forthcoming manner.... Brodeur teams up with an experienced hockey writer and author in Cox to produce a fine read."

Wayne Scanlan, *The Ottawa Citizen*

"Refreshingly, Brodeur shares many opinions that are not those of the majority, come hell or high slapshot."

Dave Stubbs, *The Montreal Gazette*

"A refreshing, candid look at [Brodeur's] career and hockey in general.... With veteran *Toronto Star* columnist Damien Cox, [Brodeur] brings the reader into his world both on and off the ice and doesn't avoid tough subjects."

Canadian Press

"A candid look at the life and career of one of the greatest goalies to ever slide between the pipes."

Daryl Slade, *The Calgary Herald*

BRODEUR
Beyond the Crease

Martin Brodeur   Damien Cox

WILEY

John Wiley & Sons Canada, Ltd.

National Library of Canada Cataloguing in Publication Data

Brodeur, Martin 1972-
    Brodeur : beyond the crease / Martin Brodeur, Damien Cox ; with photographs by Denis Brodeur.

Publ. for the Canadian market.
Includes index.
ISBN 978-0-470-15377-2

    1. Brodeur, Martin, 1972-. 2. Hockey goalkeepers—Canada—Biography.
I. Cox, Damien, 1961- II. Title.

GV848.5.B76C69 2007   796.962092   C2007-904025-X

Production Credits
Cover design: Ian Koo
Interior text design: Natalia Burobina
Project conceived by: Brad Robins, Intellectual Capital Inc.
Printer: Friesens
Cover printed by: Phoenix Color

John Wiley & Sons Canada, Ltd.
6045 Freemont Blvd.
Mississauga, Ontario
L5R 4J3

Printed in Canada
1 2 3 4 5 FP 11 10 09 08 07

Two lucky dads dedicate this book
to their beloved children

To
Anthony, William, Jeremy and Anabelle Brodeur

and
Meghann, Delaney, Dawson and Leagh Cox

Contents

Preface

THIS PREFACE IS BEING WRITTEN en route to London for my yearly pilgrimage to the All England Lawn Tennis and Croquet Club for The Championships, otherwise known as Wimbledon. This trip has become an annual opportunity to reflect upon the latest season of hockey, the sport that usually commands the bulk of my professional attention, and to get a different perspective on sport in general.

The 2005–06 NHL season was unusual in a number of respects, not the least of which was a return to a style of hockey—a style with less hooking and interference and more scoring and creativity—that I believe will improve the game's growth potential after years of sluggish growth, or even decline.

It was also unusual in that a collaboration with Martin Brodeur—a player who will surely be an automatic Hall of Fame selection in a decade or so—provided me with a priceless insider's viewpoint of the changing NHL. Having covered the league for the *Toronto Star* as a beat writer and columnist since 1989, I have watched with increasing distress as high, impenetrable walls have been erected between the media and the many terrific, personable athletes who play in the league. Partly it has been the result of the growing wealth in the game, and partly the product of the shortsighted tendency of many NHL clubs to shield their players from the demands of media. Too often, in recent years, my exposure to hockey players has been as part of a crowd of writers, TV cameras and microphones, with some team official yelling "Last question!" after three minutes.

The overall damaging effect, in my mind, has been the increasing tendency—out of necessity—for the media to portray the players in a one-dimensional manner, as sportsmen only, without the more personal touches that make them appealing to fans of the sport.

I had met Marty several times over the years, either in a post-game interview setting or a scrum with other reporters—which is to say I hadn't really met him at all. Then, in April 2005, a mutual friend, Brad Robins, brought us together for a dinner at Shakespeare's steak house in Hamilton, Ontario. Marty was in town to play in an outdoor game at Ivor Wynne Stadium during the NHL lockout, and the dinner was simply Brad's idea to bring together two people with whom he enjoyed spending time.

Over the succeeding months, with Brad's encouragement, I developed the concept of a book that would highlight not only Marty's obvious excellence as an NHL goaltender with the New Jersey Devils but also his rather underexposed presence as one of the more interesting hockey players in the world. I believed that lack of exposure was odd, particularly since he had always been one of the most accessible, open and articulate players in the sport. I have always laughed to hear about goaltenders who "don't talk on game days," a growing breed. Marty has never been that way, and even before I got to know him well, I had often felt that if I'd knocked on the Devils' dressing room door between the third period and overtime of an important playoff game, he'd have been more than willing to do a quick interview.

We met again the following autumn, this time at a Japanese steak house across the road from the Devils' practice facility. It became clear at that time the most difficult hurdle to cross was my inability to accept Marty's affirmative answers. I would ask him if he was prepared to do such-and-such to make the book special, and he would answer curtly, "Yes," or "Sure." Gradually, I learned that one of his most unique characteristics as an athlete was that when he said "Yes," he meant it, and would follow through. From a sportswriter's point of view, that is an endearing quality.

The result is a book that provides unique insight into the NHL and the sport of hockey through the eyes of a player in the absolute prime of his career and at the top of his game. The tendency is usually for elite athletes to wait until they are at or near retirement to use a book or some other vehicle to look back over their careers. The special value of this effort is that Marty chose to participate in this project during a season in which he played goal in the 2006 Winter Olympics, led his team to an NHL record 11 straight victories to close out the campaign, set an individual record for the most consecutive playoff starts by an NHL goalie and finished second in voting for the Vezina Trophy after winning it in the previous two years.

If the final effort seems incomplete in any way or falls short of expectations, the fault is mine. Not once over the months of discussions and interviews that took place in Austria, Italy, Canada and the United States did Marty ever decline to talk about a topic or refuse to say what he thought, and the result is a decidedly un-sanitized look at the game. Over the course of the succeeding pages, you will learn of his triumphs, defeats, hobbies, finances, relationships, personal philosophies and family, as well as his candid thoughts on the past and future of the game he loves. You will come to know an athlete who plays an incredibly difficult position with an extraordinary self-belief that I have seen in only one other athlete in my time covering sports, Swiss tennis star Roger Federer.

A number of people deserve thanks for helping to make this project happen, including Brad, who kept it on the rails over the months and constantly provided inspiration. Brad, Marty and I are all fathers—taken together, our children number 13—and maybe it was that bond of exhaustion that made it all work.

Graham Parley, the sports editor of *The Star* and the man with the messiest desk I've ever seen, never gave me a hard time when my mind wasn't totally focused on the paper. Karen Milner, my trusted editor at Wiley, nearly leapt out of her seat during a sushi lunch when I first mentioned the Brodeur book, and she knows that lattes and anything with blueberries soothe the irritable writer. Nicole Langlois, meanwhile, made the book better with her masterful editing eye.

I'd also like to thank the various members of the Brodeur clan, including Marty's wonderful parents, Denis and Mireille, for their warmth and hospitality. The apple surely does not fall far from the tree. Special thanks also go to Marty's partner, Geneviève, for opening up her home to me and never complaining—at least within earshot—that I was hanging around too much.

I'd also like to thank my wife, Vicki White, for letting me get away with being zoned out on those days when I needed to put fingers to keyboard. It is an enormous blessing to have a partner who believes in you so much. Her favorite line is to tell me, "Use your powers for good, not evil." I have tried.

This book is called *Brodeur: Beyond the Crease* because the idea was to give a new voice to a brilliant goaltender with insights and opinions to offer that extend beyond the happenings inside the blue paint.

I can only hope that has been the result.

Damien Cox
July 2006

chapter 1
A Company Man

PROFESSIONAL TEAM SPORTS, for better or worse, have come to be known for money disputes and constant player movement. The NHL, which has gone through turbulent change since the day I was drafted in 1990, has been no exception to this rule. But through good fortune or good planning, I've been able to avoid being part of that often messy game of musical chairs. I've been a goaltender since I was seven years old, a position that provides an athlete with the unique ability to be a crucial participant in the action and also stand back and observe the elements and moments that shape a game. Maybe, in a larger sense, that's how I've been able to look at the business of the sport and my place in it.

It was a surprise to many in the hockey world when, in January 2006, at the age of 33, I signed a new six-year, $31.2 million contract with the New Jersey Devils, the only pro team for which I had ever played. I wasn't looking to move, and I wasn't looking to be paid more than any other goaltender in the game. I had been part of the growth of the franchise, from one of the league's doormats to a three-time Stanley Cup champion, and I wanted to stay part of it. Just before I signed, a reporter asked how I had managed to handle the ups and downs of our team that season in such a relaxed, even way. I explained the importance of being a steadying influence on the team, of helping to solve problems when things went poorly instead of creating new ones. "I guess I'm a company man," I shrugged.

Some people, of course, particularly athletes and people involved in pro sports, would hate to be described as a company man. It almost goes against the grain of the modern athlete. It implies, or seems to imply, somebody unwilling to speak up and somebody easily controlled by his bosses. That's not me, and that's not how I would interpret that term. Ever since I turned pro my objective has been to work with the organization to achieve success for myself and the team. That approach has paid off. It's why I own three gorgeous rings, two of gold and one of platinum, one ring for each of the Stanley Cups the Devils won in 1995, 2000 and 2003. Only Scott Stevens, Ken Daneyko, Sergei Brylin, Scott Niedermayer and I were on all three of those teams. Each of us became Devils and stayed Devils in our own ways. My story is interwoven with theirs, and with that of the only general manager I have ever had in the NHL, Lou Lamoriello. We all came from different places and brought different talents to the table, but as a group we achieved more than any of us could have dreamed when we first began to play the game. That success also meant I was able to win the Vezina Trophy as the NHL's top goalie twice, and it positioned me to play at the highest international levels of the sport for my country, Canada. It may seem like a strange place to start telling the story of my life in the game, but from my point of view, being willing to work with the team when it came to signing contracts played a part in helping us win those three Cups and all the other success that came with them.

It was never, at least for me, just about trying to get more money than somebody else. My objective is to play for a team that wins, not a team that will pay more than any other club but then can't go out and get other good players because of one expensive contract. That approach became even more important after the lockout that wiped out the entire 2004–05 season. In the new economic era of the NHL that followed, each team had to live under a league-wide salary cap, which was $39 million for the 2005–06 season. After the 24 per cent, across-the-board salary rollback the NHL Players' Association agreed to as part of the collective bargaining agreement that ended the lockout, I made $5.237 million dollars in the final part of my existing contract. Under the terms of the new deal, no player could make more in a single season than 20 per cent of the overall cap figure of $39 million, or $7.8 million. If I had been making that amount, the difference of about $2.5 million would have made a significant impact on our team. In fact, it would have made it almost impossible for management to make the difficult choices and changes that were made in December and January that turned a losing season into a winning season. When I later agreed to a salary of $5.2 million per season through the 2011–12 season, it was with the cap and the future of the team in mind. Under the new CBA, players were entitled to receive 54 per cent of league revenues, and so it was clear that as revenues increased, the cap would go up. That meant the maximum any individual player could make would also go up. But my philosophy was to try to come up with a fair salary that would allow the team to stay strong and allow me to stay in New Jersey. My new contract eliminated the final year of the old deal, which meant the team had extra payroll room starting with the 2006–07 season, when I would have been earning $6 million but instead received $5.2 million. That salary difference gave the team flexibility, and the chance to add other players. But by the time I'm 38 or 39 I'll quite likely be making more than I'm worth. So that was the cost to the team, the trade-off the Devils had to make.

Many players don't think this way, or at least their agents don't. I don't have a problem with the way others think about their careers and the business, or if the players' association looks at it differently. But this is my view of playing hockey. I want to win, and to do that, I need all the help I can get.

I want to play for a good team, and the way in which I handle my contracts is part of achieving that goal. If that makes me a company man, I'm happy to be one. I'm fortunate in that I have been able to work for a company that embraced my talent and put me on a plateau that any athlete should want. The Devils have always backed me up on everything, personal and professional. Other than a three-week holdout in a brief salary dispute in 1995, all my relations with the Devils have been smooth, constructive and professional. Over the years I've been in New Jersey, there has been impressive stability. I've had the same GM, Lamoriello, my entire career, and the same goalie coach, Jacques Caron. In Stevens, Niedermayer and Daneyko—two guys who are going to the Hall of Fame and one who thinks he is (Can't wait until my buddy Daneyko reads that!)—I played behind the same three defensemen for a decade, something not many NHL goalies can say. When people think about the Red Wings, for years they thought of Steve Yzerman. When they think of Colorado, it's Joe Sakic. And when people talk about the Devils and the history of the team, they talk about Stevens. Or Daneyko. And me. That's special.

As it turned out, the winter of '06 turned out to be a time for goalies to sign rich new contracts. Marty Turco was the first to sign, agreeing to a four-year pact with Dallas worth $22.8 million, or an average of $5.7 million per season. Then came my six-year deal, followed by Evgeny Nabokov of the Sharks, who received an average of $5.375 per season on a four-year deal. Soon after, Washington signed its fine veteran netminder, Olaf Kolzig, to a contract extension worth $5.45 per season, although without the no-trade provision I received and valued so much. By the end of this financial flurry, the pay scale for NHL goalies was: Nikolai Khabibulin ($6.75 million), Turco ($5.7 million), Kolzig ($5.45 million), Nabokov ($5.375 million) and me, at $5.2 million per.

Other than me, Khabibulin was the only one of those goalies who had been on a Stanley Cup team, and Kolzig was the only member of that group other than me who had won a Vezina Trophy. So shouldn't I have been ticked off? Hadn't I accomplished more? Shouldn't I have demanded the Devils re-do my deal? Isn't this the way pro sports operates nowadays?

To put it simply, no. At least not for me. To me, those contracts involve those players, not me. If their club feels the need to pay them that salary, that's up to them. For me, it's what I'm comfortable with, and while I know the numbers and the salaries, I really don't compare myself to anybody. I've been the lowest-paid goalie in the league on a team that won the Stanley Cup (I initially made $81,200 for the 1994–95 season for playing 40 regular season games and 20 playoff contests), and I've been one of the highest-paid players in the game. If I start worrying about what others are making, then my priorities are out of whack. See, a salary doesn't necessarily equate with ability. Look at some of the better goalies around the league in the 2005–06 season and their contracts. Mikka Kiprusoff of the Calgary Flames was making $2.9 million, and he was as good as anybody. Ottawa's Dominik Hasek signed a bonus-laden deal going into the season that paid him a base salary of only $1.5 million. Martin Gerber, then a member of the Carolina Hurricanes, was a key reason why his team rode high in the Eastern Conference standings that season while he was earning the relatively moderate salary of $1.064 million per season. It might not have been a mind-blowing salary, but he looked like the most valuable goalie in the game in Turin at the '06 Olympics when he stopped 49 shots for Switzerland to beat Canada 2–0 in one of the biggest upsets in Olympic hockey history. The point is, a salary doesn't always reflect the quality or true value of a hockey player.

If certain goalies accomplish something important for their organization, and the organization wants to compensate them in a certain way, that's terrific. I feel I was rewarded to an enormous extent at a time when there was no limit on payrolls in the NHL. Now that there is a limit, a salary cap, there are valid reasons not to be greedy. To go somewhere else to get more money—not knowing the organization, the town or the people running the team—makes no sense to me. A quality goalie like Khabibulin did very well on a contract to leave Tampa Bay and go to Chicago, but he ended up leaving a Stanley Cup champion to join a non-playoff club. Nabokov signed his rich new deal, but by the end of the 2005–06 season and playoffs he had been replaced by Vesa Toskala as San Jose's No. 1 goalie. As far as NHL teams go, I've known just one thing, but that one thing I like.

Also, when I sign a contract, I don't have to pay $200,000 or more in fees to my agent. Why? Well, I haven't had one since 1998, an unusual situation for an NHL player. By the winter of 2006, I had negotiated three contracts on my own worth more than $87 million. The process of my financial education began back in 1990 when I signed my first pro contract with the Devils.

The 1990 NHL entry draft was held at GM Place in Vancouver, an exciting day for the existing 21 teams to plot their future. I was the 20th pick overall, taken by the Devils from the St. Hyacinthe Laser of the Quebec Major Junior Hockey League. It was an honor, looking back, to be part of one of the strongest drafts in NHL history that day. Fifteen of the 21 picks in the first round went on to meaningful NHL careers. Owen Nolan went first, followed by Petr Nedved, Keith Primeau, Mike Ricci and some guy named Jagr. If the teams could do that draft all over, Jaromir Jagr would undoubtedly be the first pick, and I'd like to think I would have gone a little higher. Trevor Kidd was the first goalie taken with the 11th selection, which actually was New Jersey's pick until a trade on the draft floor moved them all the way back to the 20th pick. After Keith Tkachuk was drafted at No. 19 by Winnipeg, I finally heard my name called by the Devils. Even beyond the first round, there were players who went on to strong NHL careers, like Doug Weight (34th), Sergei Zubov (85th) and Petr Bondra (156th). Felix Potvin, who I had known growing up in the east end of Montreal and who also had the same goalie instructor, Mario Baril, as I did as a teenager, was drafted 31st by the Toronto Maple Leafs.

At that time, Sean Burke was the No. 1 goalie with the Devils, although Chris Terreri was pushing him hard. Burke was making $180,000 per season but was looking for a new contract that would pay him almost double. Ed Belfour was starting as a rookie in goal for the Chicago Blackhawks and making about $120,000 a season. Edmonton had knocked off Boston for the Cup the previous season, Chris Chelios had been traded by Montreal to Chicago and the really big news of the off-season had seen Scott Stevens, my future teammate, rock the business foundations of the league by leaving Washington to sign a free agent deal with St. Louis for what was then considered the extraordinary sum of $5.145 million over four years. A year later, he found himself transferred to New Jersey as compensation for the Blues' signing of free agent winger Brendan Shanahan of the Devils, a transaction that would have a spectacular impact on the future of the Devils over the next decade.

Nolan signed a five-year contract right away, including a $250,000 signing bonus and $175,000 salary in the first year.

The other top picks—Ricci, Nedved and Jagr—also signed soon after being drafted, and for big dollars. It was the beginning of an enormous surge in player contracts, partially fueled by the increasing demand for players due to expansion. By the fall of 1990, 11 cities had put down $100,000 each just to be considered for NHL expansion, a process that eventually led to Ottawa and Tampa Bay being added to the league for the 1992–93 season. San Jose had been granted an expansion team the year before and both Florida and Anaheim joined a season after the Senators and Lightning. Along with the change in leadership of the NHL Players' Association from Alan Eagleson to Bob Goodenow, expansion would help fuel the wild salary inflation that occurred throughout the 1990s as the league gradually grew to 30 teams. In this environment of economic change, I had to find my place.

My first contract was signed three months after I returned to the Laser following my first NHL camp in September 1990. My bonus was $80,000, my minor-league salary was $35,000. I was scheduled to earn $125,000 for NHL work in the first two years, $140,000 in the third year and there was an option year tacked on, also for $140,000. Given what other goalies and other players were making, it seemed about right. My father, my brother Claude and I had interviewed a few agents, including Don Meehan, Jay Grossman and Gilles Lupien, and in the end we picked Lupien, a former NHL defenseman with the Montreal Canadiens who seemed like a nice guy and represented some players I knew, like Potvin and Martin Lapointe. Lupien negotiated my first contract, and it seemed to be a relationship that would last for years.

After a second training camp in 1991, one in which I once again didn't even get to play an NHL pre-season game, back to St. Hyacinthe I went to rejoin teammates like Patrick Poulin and Martin Gendron, players who would also eventually make it to the NHL. Our team was good, not great, and was in fourth place after 48 games. One day in late March, I was sitting in the stands after practice, playing cards with some teammates, when our general manager walked up and told me that I had been called up to the NHL. Just like that. No warning. Less than two years after being drafted, I was headed to the NHL.

The Devils, in those days, were a team struggling to develop into a consistent winner. The franchise had started in 1974 as the Kansas City Scouts, moved to Denver after just two seasons in Missouri to become the Colorado Rockies, and had moved east to New Jersey eight years before I was drafted. They finished second last their division their first year in the Garden State and missed the playoffs their first five seasons in the Meadowlands. In their second season in New Jersey, the Devils suffered an insult that stigmatized the club for years. Wayne Gretzky, after the Oilers beat the Devils 13–4 in Edmonton on November 19, 1983, blasted the Jersey squad as a "Mickey Mouse organization." It was one of the few truly controversial statements Gretzky ever uttered, and most believe it came of frustration at watching his good friend, Ron Low, suffer as he played the entire game in goal for the Devils that night.

In the spring of 1988, the Devils gained a measure of respectability by making a surprise run in the Stanley Cup playoffs in Lou Lamoriello's first year as general manager, a charge that was stopped by the Boston Bruins in the Eastern Conference final. It was a series made infamous by the Don Koharski "doughnut" controversy. After Game 3 of the series, Koharski, a referee, was confronted by Devils head coach Jim Schoenfeld in the hallway outside the dressing room. As the two men argued, Koharski slipped, and he believed he had been shoved by Schoenfeld. He angrily told the Jersey coach he would never coach in the league again, and Schoenfeld responded by calling the referee a "fat pig" who had lost his balance, and suggested Koharski "have another doughnut."

Schoenfeld was suspended for the next game, but the Devils fought the decision and got a restraining order that allowed him to continue coaching. When he appeared behind the New Jersey bench for Game 4, the officiating crew refused to work, and replacement officials wearing orange shirts were hurriedly brought in to call the game, a terrible embarrassment for the league and president John Ziegler. The issue was resolved when Schoenfeld, after coaching Game 4, was suspended for the next game. He was replaced for Game 5 by Lamoriello, who had coached for years at Providence University but had never been behind the bench for an NHL game. The Devils were thumped 7–1 that game at old Boston Garden, and in the end, the Bruins silenced the surprising New Jersey '88 post-season run in seven games. But after years of being a laughingstock, it was time to start taking New Jersey seriously.

The next season, the Devils missed the playoffs again. By the time I was called up for my first NHL game in March 1992, however, things were looking up. The team had made the playoffs two years in a row, and Lamoriello had drafted players like Scott Niedermayer, Brian Rolston, Bill Guerin and me, players who would help form the foundation of future championship teams. Partway through the 1991–92 season, both of the club's goalies, Craig Billington and Terreri, had been injured, and after minor-league callup Chad Erickson had played a couple of games, they decided to give me a chance, calling me up on an emergency basis without even having played an NHL exhibition game. I was a 19-year-old with only a decent grasp of English, heading to Newark airport for my first shot at the big time.

On March 26, 1992, I went to the morning skate after staying at the Turtle Brook Inn near the Devils' practice rink, and afterwards the head coach, a tough guy with a gravelly voice named Tom McVie, called me into his office. "Where were you last night?" he said with a stern look. "I tried to call you." I didn't know what to say. Then he started laughing, and said, "You're in tonight, okay?" Robbie Ftorek, who would later become head coach of the Devils, was also in the office, and he said, "Kid, it's a big day for you. Make sure you call your family. Try to get everybody in here because it's your first NHL game." As fast as I could, I called my dad, my girlfriend, my buddies, my brothers—and they all came, making the six-hour drive from Montreal. The game was at home against the Bruins. The Devils were still wearing their old green, red and white jerseys and No. 29 was hanging in my locker rather than the No. 30 jersey I would later come to wear. Kerry Fraser was the referee, Billington was my backup, and Andy Moog played goal for the Bruins. We won 4–2. Joe Juneau was the first NHLer to score on me, at 8:38 of the third period, Steve Leach beat me on the other goal and in all I made 24 saves for my first NHL victory. Back then, as a temporary NHLer, I was making $700 a day, a whole lot better than the $44 a week and $18 in gas money I was receiving from the Laser. I don't remember that much, but I do remember making a big save on Vladimir Ruzicka, who in the 2004 World Cup nearly coached the Czech Republic to a huge upset victory in the semifinals over Team Canada when I was out with a sprained wrist and Roberto Luongo had to step in to save the day.

Two nights after the Boston win, I played again at home and we beat the Québec Nordiques 5–2. One of the goalies I'd known well from the Montreal area as a teenager, Stéphane Fiset, was in goal for the Nordiques. The day after that I played part of a

5–4 loss to the Flyers in Philadelphia after Billington re-injured himself in the first period. The game was at the old Spectrum and I made my first big giveaway for a Flyer goal while trying to make a fancy play with the puck. I was starting to enjoy being an NHL player when—boom!—on April 1, by a vote of 560–4, the players' union called the first full-scale strike in NHL history. There was great fear the Stanley Cup playoffs would be canceled, but that disaster turned out to be still 13 years away. This strike lasted only 10 days before a new collective bargaining agreement was struck, but by the time it ended I was already back in junior. As soon as the strike was called, Lamoriello had put me on a private jet back to St. Hyacinthe for a playoff game that night against Collège Français de Verdon. I arrived with 10 minutes left in the warmup, and even my teammates didn't know I was coming until I walked in the dressing room. It was like a story out of a book. I jumped on the ice, the fans went wild and we won that game—but then lost the next two, and the series.

—⋙—

After the strike was over, I got called up again. I played in one more regular season game, facing nine shots after entering the game in relief in a 7–0 loss to the New York Islanders, went to the minors for one day and then backed up Terreri in the first round of the playoffs when we lost in seven games to the Rangers. In Game 5 of that series, we fell behind 4–0, with Mike Gartner of the Rangers scoring three times. After Doug Weight made it 5–0, Terreri was pulled and in I went for my first taste of NHL playoff action. Before I could get warm, Kevin Todd and Alexei Kasatonov scored for us, and we were creeping back into the game. By the four-minute mark of the third period, we had cut the lead to 5–4, and the kid from St. Hyacinthe was feeling pretty good, although with one eye on the bench, thinking McVie was going to put Terreri back in to try and win the game. Well, let's just say the Ranger offense got rolling again. First Kris King scored. Then Adam Graves. Then Graves again, the third goal I'd given up on 15 shots. Final score: 8–5 Rangers.

The next game, we beat the Rangers at home, with Terreri beating Mike Richter. John Vanbiesbrouck was the New York backup goalie, and right near the end of the game the Rangers decided they were going to jump Claude Lemieux, and both benches cleared. It was an old-style brawl. Richter was just annoyed with the game and went to the dressing room, leaving me, Vanbiesbrouck and Terreri out there on the ice. I was just listening, and those two guys weren't even talking about the brawl going on. They were talking about golf! They were big golfers and good friends. Nearby, Joey Kocur, a really tough player on the Rangers, had moved in to make it two-on-one against Lemieux, who's fighting for his life. So Terreri says, "Marty, you gotta get in there!" I dropped my gloves and skated over to grab Kocur, one of the most feared fighters in the league.

He turned around and said, quietly but firmly, "Let me go."

I just lifted my hands in the air and said, "There you go, buddy." I followed him around, but I sure wasn't touching him again. As the years passed, looking back at the situation, I realized I could have got killed because of Terreri. He loved to tell jokes about that night.

After those playoffs, I was really excited about training camp the next fall, figuring I had my foot in the door. I was cashing $6,000 checks, and I couldn't believe they were paying me that much money to play hockey, although I definitely wanted to keep it coming. If I thought I was in the NHL to stay, I got a rude awakening the following September when, without even playing an exhibition game, I was demoted to the farm club in Utica.

Right to the minors. Lamoriello had always maintained I was going to play a full season in the minors, and that wasn't going to change because of a little playoff experience. He had a plan for me.

By the fall of 1993, I was finally in the NHL for good, and by then, I wanted it more than ever. A year in Utica had probably been good for my development, but I really wanted the opportunity to prove I could play in the NHL. Jacques Lemaire was the new head coach, taking over from Herb Brooks, and that meant new opportunities for players. Lemaire had brought in Jacques Caron as a goaltending instructor, and he had seen me play the previous year in the minors and was familiar with my game. By January, Terreri and I were basically sharing the job and the Devils had allowed the fewest goals-against in the entire NHL. Peter Sidorkiewicz, who had shoulder problems, had become the No. 3 goalie. The Devils finished with 106 points, a team record, and then in the first round of the playoffs we got past Buffalo in seven games, including one game that went into a fourth overtime before Dave Hannan of the Sabres won it. The next round, with Terreri and me sharing the work, we knocked off Boston in six games, putting us into the Eastern Conference final against, of course, the Rangers. The Rangers won the series four games to three, but I played all seven games and all but a few minutes in the series. We lost in double overtime of Game 7 on Stéphane's wraparound goal, a crushing defeat but also an enormous achievement for our "Mickey Mouse" franchise. At 22, I had established myself as the Devils' No. 1 goalie and won the Calder Trophy as top rookie, beating out Jason Arnott of the Edmonton Oilers and Mikael Renberg of the Philadelphia Flyers. The awards evening in Toronto was spoiled a little, however, when Quatre Saisons TV in Montreal somehow gained access to the list of winners and broadcast them two nights before the actual ceremony.

Despite the Calder, I was the second-lowest-paid player in the league at $140,000 per season, although I did get a $50,000 bonus for winning rookie-of-the-year honors. There was still the option year of my contract left at $140,000, and Lupien, my agent, pushed hard for a new deal over the summer that would put me among the top 10 goalies in the league. He threatened a training camp walkout, but the Devils wouldn't budge. That summer, Stevens had signed a monster five-year, $17.1 million contract with the Devils, but I would have to wait. A lockout wiped out the first four months of the season and left the NHL with only a 48-game schedule. While earning a pro-rated $81,200, I played 40 regular season games, then all 20 playoff games, winning 16, as the Devils won the first Stanley Cup in franchise history. It was a thrilling achievement, particularly the four-game sweep of Detroit in the Cup final, and it touched off the first of what would be three Stanley Cup celebrations back at my family's home in St. Léonard, Québec.

But business was business. After the season, under the terms of the new collective bargaining agreement, I qualified for "retro-active arbitration" and eventually received back salary for the '94–95 season worth $850,000, a sizable raise. But I still had to work out a new deal with the Devils. After failing to come to terms on a new contract over the summer of 1995, I held out for the first three weeks of training camp. It was a very difficult thing to do when what I really wanted was to make sure I was out on the ice when our Stanley Cup banner was raised. Still, I held out because Lupien strongly believed I should get more money than the three-year, $3.6-million contract the Devils were offering. The offer gradually improved, however, and finally I decided I wanted to sign. Lupien was really disappointed, and refused to go with me to sign the contract, which was worth $5.3 million ($1.5 million, $1.8 million, $2 million) over three years. Lupien was unhappy with me because he felt I should get more, even if it meant forcing a trade to another team. But I wasn't mad at him. He believed what he believed, and it wasn't his fault I didn't want to follow him. To me, it was always about more than money. It was about being accepted in an organization, about being successful in an organization, about being comfortable in a city and being reasonably close to my family in Montreal. I had started to understand what I had, and I didn't want to mess it up.

The next contract negotiation started during the 1997–98 season. I was sitting in a bar with my goalie coach, Jacques Caron. He and I were close, and over the course of my career I often felt he was the person who could occasionally act as a go-between when there was a need for Lamoriello and me to communicate but the subject matter might be delicate or awkward. For example, just before the 2006 Winter Olympics, after Lamoriello had taken over as coach of the Devils following Larry Robinson's surprise resignation, it was Caron who came to me and wondered what I would think if Lamoriello continued as head coach. Maybe it was just too awkward a question for the GM to ask his goaltender. I gave Caron a favorable response—after all, we'd been winning after a terrible fall—and before I returned from Turin, Lamoriello had announced he would coach the team for the rest of the season. If Lamoriello wanted to know my opinion on something, it often seemed to me that he would use Caron to get my thoughts.

In the case of my contract talks in the middle of the 1997–98 season, I was in the final year of the deal I had agreed to after my brief holdout two years earlier. I told Caron during the course of our conversation that if I could get $16 million for four years, it would be a contract that would satisfy me. In my mind, not only would it put me in a certain level with other goalies, but it would set up my life. I would never have to work a day after this contract. Caron passed the information to Lamoriello, who then approached Lupien about trying to get a deal done on those basic terms. Lupien, however, believed I should get $5 million a season, and so they started fighting again over dollars. Finally, Lamoriello came to me and said simply, "I'm not going to deal with Lupien anymore. Do whatever you want." He was mad, and I wanted to get something done. I felt Lupien was being greedy, and so I decided to try to negotiate a deal myself. Lamoriello and I had lunch once, then we met in his office once. We worked on numbers and bonuses for winning awards. I had concerns about the deferred money he wanted me to accept, particularly the fact he didn't want to give me interest on the monies deferred. As a compromise, he gave me more on bonuses, and those monies were always added on as part of my salary if I cashed in. In the end, the contract ended up being worth more than the $16 million I originally wanted—about $17.1 million, in fact—and I had cut the deal myself.

Now I had to work out my differences with Lupien. He came down to New Jersey and we had lunch at a little Italian restaurant I liked in Secaucus. I told him I was going to sign this deal I had negotiated, and asked him, "How much should I pay you?" He pulled out a napkin and a pen, wrote a figure down and slid the napkin over to me. I looked, and saw that he had written a large zero. He was very angry, probably both that I had done a deal without him and because I had settled for less than he believed I was worth. I offered him $100,000 just to maintain our business relationship as agent and client, and said I hoped he would be able to negotiate my next contract. After all, he had been my agent since 1990, and I really didn't want to fire him. The honorable thing to do, it seemed to me, was to offer him what I had, but he didn't take it. I still owed him about $90,000 from our previous agreement, and I gave him a check for that amount soon afterwards, following a game in Montreal. For the next year and a half, we didn't talk. I no longer had an agent.

There was gossip within the players' association and among other agents that I had settled for too little, and in doing so had undermined the negotiating power of other goalies and other players. At that point, salary escalation was really getting revved up, and the players' association was working to push hard on every single contract negotiated. I heard the chatter, but nobody in the union ever said a word to me. Really, I couldn't have cared less. It was my business, and I believed building my relationship with the organization was more important than an extra $500,000, or whatever. At 26 years of age, I believed in what I was doing.

—⁓—

That contract took me through our second Stanley Cup victory in 2000 and a trip to the Cup final in 2001, where we lost to Colorado in seven games. The following season, just as had been the case in the final year of my previous contract, we started talking about a new one. The three contracts I negotiated—in 1998, 2001 and 2006—were all initiated during the early part of a season, which meant I was never under pressure, or up against a deadline, or in a situation where I needed to have a strong season to get the contract I wanted. They were always the product of a mutual negotiation and a mutual willingness to reach a new agreement. While I had my high school diploma, I hadn't attended university or taken any finance courses, but still I was never intimidated by the process of negotiating a contract for millions and millions of dollars. Why? Well, first of all, don't give the agents too much credit. It's not that hard. The numbers are there, you know what other players are making, and it's not all that complicated. Second, it's actually easier because I just have to look out for myself.

An agent, on the other hand, might have other players on the same team, or in the organization, or there might be players he would like to see drafted by that club. In that situation, a general manager might ask an agent to give him a break on one contract, and he might be able to help a player in the minors get a shot in the NHL, or get a one-way contract. Bad blood between a team and an agent could make contract negotiations very difficult. I don't think, for example, that New Jersey ever drafted a Lupien client out of junior after the trouble he and Lamoriello had.

—m—

For me, then, doing a contract was much simpler because I didn't have to worry about the impact of my deal on any other players. I was just doing my own thing.

My personal lawyer, Susan Ciallella, often helped me with issues related to the contracts, along with a variety of other issues involving my career. On the deal I negotiated in the fall of 2001, I was a year away from unrestricted free agency and there was also the possibility of arbitration the following summer. At one point, I shopped around a little for an agent, thinking I might need one if I ended up in arbitration, and I even talked to powerful agents like Don Meehan and Mike Barnett. Eventually, however, without an agent, I agreed on a deal with the team worth $40 million over five years. My not having an agent left the union unhappy. By having only union-certified agents represent players, the union could control the flow of information and influence certain deals. Union officials filed a grievance, arguing that Ciallella had actually negotiated the contract but wasn't a certified player agent. By the spring of 2006, the grievance was still pending, and it still seemed ridiculous to me. After all, these were the same people who had certified David Frost as an agent, the man who became notorious for his relationship with St. Louis Blues forward Mike Danton—briefly a teammate of mine with the Devils—after Danton hired a hit man to kill Frost and eventually went to jail for the offense. And they were grieving my use of my own lawyer? Are you kidding me? It really bothered me that the union never approached me about the issue, never confronted me with any questions, but then went and filed a grievance.

Starting with the contract I negotiated in 1998, I began deferring money. I had seen Bobby Carpenter do that, and while he was in New Jersey he was still getting paid from his contract in Washington. I don't need all the money now, and I have long felt that it gives you a buffer at the end of your career. It's not easy to go from making millions to zero, and deferring money to later years gives you an ease-in period. With the contract I signed in 2001, about 20 per cent each year was deferred except for the last year, when I was scheduled to receive a flat $8 million. Each year there were also "guaranteed bonuses," extra payments I would receive immediately if, for example, I won the Vezina. If I didn't win, the money would still be paid out, but several years later in a deferred payment.

More than with any of my contracts, I was thrilled with this one. Before, I was establishing myself and taking care of my family. This was something else, this was gravy, really big money. To celebrate, Susan and I went to Ken Daneyko's restaurant, Mezzanote, and had champagne. This was as big as it was going to get, and I could afford whatever I wanted. I chose to build my dream cottage in St. Adolphe d'Howard, just north of Montreal. I bought the land and had a main cottage and a guest cottage built, and my parents eventually sold their cottage and moved into that. There is a tennis court and a saltwater pool on four acres of land, and many of the ideas I took from a cottage that Carpenter had built in New Hampshire. Eventually, worried that somebody would buy the adjoining land and develop it, I bought another 440 acres, much of it mountain, which allowed me to make my dream cottage on Lac Ste. Marie very private. My children love it, it's where I retreat to in the summer and it was an expression of what I had achieved with this new contract.

Unfortunately, I didn't realize the entire value of the contract. The third year of the deal was wiped out by the 2004–05 lockout, which had the same effect on every NHL contract. And with the 24 per cent across-the-board salary rollback negotiated by the players' union as part of the settlement, I lost another $1.5 million or so on my 2005–06 salary. At the time, I was also in the middle of a divorce settlement from my wife, Mélanie, and there was a substantial cost incurred. Finally, I was due about $6 million in the final year of the contract, 2006–07, reduced from $8 million because of the 24 per cent rollback, and instead I chose to merge that into the new contract I signed in January 2006, which meant the salary was reduced again to $5.2 million in the first year of a six-year agreement. Some of these were choices I made, and some were made for me as a member of the players' union, but suffice to say the contract I negotiated in 2001 was not completely reflected in the paychecks I received over the next five years.

After the lockout, I was 33 years old and heading into the 2005 training camp with the Devils. Just prior to that, Lamoriello approached me, knowing there were still two years left on my existing deal, to ask me what I wanted for my future and whether I wanted to stay in New Jersey. He said he wanted me to be a big part of the team's leadership in the coming years, and after 15 years in the organization, three work stoppages and three Stanley Cups, I was certainly inclined to stay. The next thing I knew we were working on another contract. He asked how it would work with my personal life and finances, since he knew I was working on a divorce settlement. For him, it became pretty clear early in the season that the Devils had cap problems that had been made worse by the performance of Alexander Mogilny, Vladimir Malakhov and Dan McGillis, three expensive free agents signed the previous summer. It was easy to understand that the team was going to face trouble in the immediate future if it allocated too much money to one or two players, but at the same time the news trickled in that the cap would be rising for the next season from $39 million to $42 million, possibly more. Initially, I wanted a five-year deal, and he wanted six. I probably could have signed for two years at $7 million per, but I worried what that would do to the team and what would happen to my earning power after that contract expired.

The Devils eventually waived Mogilny and McGillis, sending them to the minors, and Malakhov retired, although news reports said he tried to change that decision afterwards and it became a contentious issue. The Devils had managed to get away with some pretty serious and expensive personnel errors, but I could see the future meant teams with the most cap flexibility would consistently do the best. As it was, I knew that some of these Devils contracts were already going to count against the cap for the next season, so the concept of taking less myself would allow the team to add other players. Locking the Devils into a contract that paid me a large salary would hinder the club, and I knew I would rather make less and play on a good team than make more and risk playing on a weaker team. I valued the luxury of winning more than money. So I signed the new deal, agreeing to a salary of $5.2 million from 2006–07 through to the end of the 2011–12 season with a no-trade clause included. By the playoffs of that final season, I would be 40 years old.

Perhaps I was afraid of the possibility of change. I can say I didn't want to gamble with something that has worked so well for me. As well, I didn't want to risk moving to another team and being away from my four children—sons Anthony, Jeremy and William, and daughter Anabelle—because I knew they would stay in New Jersey with their mother. I could do it if I had to, but I've always wanted to build close relationships with my children. At the time I signed the contract, Anthony was 10, the twins, Jeremy and William, were nine, and Anabelle was just four. If you notice on the back of my mask, I have the letters J-A-W-A in honor of my kids, and I often use JAWA as a code for e-mail and other business matters. I knew the future I wanted was to be close to them, not playing in an NHL city far away. It helped with my decision that in the course of the negotiations it was made clear that if I was interested in staying with the Devils, in another capacity after my playing career was over, there would be an opportunity for me.

When it was all done, there was something about this contract that felt sad, different from the sense of triumph with the contract five years earlier. It was the third time I had negotiated my own deal, and this was probably the last contract of my career. The likeliest scenario is that I will finish this one off, and then my career will be over. At the other end lies the real world.

On the positive side, this contract also meant I would be around to play in the new arena the club plans to open in downtown Newark for the 2007–08 season. I wouldn't have wanted to play all these years in New Jersey, then move away when the team finally got the new building it has needed for a long time. I was asked to give my input into some of the details of the arena, and this place will be special. There will be two rinks, one just for games and one just for practices, as well as one game dressing room and one practice dressing room. The concept behind that is when we have a game, it should have a unique feeling and atmosphere. There will also be a gym and swimming pool, as well as luxury suites, restaurants—basically, everything we don't have now. In our current arena, you buy a ticket for $95 per seat and you still have to walk up 40 steps to get a drink. People demand more than that now, and this new rink will be different. It will make the franchise better and I want to be part of it. I've been part of the process of building this organization, a team that during the 2005–06 season finally retired its first two jerseys in recognition of Stevens and Daneyko. We need people to start relating to the organization more, and people like Daneyko and Stevens are the perfect role models for the franchise. We had built a mini-dynasty by winning three Cups, but it seemed we were still the junior sidekick of the big-city Rangers with nothing tangible to show for all the team's success except the banners hanging from the roof of the Continental Airlines Arena. The new building, I hope, will change that, and begin to establish the Devils as a franchise with real roots and real staying power.

In the end, I guess I didn't want to know anything else. This is what I believe in. Being a Devil.

The Toughest Shooters

(and how many times they beat me)

ALEXEI KOVALEV

68 games, 19 goals*

A left-handed shooter with an unbelievable level of skill, Kovalev is a player I have played a lot, when he was with Pittsburgh, the New York Rangers, Montreal and in international competitions. I even watched him play as a minor-leaguer, a time when he would sometimes deke the same player twice on one rush. He is able to play with the puck very close to his skates, either because he uses a short stick or a very high lie. He can make all the moves at full speed or while cruising. He has always been dangerous.

Source: Elias Sports Bureau. Statistics combine regular season and playoffs and are current as of conclusion of 2005–06 season.

chapter 2
Turmoil

SINCE THE EARLY 1990s, chaos, uncertainty and confusion had not been the signature characteristics of the New Jersey Devils. For the most part, these were ways in which other NHL teams were described, the reasons why those clubs floundered, missed the playoffs or misfired on trades, with free agents and on draft day. Since the day Lou Lamoriello had arrived as president and general manager on April 30, 1987, there had been a plan in New Jersey and a careful, logical manner of achieving that plan. There had been controversy, sure, and players such as Bill Guerin and Claude Lemieux had left town after angry contract disputes. At one point, it appeared the Devils and owner John McMullen might even depart the Meadowlands for Nashville because of a lease dispute at our home arena. Coaches had been fired, including Robbie Ftorek, who was removed with only eight games left before the 2000 playoffs, the year we turned our season around under a new coach, Larry Robinson, and eventually won the Stanley Cup over Dallas.

For the most part, however, the Devils had been the definition of stability, and three Stanley Cup championships over an eight-year span were proof that being predictable and organized rather than flamboyant and erratic made for winning hockey, if not necessarily a fan base to rival the nearby Rangers.

Well, by Christmas 2005, we suddenly weren't that team any-more. In the wake of the previous year's destructive lockout, a labor dispute that had cost us all a year's pay and left the NHL without a Stanley Cup champion for the first time in 86 years, it was as though the Devils had lost the organizational personality that had made us so successful. Veteran players had been signed to expensive contracts, then benched or cut, while other experienced Devils were missing from the dressing room for the first time in years. A coach had been fired after calling our team "the strangest he'd ever been around," the team's best offensive player hadn't played a game because of a mysterious illness, young players had been advanced to the NHL but weren't ready and, after years of being one of the most durable goaltenders in the league's history, I'd been hurt and hadn't dressed for a game for the first time in more than seven years.

Rock bottom came with a thud on New Year's Eve, when an announced crowd of 11,971 turned out at the Meadowlands to see us lose a messy 6–3 decision to the Toronto Maple Leafs, a team we had dominated in the playoffs for years. Suddenly they were finding it easy to score on us, as easy as a knife slicing through warm butter. We hadn't elected a captain to replace the retired Scott Stevens, and questions swirled about the leadership and cohesiveness of our team, even suggestions that there was dissension in our dressing room as we tumbled out of the Eastern Conference playoff picture with a lousy 16–18–5 record. As a team, it seemed we were having a lot of trouble adjusting to the NHL's new interpretation of some fundamental rules, such as hooking and interference. The red line for two-zone passes had been removed, players could no longer shoot the puck over the glass in their defensive zone and teams that iced the puck could no longer change players before the next faceoff. It was a lot to digest, and we were having trouble.

As well, some strange things were happening internally. Down with our farm club in Albany, New York, my former backup, Chris Terreri, had been forced to come out of retirement after four years and eight months and start a game at 41 years of age because the starter, Ari Ahonen, was injured, and his backup, Frank Doyle, was worn out. It was a funny story, in some ways, as Terreri was so tired after the first period he had to rest during the second so he would have enough energy to play the third.

Meanwhile, the rest of the league was having a few chuckles at our expense. Not only were we struggling as a team, we seemed dangerous to be around. Larry Robinson, our coach to start the 2005–06 season, had become physically ill as he dealt with the pressures of NHL coaching. On November 23, during a game in Florida against the Panthers, referee Don Van Massenhoven was hit by a deflected puck in the corner in our zone and suffered one of the worst injuries I've ever seen. Our trainer, Bill Murray, was there in an instant, but there was blood everywhere. The shot had driven the septum of Van Massenhoven's nose into his brain, broken both orbital bones in his face and required seven hours of surgery and seven titanium plates to repair. Incredibly, Van Massenhoven came back to the NHL in early January, and even refereed at the Turin Olympics.

Interestingly, he was also the referee who called me for playing the puck outside the "trapezoid" in a game against Ottawa on February 1, 2006. The league had drawn two lines from the goal line to the end boards, and goalies were no longer able to play the puck outside that area. After years of being creative with playing the puck, I felt it was a rule aimed at me. The penalty was a two-minute minor, and when Van Massenhoven whistled it against me, I thought he was wrong, that the puck was on the line when I played it. Even worse, he made the call from outside the blueline. To be honest, I had to resist making a smart aleck remark about how he couldn't see it because he was wearing a visor, as many of the referees had started to do after his accident. I've been friendly with many of the officials over the years, especially the veteran referees and some of the French-Canadian linesmen. I really liked Stéphane Provost, a linesman from my neighborhood in St. Léonard, who was killed on his motorcycle during the 2004–05 lockout when he ran into a standing tractor-trailer in Florida. He wore No. 72, and the officials wore that number on the shoulders of their uniforms in his honor afterwards.

Van Massenhoven's injury was one of those that really make you think how dangerous our game can be. I'd seen some nasty things over the years, like the night Jason Arnott took a slapshot in the teeth in St. Louis, and a game in Chicago when Mike Peluso was flipped in the air after trying to bodycheck one of the Blackhawk players and accidentally kicked our Devils teammate, Randy McKay, in the face. I'd seen Ken Daneyko crosschecked in the mouth, and when he took his mouthpiece out, there were two or three teeth in it. Just after the '06 Olympic break, Islander defenseman Radek Martinek turned and accidentally fired a slapshot right into our bench. None of our players were really watching, and the puck hit Sergei Brylin in the side of the helmet. The shot shattered the helmet and cut Brylin, and you had to think of the damage that could have been done if it had hit someone in the face, as the puck did that night with Van Massenhoven.

The problems with the first half of the 2005–06 season in New Jersey were varied and complicated, but they really could be traced to the previous summer, when defenseman Scott Nieder-mayer left as a free agent to join the Anaheim Mighty Ducks. Ken

Daneyko had retired after the 2003 Stanley Cup. Scott Stevens had suffered a serious concussion during the 2003 playoffs when he was hit in the head by a shot off the stick of Tampa Bay's Pavel Kubina, and during the 2003–04 season he missed the final 44 games with post-concussion syndrome. By the summer of '05, Stevens hadn't officially retired, but it didn't seem likely he was coming back. He had all but disappeared, and we had already started to adjust to life without him. But Niedermayer was another case altogether.

He was free to sign with the highest bidder, but with Daneyko and Stevens gone, we needed him more than ever. I called him a few times after the 2003–04 season, and spoke to him at the 2004 World Cup, but it didn't seem like he knew what he wanted. I think the Devils tried to play it smart by seeking a trade for his brother, Rob, who already played for Anaheim, but the Ducks' new GM, Brian Burke, wouldn't make that deal. That may have made the difference. Niedermayer waited so long to announce that he was signing with the Ducks that I think Devils management really believed he would stay in New Jersey. When he did sign with Anaheim, he said getting the chance to play on the same team as his brother—they had played against each other in the 2003 Stanley Cup final—was a big reason behind his decision.

When it became official Niedermayer was leaving, Lamoriello immediately called to assure me he had a backup plan. Within a matter of days, he had re-signed Brian Rafalski for $4.2 million per season, and he had also gone out and picked up free agent defensemen Vladimir Malakhov (two years, $3.6 million) and Dan McGillis (two years, $4.4 million). Those contracts, really, were the reaction to Niedermayer leaving, and the Devils probably overpaid because of it. Soon after, Lamoriello also went out and signed winger Alexander Mogilny, who had played for the Devils for two seasons and been part of the 2000 championship team. He was 36 years old, and one of the few players who had been paid in full through the lockout because of a hip injury he had suffered while playing for the Leafs. With us, he got a contract worth $7 million over two years, and that seemed like an awful lot of money, too, particularly under the new cap system.

Those contracts meant that from the beginning of the season we were theoretically well *over* the new $39 million cap already, at least in terms of the players that were under contract to the Devils. But that was only true in theory. Winger Patrik Elias had signed a one-year, $4.18 million deal in August, but he was not likely to play for a few months since he was still recovering from hepatitis A, which he had contracted while playing in Russia during the lockout. His salary wouldn't count against the cap until he was activated. But that also meant the entire team knew there would eventually have to be changes. Somebody would have to go to make room for Elias, a talented forward, and it had an unsettling effect. Players know what other players make, and pretty soon players were doing the math on which of their teammates would have to go to get the Devils under the cap. Under the NHL's old system, this wouldn't have been an issue, but in the post-lockout world, suddenly the Devils were under severe financial duress.

The first casualty of this new order was Krzysztof Oliwa, an enforcer who had been part of Calgary's 2004 Stanley Cup finalists and had played for us before. Oliwa signed a $700,000 per year deal with the Devils during the lockout and came to camp in September 2005. But on October 25, after only eight games, he was put on waivers. Darren Langdon, who had signed four months after Oliwa for $450,000, was obviously cheaper, and in the new, faster NHL, it was apparent that one enforcer was enough. The new rules for recalling players from the minors were complicated, particularly because experienced players had to clear waivers going down and coming back up, and, if claimed by another team on the way back to the NHL, half of that player's salary and cap figure would count against the team that had lost him. So with Oliwa, the Devils just sent him home, rather than assigning him to the farm club in Albany. He was there one day eating lunch in the same Japanese steak house up the road from our practice facility as me, and then, suddenly, he was gone.

Along with Elias' impending return, another symbol of the roster changes that were inevitable was Tommy Albelin. He was 41 and had played with us twice before, including on the 1995 and 2003 championship teams, but he didn't have a contract coming out of the lockout. Instead of leaving town, or going to the minors, he just hung around. We called him "The Stalker." He was, unofficially, our eighth defenseman. He took part in practices, even those in which extra players were simply skated to exhaustion, and because he was so fit—but at the same time not tired from playing in the season that had just started—he looked terrific during scrimmages. Nothing was said and there was no definite plan. He was just there. Waiting.

What backfired on us was that everybody expected things to be the same with a cast of new players. Well, it wasn't the same. There were lots of new faces and we just didn't know each other very well. Suddenly, players had to take different roles than those in which they had shone before. I knew Malakhov and Mogilny, of course, from their previous tours of duty with the Devils. Langdon I had never met, and he turned out to be a terrific guy. He's from Newfoundland, and it was unbelievable the way he spoke. Me this, me that. "Me stick no good," or something about "me mudder." At the start, I just couldn't understand what he was saying, but we became good friends and I set up my phone so that each time he called a Miller Lite logo would pop up on the screen. The images of Langdon and beer just went together. Unfortunately, later in the season, the Devils decided he was no longer in the plans and sent him home as well. Like Oliwa, one day he was just gone.

Richard Matvichuk was a player I knew a little bit. We had been taken in the entry draft the same year, 1990, and we had both competed for a place on Team Canada at the 2002 pre-Olympic camp, but I had never played with him. McGillis was somebody I had never met before. With all the changes, and with so many games packed into the early part of the schedule, it was tough to get the feel of being together. It seemed we were just in and out of the arena without much time together, and that sense of together-ness just wasn't happening. Other years, we hadn't had to worry about gelling as a team because the core had remained the same and we knew each other so well. The salary cap problems—which we knew weren't going away—made it all the more difficult.

—ᴍ—

We looked good on opening night against Pittsburgh in Sidney Crosby's NHL debut, beating the Penguins 5–1. But our overall start was slow: after eight games, we were 4–4, and Brian Gionta was probably our brightest light, with five goals. We were giving up more goals than we were used to, 27 in those first eight games, and while we were scoring quite a few ourselves, the NHL's new style of rule enforcement seemed to be causing the Devils to play a very different style.

On October 15, Carolina bombed me for five goals on 19 shots over two periods before I was pulled for the third, and my numbers sure weren't what I was used to. Since becoming a full-time NHLer in 1993, my goals-against average had never been higher than 2.57 in a single season, and my save percentage had always been .906 or better. Going into the season, I had 75 career regular season shutouts, and now the concept of a shutout seemed like a distant dream. It was difficult, because in those situations, the focus always turns to the goaltender, and it was naturally assumed I was having a slow start. I certainly didn't feel that was true.

In the ninth game, against Tampa Bay, my season took an unusual turn when I went down with an injury, a twisted right knee. I'd been very fortunate with my health over the years, although I had suffered a sprained wrist in the quarterfinal of the World Cup 13 months earlier and a shoulder injury in the world championships the following spring. But over the course of my career, my reliability and durability were parts of my game of which I was very proud. I liked to play, and I liked to be counted on. In the 1994–95 season I had played 40 of 48 games in the lockout-shortened regular season, and since then I had played at least 70 games every season except for the 1996–97 season, when I played 67.

I was injured against the Lightning when I tried to move post-to-post across the crease with what I called my "Billy Smith" pokecheck and just went over on my right knee. I ended up missing six games, which I figured would have been only four in a regular season, but we were playing a compressed schedule to make room for the Olympics later in the season. The Devils recalled goalie Ari Ahonen from the minors to fill my spot on the roster, and for the first time since April 16, 1998, I wasn't in uniform as Scott Clemmensen started at the Meadowlands against the Buffalo Sabres. It gave me a chance to sit back and watch in streetclothes, a chance I hadn't had in more than seven years. As I watched, it seemed clear the team wasn't that close. As I watched the bench, I could see there wasn't much going on, and certainly not a lot of emotion. Players were making mistakes, but they weren't feeling those errors as if they were really costing the team. They were just individual mistakes made by a team of individuals, or so it seemed. It also gave me some time to look at what was going on around the league as the NHL got back to work after missing an entire season.

I watched every single game on TV I could, which wasn't much different from my usual routine. If you come to my house, almost all the time you'll see the TV on in the background, either tuned to a game or ESPN. I'm constantly looking for information on the NHL or hockey in general. To be the best, you have to look at other people, at trends and everything that's going on. The more you can find that will give you a little extra knowledge or a special edge, the better off you'll be. If you're blind about what's going on around you, then you're not doing your job. For me, to get to the rink and see somebody who doesn't know if the Flyers won or lost the night before, or how the Rangers or the Islanders did, that's garbage. Every player on our team should know those things. It's their job, and for the most part, players do stay on top of those things. You don't necessarily need to know who scored, but you need a general idea of what's going on around you, and in the case of the Devils, what's going on in the Eastern Conference specifically. How can you get up for games if you don't understand the importance of each one? I think I'm probably more aware than most players. I watch more games than most, and it's crucial to me to understand the events that are taking place in the league and the sport.

When I was out with the knee injury, I saw how the speed of the game had increased and the new ways in which attacks were being generated. There really was a startling difference. The red line was out, the bluelines were further away from the net and certain types of fouls that used to be called only inconsistently, like hooks on the puck carrier, were being called. Scoring chances were coming from different areas and out of different kinds of offensive plays, and it was very noticeable how much more "swimming" goalies were doing compared to before, how much more they were being forced to scramble and lunge for pucks. The position, clearly, was becoming even more physically demanding, with the goalies forced to worker harder and stay in the crouch longer as teams earned greater time with the puck in the offensive zone. It became clearer to me why the Devils were having so much trouble. We were out of position much of the time, and it meant we were having to skate so much more just to get the puck. That was leaving players tired and even more frequently out of position. If we could improve our positioning, it would improve all parts of our game, and in particular our players would be fresher when they got the puck and could make smarter and more creative decisions.

In the six games I missed, we won two games (one by a shootout), lost two games in regulation and lost two more, one in overtime and one by a shootout. Poor Clemmensen—we scored only 16 goals for him in six games, five of those in a shootout win over Boston. Then, as soon as I returned, the team started scoring like crazy. We scored five against Montreal, four against Ottawa, five against Florida and eight against Tampa, and suddenly we had six wins in eight games and, for a moment, it looked as though some of the Devils' problems had been solved, at least temporarily.

Playing for the Devils throughout my career had meant that most nights I jumped on the ice, I had a chance to win. There were many nights when we didn't draw a lot of fans, and the Rangers were always the sexier team. But we knew that for our team, winning was the primary goal. That said, we valued defence more than offence. Sometimes it seemed that we were so committed to a defensive style of play that we would rather lose a game 2–1 than win 6–5. That was just the way Lamoriello teams had always played because he believed in putting the team first, no matter what. It fit perfectly with his love for Vince Lombardi and the Green Bay Packers, and certainly with the Montreal Canadiens. In fact, starting with Jacques Lemaire, we had a long line of coaches and assistant coaches with links to the Canadiens, including men like Robinson, Jacques Laperrière and Pat Burns. That singular approach was why we had been so consistent. Other teams went on bad losing streaks, but it never happened to us. Every day we knew with the system we were going to play we had a chance to win. Physically, that made playing the game, and playing a lot of games, easier on me over the years than it would have been playing with other teams. In the first part of the 2005–06 season, however, it seemed like we were playing crazy games every night. There were more power plays, which meant more side-to-side movement and more physical stress on goaltenders. If I'd been required to play the same type of games from the start of my career, it's unlikely I would have been able to maintain the same level of durability.

The introduction of the shootout to NHL competition may have added excitement for the fans, but it just added another burden to the league's goaltenders. We had been told to wear smaller equipment and forced to work harder, and now there was an extra session of acrobatics required some nights if 60 minutes of regulation play and another five minutes of overtime couldn't produce a winner. In fact, in one of the first shootouts during the pre-season, goalie Brian Boucher of the Phoenix Coyotes pulled his groin and missed many weeks of playing time.

During the lockout, there was debate over increasing the size of the nets, which I believed was a ridiculous idea. One of the arguments against doing so was that it would make the NHL history books meaningless by giving modern shooters a larger target. Well, adding the shootout meant that every game would have a winner for the first time in the league's history, which also meant that goalies who had put up strong win-loss records over the years would have those records compromised. Patrick Roy, for example, retired with 131 regular season ties. If, say, 65 of those had been wins through OT or the shootout, Roy would have 616 career wins, and his NHL record would be a lot harder to catch. If you look at a young goalie like Henrik Lundqvist of the Rangers, he's going to have 10 years or more of playing under these rules to pile up win totals. But nobody seemed to care as much about that as they had worried about the records of the game's greatest goal scorers. I disagreed with the shootout when it was instituted, and while as the season went along I became one of the best shootout goalies in the league, I still didn't like them, maybe because the Devils had always played such a team game and the shootout was a process that allowed only a handful of players to participate.

My first shootout was on December 3 against the Minnesota Wild, when a 2–2 tie remained unbroken after OT. The Wild must have thought my knee was still sore because Todd White, Brian Rolston and Marian Gaborik all tried to beat me with low shots. Rolston tried to surprise me with a slapshot, while Gaborik carried the puck wide and then tried to tuck one between my legs. I stopped all three, and Viktor Kozlov began the process of establishing himself as our best shootout man: He scored the only goal, and we won. I picked up a career victory that, frankly, I didn't feel I deserved, and I sure didn't feel it was right that the Wild lost a road game like that. But the fans loved it, that was undeniable, and we're in the entertainment business. My goals-against average was still over 3.00, my save percentage was below .900, but I had made 37 saves in what had probably been my best game of the year.

—ᚦᚦᚢ—

I was back and playing well, but the team was still unsettled and a number of issues were simmering on the back burner. Elias, for example, had still not returned to play after suffering a strained abdominal muscle during training. He was still weeks away from returning. As it turned out, an even more significant problem was about to come to a head.

Larry Robinson, who had coached us to the 2000 Stanley Cup after taking over from Ftorek, and to the 2001 final as well, had left after the 2002 playoffs. He returned for the 2005–06 season as the successor to Pat Burns. Burns had been diagnosed with colon cancer after the 2004 playoffs and, when the cancer came back in the summer of 2005, he was forced to step down as Devils coach. It became clear during the early months of the 2005–06 season, however, that returning as head coach of the Devils was taking its toll on Robinson. He missed the shootout win over the Wild with a severe throat infection, and assistant coach John MacLean, an old Devils teammate, coached us. MacLean was behind the bench again three nights later in Detroit, a city we hadn't won in for nine years, and we gave up 44 shots with Clemmensen in goal and got whipped, 5–2. Brendan Shanahan, MacLean's old linemate in Jersey, scored twice for the Wings.

We went home to face Calgary, and the Flames started their backup goalie, Philippe Sauvé. It seemed more teams were doing that—Ottawa had used Ray Emery against us instead of Dominik Hasek three weeks earlier—and I found that depressing, a sign that other teams no longer feared us as much. We lost 4–1, and I gave up three goals on four shots with Team Canada executive director Wayne Gretzky in the stands watching. Gretzky was on a brief tour to evaluate prospects for the 2006 Canadian Olympic team, a squad I badly wanted to be part of. So the mood of the team was down that night, and so was mine.

After the game, Robinson, who had returned from his throat problem, suggested the team was in disarray, and remarked that the absence of former captain Scott Stevens was noticeable. "It's the strangest team I've ever been around," he told reporters. "They're a different group. A leader would probably help. Most great teams have somebody that will step forward. We have a bunch of guys and not one particular guy to come forward and step in front if things get out of hand."

It was clear our team's confidence was really shaky. We were up and down every night and we just weren't in a position at that point to compete with the two teams that had just beaten us, the Wings and Flames. When adversity came, we didn't seem to have the ability to brush it off like the championship team we had been. But when Robinson made his public comments, I was disappointed, particularly since I felt that I was very much a leader on our team. He should have known better, and known that our struggles were part of the growing process after the team had changed so much. Robinson had played in the NHL for years, and was regarded as a player's coach, so his comments seemed out of character to some extent. Still, after the loss to Calgary, we were sitting 10th in the conference and the season was looking grim. The Devils had only missed the playoffs once in my tenure with them, the season after we won the Cup in '95, and suddenly that possibility was staring us in the face.

Colorado continued this new tradition by starting their backup goalie, Vitaly Kolesnik, against us at the Meadowlands two nights later. We responded to Robinson's challenging words poorly, falling behind 3–0 after one period. But with goals from Mogilny, Gionta—his 17th in 28 games—and Gomez, we fought back to tie the game and ultimately forced a shootout. It went on forever, with each team getting seven shots. Kolesnik, a 26-year-old rookie from Kazakhstan, was pretty good, stopping Kozlov, Gionta, Gomez, Mogilny, Sergei Brylin and John Madden all in a row. I made six stops as well until Antti Laaksonen beat me, and then Kolesnik stopped Jamie Langenbrunner to clinch the win for the Avs. Our comeback was encouraging, but a loss was a loss. McGillis, who had been struggling to adjust to the league's new emphasis on speed, was scratched for the fourth straight game, an unsettling story in the background given that he was a well-paid 33-year-old veteran, not some rookie.

Two nights later, we lost 3–2 in overtime to the Blue Jackets in Columbus, despite holding a 2–1 lead in the third to a team that in five seasons in the NHL had come from behind in the third period to win only nine times in 170 games. We went 0–7 on the power play and gave up 39 shots to the Jackets, who didn't even have their best forward, Rick Nash, due to injury. On the winning Columbus goal in overtime, a shot that was going 25 feet wide bounced off our winger right on to the stick of Bryan Berard, who buried it. Over and over, things like that were happening to us, the kinds of things that had never bothered us in other years because we were so consistent. With so many new faces on the 2005–06 team, we were starting to find out how players—and coaches—would react when things went wrong.

The tension was building internally as we sunk in the standings, and Robinson was quoted as saying I was having a "good, not great" season. At the end of the day, everybody gets questioned when things aren't going well, and I was no exception. Everybody also has their own feeling about why things aren't going well, and sometimes things are said that the speaker doesn't really believe. When a coach is asked "what's wrong?" day after day, he has to say something different so as not to be boring.

Outside the dressing room, I had been added as the only goaltender to the league's new "competition committee" about a month earlier, an appointment I embraced as a chance to make the concerns of goaltenders throughout the league heard at the highest levels. Until this point, NHL players had never had a formal role in the consideration of rule changes. Every year, first the league's general managers would meet to consider any alterations, and the GMs would make recommendations to the league's owners—the board of governors—and those changes would usually be rubber-stamped. But the new collective bargaining agreement between the owners and the players signed in the summer of 2005 included a provision for a 10-man competition committee that would include representatives from the ranks of players, general managers and owners. Initially, no goaltenders were invited to be part of the group, an obvious oversight that was corrected when the union nominated me to join the committee.

For weeks, I had been noticing that, with more speed in the games and a reduced ability of defensemen to use their sticks and bodies to either get players out of the crease area or intimidate players from going there in the first place, goalies were getting hit a lot more by forwards. During a game between Vancouver and Anaheim, for example, the Canucks goalie, Dan Cloutier, had been injured and knocked out for the year with a knee injury after a collision with Rob Niedermayer of the Ducks. It made sense to me that there were going to be more collisions and more injuries.

We hosted the Atlanta Thrashers on December 15, and I learned more about this new trend the hard way. The game went to overtime tied 2–2—the fourth game in a row to do so for us—and partway through the extra period Atlanta's big winger, Marian Hossa, roared down the right side and was hooked down by McGillis, who had returned to the lineup. Hossa crashed into me, knocking me flying into the net. It felt like I blacked out, and I was definitely down for several minutes. As I was regaining my senses, I joked to our trainer that he'd better get Clemmensen ready. "You want him to take the penalty shot?" he said. Then it was my turn to be surprised. I didn't realize that Hossa had been given a penalty shot when McGillis pulled him down. Once I got back on my feet and readied myself, he steamed in, and I managed to deflect his wrist shot over the crossbar with my glove. Just over a minute later, however, Marc Savard scored for Atlanta, and we'd lost another one.

With the knee injury and all the extra OT work, the shootouts and now this collision with Hossa, I was feeling every one of my 33 years. The good news was that we had hired a new massage therapist, Tom Plasko, and he was really helping me. He had worked for Pittsburgh and with Mario Lemieux, but the Pens had let him go during the lockout. I met him while he was working for Team Canada at the 2002 Olympics and the '04 World Cup, and at the World Cup he'd helped me with a groin problem and worked on Niedermayer's back with good results. When Pittsburgh let him go, he called me, and I recommended to management that we hire him. We did, and early in the 2005–06 season, I was pretty happy that we had.

The Atlanta loss was our fifth in six games, and Robinson was struggling to maintain his sense of calm and keep the team together. McGillis, who hadn't been able to fit into the lineup comfortably, was put on waivers and sent to the minors. This was the first indication that the wheels were starting to turn in the background. Robinson, meanwhile, just seemed out of character much of the time with the way he was acting, yelling at players and getting all over them for petty things. It was as though he was being forced to be somebody he wasn't. All his life he had been a nice guy, and suddenly it seemed that he was forcing himself not to be so nice. He was trying to get players to be accountable to the team and each other, but it wasn't working. We were leading the league in meetings, our power play was terrible and players were constantly getting weighed to see if they were at or below their designated playing weight. For example, the coaching staff was all over Gomez for being too heavy, and despite being forced to lose weight Gomez didn't seem to be producing as well as he had in the past. I was also getting weighed almost daily, and it was becoming a nuisance.

It was almost as if Robinson was in pain, and during games the bench was getting more chaotic. In one game, with a faceoff in our end and just a few seconds left, he put out our fourth line and the other team got two good scoring chances. Another night, he called defenseman Sean Brown's name, and Brown wasn't even dressed. Two nights after the Atlanta game, we were playing Carolina and with a minute left in the period he put our fourth line out against Carolina's top line centered by Eric Staal, which was just not the way we did things. When the other team was using its top line, we always used our best checkers, usually John Madden and Jay Pandolfo. Robinson benched both Mogilny and Gomez during that game, which we lost 4–1 to the Hurricanes. For Gomez, it was really disheartening, because he was hoping to play for the U.S. at the Olympics and Carolina coach Peter Laviolette was the American Olympic coach. Gomez wanted desperately to impress Laviolette, but he ended up sitting on the bench for the third period. At one point in the game, we had a power play, and Robinson thought it was still five-on-five. The players wanted to know who was going out, and it took him a long time to answer. That was the last game he coached.

Two days later, on December 19, Robinson announced he was stepping down. The night before, at our team Christmas party, he had seemed very emotional, so I wasn't surprised when he made the announcement. After the party, he had spent the night having a few drinks with our goaltending coach, Jacques Caron, and his wife, Marjorie. Caron and Robinson were close. Caron had cut back his everyday coaching duties earlier that season, partly out of concern for his wife's health, and that had to have influenced Robinson, who had been struggling with his own health for weeks. At practice the next day, he told us of his decision, how he had been suffering from headaches and couldn't sleep, and that he'd been to doctors for a CAT scan. He said that he had promised his family he wouldn't make himself sick over hockey and that he had two grandchildren he wanted to see grow up. He was very candid, and very personal. It's hard when you see somebody who is such a nice person hurt like that, suffering from such stress, and the players just seemed stunned. Nobody could really say anything.

"Nothing is worth being sick over," Robinson told reporters. The only happy part was that almost immediately after he finished telling us, you could see that he was back to his old self. It was that quick. The weight was all gone.

His resignation was only one element of the craziest day I had ever experienced with the Devils, 24 hours of mind-blowing change. Robinson's replacement, for starters, was Lamoriello, who at 63 had only coached one other NHL game in his life. He came out for practice on that first day wearing suit pants and a bomber jacket, like right out of the 1970s. There were more changes. Elias practiced for the first time all season. McGillis was recalled from Albany. Albelin—"The Stalker"—was signed to a one-year, $450,000 contract. Finally, in the biggest surprise, Malakhov packed up his skates and retired. All this in one day!

The story on Malakhov was he had supposedly turned down $2 million a year to play with the Flyers, but had come back to New Jersey because the Devils were willing to pay him $3.5 million a year. It's hard to play for money. Still, nobody on the team really understood what he was thinking. Malakhov had played on our 2000 Cup winner after coming over in a trade with Montreal during the season, but immediately afterwards signed a free agent deal to play with the Rangers. He was quiet and a bit mysterious. From management's point of view, Malakhov's retirement was helpful news because it would save the team all of his salary in cap room, just as had been the case earlier in the season for Phoenix when Brett Hull had decided to quit. It wouldn't create quite enough room to make way for Elias when he was ready to play, but it was a start. Within a few days, however, Malakhov's agent said he believed there had been a miscommunication, that Malakhov only wanted a "leave of absence," and the fight over that issue went on for months.

In the wake of Robinson's resignation and the flurry of personnel moves, our record was a mediocre 14–13–5 and it seemed that we were in complete turmoil as we headed into two games in the next two days, one against our archrivals, the Rangers, and the other against the Islanders. Still, there was reason for optimism. Elias was coming back, getting rid of the contracts for Oliwa and Malakhov meant there had been some cap relief, and nine days later McGillis was again sent to the minors for good. David Hale was recalled and given McGillis' No. 2 jersey, and his $650,000 salary meant more than enough space had been cleared for Elias' return.

I thought Lamoriello's decision to take over, even on an interim basis, was a good one because it would make the team more accountable. Everyone knew their job could be on the line, and now the person making that decision was standing behind the bench, not in an office upstairs. "We went from having one of the nicest guys to one of the most intimidating people in hockey behind our bench," said Gomez. "And don't think we all weren't nervous about it." Right away, the attitude seemed to improve.

They stopped weighing Gomez all the time, and he started scoring. Lamoriello was like a college coach, and his emphasis was less on systems and more about attitude, giving the player next to you the chance to be successful.

Visually, it took a while to get used to. He wasn't a very good skater at practice, and during games Lamoriello just looked so small behind the bench. But his decision took guts. He had hired Robinson after Burns had become sick, and when it wasn't working out, he decided it wasn't fair to make somebody else deal with the problem and went behind the bench himself. But he also said the move was temporary. That set off a bunch of rumours that suggested people from Brent Sutter to Rick Dudley to Paul Maurice to Ted Nolan to Walt Kyle were soon going to be taking over.

We had been such a boring, successful organization, and people in hockey were shocked that this was happening to us. The weird part was that we were a mess, while the Rangers, who hadn't made the playoffs for seven years, seemed organized and confident. So much still seemed uncertain, but I knew it was important not to seem bothered by all the changes and that it was important to seem confident and composed in front of my teammates and the media. I needed to show confidence that the boat was going in the right direction, and in games it was important that I didn't start losing my temper or behaving out of character.

Things sure didn't get better right away, although we beat the Rangers 3–1 in Lamoriello's first game in place of Robinson. The only immediate lineup changes were that rookie Zach Parise was put on a line with Gomez and Gionta, and Mogilny was shifted to the point on the power play. We then lost three in a row to the Islanders, Thrashers and Leafs, and during the game in Toronto at the Air Canada Centre there was the strange sight of Lamoriello losing his balance and falling behind the bench. We went 0–6 on the power play in that game, dropping us to 4–100 for the month. Trade rumours began to circulate about the team acquiring an offensive defenseman, some focusing on Berard of Columbus or Pittsburgh defenseman Dick Tarnstrom.

The year ended terribly, with a 6–2 loss in Pittsburgh with Clemmensen in goal and then the New Year's Eve disaster at home against the Leafs. We felt desperate, but we'd felt that way for a while. "It was a bad 2005 for the Devils, and a lot of people around the league are loving it right now," Gomez told reporters. Lamoriello was 2–5 as coach, but he was still insisting we would get things turned around. We did, or at least started the process. On January 3, I picked up my first shutout of the season against Florida, 3–0, and for the first time all season it seemed we were finally playing our game.

The next day at practice, there were two more surprises. Mogilny was gone, put on waivers and sent to the minors. Lamoriello made it clear that it wasn't a cap move despite Mogilny's $3.5 million salary, but instead was about ridding the team of passengers. I always felt "Almo" was a good player on a good team, but on a struggling team he was exposed for his tendencies and habits. I had thought he would do better when Elias returned and Mogilny was put in a lesser role, but he never got the chance. I felt bad for him as a hockey player who had accomplished a lot, including one 76-goal season with Buffalo. He was close to 1,000 games played and needed only 27 goals to hit the 500 mark for his career. Suddenly, he was in the minors for the first time in his career. The new system had hurt him. Under the old rules, a rich team like Detroit or Dallas would have picked him up, but those teams didn't have salary cap room anymore. And, if he was recalled and another team claimed him in the process, half his salary would be applied to the Devils' salary cap number, which wouldn't help New Jersey. So he was sent down, and it was almost assured he was going down for good. It had seemed strange to me that Mogilny had played for us before, left us for Toronto and more money, and then returned a few years later after hip surgery had slowed him down. Only then were the Devils willing to pay him big bucks. Not surprisingly, it hadn't worked out.

The other big news that day was that Scott Stevens had returned to practice, not to play but as a "coaching consultant." In his last few seasons, he wasn't the player he had once been, and the new rules would have been tough on him. But we had missed his work ethic and his passion for the game. That was his form of leadership. He led by the way he played. In the dressing room he was never a rah-rah guy. He held other players accountable by his presence, his expressions and his demeanor, not by making speeches or helping guys with problems away from the rink. It was good to see him back.

We beat Montreal the next night 5–4, then knocked off the Sabres 3–2 in Buffalo and then, on January 9, beat the first-place-overall Flyers on home ice, 3–0. That win tied us for the eighth and final playoff spot in the east. We were leaner, about $11 million worth, and meaner, having survived more changes in a half-season than we had experienced over the previous five. The chaos and confusion, at least for the moment, were over.

The Toughest Shooters

(and how many times they beat me)

JAROMIR JAGR

59 games, 17 goals*

Jagr has long been a player who can do things other players can't. He can go from first gear to fifth in an instant, and his long reach and long stick give him the ability to make plays with opposition players hanging on his back. Every time you think he's done with a play, he has a little something left, or another idea you haven't thought of. He can beat you with a shot or with a deke, and may be the best one-on-one player I've ever seen.

*Source: Elias Sports Bureau. Statistics combine regular season and playoffs and are current as of conclusion of 2005–06 season.

chapter 3
Forty Days and Nights

IT WAS, I SUPPOSE, A MOMENTOUS DECISION. It just didn't seem that way at the time.

Growing up in St. Léonard, at six years old I was playing forward for a team at Hébert Arena, not far from my house. A team of older players needed a backup goalie for their games, and although I was mostly a forward, they asked me to play, which then put me on two teams that season. Just what every kid wants, right?

On the first day of the next season, the coach asked me which position I preferred to play.

It was just me, at seven years old, and him. My dad wasn't around to calculate what such a decision might mean to my "career." My older brother, Claude, who would often be the one to drive me to games throughout my younger years, wasn't there, and neither was my brother Denis or my sisters, Line and Sylvie.

Just me and the coach.

"Sure, I'll be the goalie," I said.

It was just that simple, perhaps because it was a simpler time. I came from a sports family—my father had played goal for Canada in the Olympics, my brother Claude would later pitch in the Montreal Expos system—but there was no pressure on me to become an athlete or a hockey player or a goalie. In fact, I loved to be a forward. Just loved scoring goals. Even in street hockey I was only the goalie some of the time. Even after I became a full-time goalie, if I was late for a game they would dress somebody else and I would play forward, wearing my goalie skates, and score a couple of goals. To this day, I still love to play forward for fun.

I certainly never regretted the decision to move inside the crease, although Claude did have to convince me not to quit hockey in favor of downhill skiing when I was 14. By the end of the 2005–06 season, the choice meant I had played the equivalent of 40 days and nights guarding the net in the National Hockey League, which certainly wasn't my objective at age seven.

In those 57,409 minutes of NHL regular season and playoff competition, I have faced 23,770 shots, equivalent to about 594 shots for each of those 40 days. I've been beaten for goals 2,060 times, been credited with a playoff or regular season victory 535 times and saddled with defeat 311 times. I've shut out my opponent 101 times, or about once every 10 ½ starts. All of this doesn't include the 25 games I've played in a Team Canada uniform at the Olympics, World Cup and world championships, or the various exhibition games and charity events for which I've strapped on the pads.

All this because of a seven-year-old's first impulse.

Of course, maybe that seven-year-old knew exactly what he was talking about.

To my mind, being a goaltender in the game of hockey is to be the most creative player on the ice. It is a position that demands innovation and imagination, an ability to adapt and consider alternatives in a split second, the capacity to generate multiple answers to the same, or similar, questions. It's about shooting the puck, not just being shot at, and sometimes even scoring. It's about being willing to try anything, even throwing away your stick if that's what it takes to make a save. If the pieces of equipment worn by a catcher in the game of baseball are the "tools of ignorance," then the pads, body armor, gloves and mask of a goalie are the artist's paint and paintbrush.

That's how I see the game and the position. That's why I dislike, or reject, the dominant goaltending technique of the modern era, the "butterfly" style. More precisely, I don't see the butterfly—on the knees, feet spread out to the corners, body erect, arms pulled in to take away the highest percentage shots—as the total answer. It can play a role in any goalie's arsenal, but only a limited role. The ability for a goalie to be many things at different times has become even more important in the vastly altered NHL that emerged from the lockout that wiped out the 2004–05 season.

People who study goaltending call me a hybrid, and that sounds about right. I know how to make saves a certain way, but I don't lock into a certain way. I have a lot of weapons to throw at a shooter and I like to use them all. In fact, my approach is to beat the player with the puck, not just prevent him from beating me. I want to make a move and pressure him to do something. Brendan Shanahan once told me when I was younger that on a breakaway he never knew what I was going to do to him. That stayed in my mind, particularly since conventional thought has always been that the shooter should wait for the goalie to make the first move. I didn't mind making the first move if that meant I could dictate the moment. From the first time I was ever coached how to play the position, the one thing I didn't like was doing the same thing over and over and over. I have to get in somebody's head and not ever be predictable. Hopefully, fans and hockey people see a lot of things out of me they don't see anywhere else.

As a basic concept, I believe that when the penalty boxes are empty and two teams are playing at even strength, I'm playing against 10 players on the ice. My five and their five. If we make a bad line change, I have to be aware of it and compensate. I need

to know where all of those 10 players are, and have some understanding of what they may do at any time. A goaltender is making
decisions all the time, depending on how he reads the play. You put
yourself in a different position depending where the puck is coming at you, and it's all happening very quickly. I try a lot of things.
If a player shoots from the blueline, but not that hard, maybe
I'll put my stick at an angle and direct it somewhere, or maybe I'll
try to catch it with my blocker. I'll do stupid stuff in practice just
to try it and make the position a little more challenging.

Have I changed a lot over the years? A little, but in my general approach I'm about the same as I was when we first won the
Stanley Cup in 1995. The difference is that expectations of me
are now greater. In '95, nobody expected anything.

—⚹—

Having a father who was a goalie didn't mean I had a built-in
teacher. My father, wisely I think, let me learn to play for fun, and
I remember using his old goalie equipment for road hockey even
though he caught with his right hand and I catch with my left. I
remember him actually showing me some of the finer points of
the game on only one or two occasions. The rest of the time, he
was just my dad.

The only book on goaltending I ever read was Grant Fuhr's
Fuhr on Goaltending, which was published in 1988. The first person to really start teaching me was Mario Baril, who is still managing the Martin Brodeur Arena in St. Léonard. As soon as I
had chosen to be a full-time goalie, I started attending Saturday
morning clinics that Baril organized. By the time I was in my
teens, he was officially my goaltending coach. From the start,
he encouraged me to diversify the way I played the position. By
the time I was 15 or 16, Patrick Roy was dominating the NHL
and revolutionizing the position with his butterfly style. But that

wasn't the way Baril encouraged me to play. He wanted me to keep the shooters guessing all the time. He wanted me to be able to do the butterfly, but also to stand up, to be able to pokecheck and to do many different things in the net. Naturally, I started watching other goalies to see what they did, and that open-minded approach has stayed with me always. You have to be open to trying different things.

As I got older, I attended two different goaltending schools, one run by Quebec goaltending guru François Allaire on the north shore of Montreal, and the other by former Soviet goaltending great Vladislav Tretiak in nearby Brossard. I preferred Tretiak. In fact, going to Allaire's school made me realize that what I was already doing was more than acceptable. In fact, it was the right thing. I hated the Allaire school and only spent one week there. Everything was about playing the percentages, and everything was planned. I have a lot of respect for Allaire and the goalies he has developed. In fact, when Roberto Luongo, a student of Allaire's and a neighbor of mine in St. Léonard, was negotiating a new contract with Florida in June 2006, one of his conditions was that the Panthers hire Allaire once his contract ran out with Anaheim. The Panthers didn't go for it and traded Luongo to Vancouver, but the point is many goalies believe that much in the people who taught them to play.

But while Luongo loved Allaire, that approach wasn't for me. I was so different. I needed to be able to pokecheck, to stack the pads and to play the puck behind the net. I didn't believe in the butterfly then, and I still don't. That's not how I want my boys, Anthony and Jeremy, to play the position, and they don't.

On the other hand, I loved Tretiak's school, and I spent four years there, three as an instructor. In fact, it was there that I met José Théodore as a student, and when he got older he helped me teach. Maybe I liked Tretiak's school better because he had played the game, and because international hockey was very important in my family, with my father having played in the Olympics. In fact, my father was there with his camera taking photographs for a Montreal newspaper during the famous 1972 Summit Series between the Soviets and Canada in which Tretiak was such an important figure. Like Baril, Tretiak taught different techniques and approaches, not just doing the same thing repeatedly. By approaching the position that way, I became a student of the game, and the way in which I would eventually play goal began to develop.

—⟋⟍—

The year after Patrick Roy hit the NHL like a storm and won the 1986 Cup with the Montreal Canadiens, another rookie goaltender named Ron Hextall emerged with the Philadelphia Flyers and began to set the game on fire in a very different way. My dad came back from the Montreal Forum one night and told me I needed to watch Hextall, who he said played the puck frequently and acted like a third defenseman. Others had done it before, but Hextall did it more creatively and aggressively, and he was my inspiration for becoming as well known for stickhandling, passing and even scoring goals as I was for staying in the crease and stopping the puck. I admired Hextall, Sean Burke and Kirk McLean growing up, mostly because they were big goaltenders. I asked my father for pictures of all three in a frame for my room, and my first goalie mask was modeled on the same design as McLean's. But it was Hextall that I wanted to emulate. He influenced me, and then I influenced a generation of goalies that came after me.

Before Hextall arrived on the NHL scene and became a goalie I couldn't take my eyes off, I hadn't really played the puck very much at all. When I graduated to midget AAA at the age of 16, I had started shooting those weighted orange pucks in practice to improve my strength. By the time I had made it to St. Hyacinthe and the Quebec Major Junior Hockey League, I had started to get pretty good with my stick, and became more confident and more aggressive. When I was drafted and moved up to the American Hockey League, I toned it down for a while and became more tentative playing against much older players. It took a while to get back to it, but I did, and eventually it became my trademark, something people expected as part of the entire package.

The natural dream for any player is to score a goal, and that certainly also applies to goalies who develop an ability to shoot and pass the puck. Hextall scored two goals over the course of his career, and by my eighth season, I had matched that. The first I scored was the most memorable, a 200-footer against the Montreal Canadiens in a first round playoff game on April 17, 1997. I'd come close before that, but had never hit the net. The score was 4–2 late in the third when the Canadiens pulled their goalie for a sixth attacker. Dave Manson dumped the puck into our zone. I stopped it behind our net, turned around and let it fly, high over the head of everybody on the ice. It landed in the middle of the Montreal net, and I just started jumping up and down with excitement. I had dreamed about doing it for so, so long. I was laughing so hard, mostly out of disbelief. It was the fifth goal ever scored by an NHL goaltender.

The second goal came against the Philadelphia Flyers on February 15, 2000, and it actually turned out to be the game-winning goal. I made a save, and Flyers center Daymond Langkow grabbed the rebound and was slashed, producing a delayed penalty call. Langkow then tried to pass the puck to a teammate but missed, and it slid all the way down into the Flyer net. As the last Devils player to touch the puck, I received credit for the goal, which put us ahead 3–1. When we won 3–2, it was also officially the winner. People kid me that it wasn't really a goal, and my answer is straightforward. When Pavel Bure bagged 59 goals one season for the Florida Panthers, a bunch of those were empty-netters and they counted. In my mind, they all count.

Scoring goals, however, is a rarity. Being active with your stick and helping your team game after game is what matters. Over the years, I've been able to develop three different kinds of wrist shots for different situations. When I want to clear the puck high, for example, my weight is on my back skate, and the puck moves from the heel to the toe of my stick. When I want to make a pass, on the other hand, the weight is on my front foot. The Devils have always encouraged this part of my game, and I have always wanted to be active with my stick, cutting off passes, intercepting shoot-ins to move the puck to my defensemen and being an effective pokechecker when the situation calls for it. Rarely do I try anything particularly bold or aggressive, and when I picked up an assist late in the 2005–06 season, it was my first point in three years.

In general, I have always touched the puck more than the vast majority of NHL goalies, and when I study the games I have played, one of the areas I always focus on is the number of times I play the puck and what I do with it. It has to always be done in the context of helping the team, not showing off. Ed Belfour was always very good at it, very honest about playing the puck. He didn't look to create, he just looked for ways to help his teammates.

—⚉—

Stability and continuity are not necessarily part of every NHL player's life. So one of the greatest blessings I've enjoyed as part of the New Jersey organization has been having the same goaltending coach since 1993, the first year I was in the NHL on a full-time basis.

When Jacques Lemaire took over as head coach of the Devils, he hired Jacques Caron out of a group of candidates, after first coaxing Caron to apply. Caron had played professional hockey at a variety of levels, starting his career in 1959 with the Washington Presidents of the old Eastern Hockey League and ending it with a 19-minute stint for the Binghamton Whalers of the American Hockey League in the 1980–81 season, at the age of 40, when he was already officially retired as a player. That final appearance was an interesting moment that summed up his long, unusual career. Ken Holland, who eventually would become the general manager of the Detroit Red Wings, was Binghamton's No. 1 goalie that season, but in a game against Maine he suffered a knee injury when he was hit by an opposition player behind the net while trying to play the puck. In a strange coincidence, that play enraged one of Holland's defensemen, who chased the enemy player all around the ice. That defenseman was none other than Gilles Lupien, who would one day be my agent.

Caron was the general manager of the Whalers, a team that had gone through five different backups that season. Whoever was supposed to be the backup on this night, however, hadn't even dressed because of a 104° fever. With no other place to turn, Caron was stuck with the option of going in himself even though he hadn't played a game in almost three years. He quickly signed himself to an AHL contract, faxed it to president Jack Butterfield at league headquarters and donned the pads with the Whalers trailing 3–1. They eventually lost the game, but it made for one of those great hockey stories.

Caron's career had taken him to many unusual places and situations. During the 1960s, he played for Eddie Shore and the Springfield Indians of the AHL. He admired Shore as a coach but disagreed with many of his management techniques, and along with teammates like Brian Kilrea he was part of a group of players who went on strike against Shore in the 1966–67 season.

Alan Eagleson, who eventually became head of the NHL Players' Association, interceded on the players' behalf, and eventually Shore backed down. It was a courageous action to take for Caron and his teammates at a time when players in minor pro hockey had very few rights compared to today. With only six NHL clubs and goaltenders such as Johnny Bower and Terry Sawchuk still playing into their forties, a lot of good goaltenders played their entire careers in the minors, at least until expansion in 1967. Caron did eventually play 72 games in the NHL with Los Angeles, St. Louis and Vancouver. By the end of his career, he had played for 12 different teams in five different professional leagues, and it was probably fair to say he'd seen it all.

From the day Caron and I started working together, it was a productive partnership. We spoke to each other in French, which added to the sense of a partnership and a collaborative effort. Anyone who speaks another language from birth will tell you it's always easier to express ideas and emotions in that first language. On a team that has had few French-speaking players, we were always able to speak freely without worrying that others might listen in and misinterpret what we were discussing. Caron had never been a full-time goaltending coach, but he had seen me play in the minors with Utica and he had spent years, after the end of his playing career, talking to the greats of the game—goalies from Jacques Plante to Tony Esposito—and finding out what had made them great. Combined with his own experiences, it gave him a unique perspective on the game, which worked well with my own.

From a technical standpoint, Caron always encouraged me to stay on my feet—to stand up rather than flop to the ice—even more than I did when I first started pro hockey, which worked well with my anti-butterfly beliefs. He saw that in my crouch I was set lower than I had to be, and with my body, arms and legs spread out. He believed my feet needed to be under my body more for balance and position. I started pro using my skates to shuffle across the crease, but he preferred a method that allowed me to push and move, covering more of the net. That's what I try to teach everybody myself now, to grab some ice by digging in your skates to move laterally. If you watch me when I skate, I push to move and lift my skates. My heels are moving, and I don't just shuffle. It's a lot different than the technique a lot of goalies use, and you can trace it back to the early days with Caron.

In practice, he always preached never allowing two goals in a row, even in drills. To him, if you started approaching practice with that philosophy, you would then start having good practices. He loved to say that practice didn't make perfect, perfect practice does. One day, Caron asked me, "Do you really watch the puck?" He told me just to look at the puck all during practice that day, and the lesson was that when you start looking at the puck, you're always in position to stop it. You always have your stick in front of where the puck is, and then your body and head follow. If you're really watching the puck, he says, the instincts and muscle memory of all your hours of practice will do the rest.

The entire time I have known him, it's those little things that have mattered the most and made me a better goaltender. I was receptive, and I think he liked my passion for the game and willingness to learn and try different things. He believed it was up to the individual goaltender, not the coach, and would say things like, "I'm not Jesus Christ. I may have the same initials, but I'm not him." That meant a coach couldn't work miracles. When he played for Shore, Shore made him go to local schools and give goaltending clinics, saying it would help Caron remember what Shore was teaching him. Maybe, in the end, that's exactly how it worked out.

After we won the Cup in 2003, Caron started to cut back his active work schedule with the Devils, partly because his wife,

Marjorie, has been ill for years with lupus. By the 2005–06 season, his contract called for him to actually be with the team only 12 weeks per year. Still, we continue to talk almost every day. I still need him, and need that frequent conversation and those reminders. Usually, we don't talk about what I'm doing wrong, but instead about what I'm doing right. We talk about the team's defense, and where I feel my game's at. He still reminds me to make sure I'm watching the puck. There isn't much he can teach me anymore, but there are many ways he can help me. After so many years of playing the position, I know what I do well and what I don't do well. But it always helps to have his eyes and his ears.

Even though his work schedule was reduced, the 2005–06 season was hard on Caron. His wife was struggling with her health, and as a close friend of Larry Robinson, he felt Robinson's pain when the team played poorly in the early part of the season. Making matters worse was the fact that, in the opening weeks, I wasn't getting the results and stats to which he and I had grown accustomed. On December 7, I allowed three goals on four shots in a 4–1 home ice loss to Calgary, and for the first time in a long time those in attendance, less than 14,000 customers, started booing me. Four days earlier when I had stopped all three Minnesota shooters in a 3–2 shootout victory, the same people had been cheering wildly. I didn't like the boos, and I didn't think it was fair, but many people don't know any more about the game than winning or losing, and they don't like losing. I've built myself up to be a certain goalie, and when I don't meet that, I expect people to be disappointed.

Wayne Gretzky, in his role as executive director of Team Canada for the 2006 Winter Olympics, had been in attendance at the game, looking at various Olympic candidates during a brief tour of a few cities. The next day at practice, Caron mentioned it in our conversation, and said he couldn't believe I'd played so poorly with Gretzky in the building. Maybe I took it the wrong way, but I barked back. "I don't play for Gretzky. He watches me on TV all the time and knows what I can do. I play for the Devils!" When Robinson quit as head coach eight days later and mentioned Caron in his farewell speech, some people thought he was going to leave as well or that something was wrong between him and me. It wasn't true. We had disagreed, and perhaps argued, but we were as close as ever. He has always supported me, and was one of the reasons I became the NHL goalie that I did. He always supported me with different head coaches and when I was negotiating new contracts. When I was preparing for the 2004 World Cup, he came to my cottage north of Montreal in August and stayed for a week to help me prepare after being away from competition since the NHL season had ended in April. He's all I've ever known as a pro, and I wouldn't have it any other way.

He often says, "I only have a daughter. Marty's my son," which shows the relationship we've built. Together, we have won the Calder, Vezina and Jennings trophies, as well as three Stanley Cups. Teammates call him my "dad," others just call him "Coot." I've tried to show my appreciation along the way with gifts. After the Devils won the Cup for the first time in 1995, I knew he was interested in a used Cadillac at a local car lot. So I went and made a deal with the owner, and when he showed up to buy the car, it was already paid for. When I won a gold medal with Team Canada at the 2002 Winter Olympics in Salt Lake City, Utah, it was the first time since I had turned pro that I had won anything of significance without him by my side. As well as medals, we received rings for winning the gold, and I had an identical one made for him. He was touched by that, I think. Even though he wasn't part of Team Canada, he was part of me.

—∿—

To see a goalie pulled from a hockey game, at least from the stands or from the living room watching on television, is to see a goalie being singled out, with all eyes on him as he skates slowly to the bench and his replacement skates into the crease. It is one of the challenges of playing the position. If another player is having a bad night, you just don't see him out on the ice anymore. He sits on the bench. But unless it happens between periods, everybody in the building watches as the coach signals to the backup to get his mask on, and gestures to the goalie to come to the bench.

I'm one of the few who knows what it's like to get pulled in a Stanley Cup final game. That happened in front of a roaring, approving crowd at the Arrowhead Pond in Anaheim in Game 6 of the 2003 final, but it was very different than what people at home would have perceived. Moments before I left the net, I had made eye contact with Pat Burns, who was our head coach at the time, and let him know that it was okay to give me the hook. With 11 minutes left, we were losing 5–2 and he pulled me and let Corey Schwab play the final part of the game. I was disappointed, sure, because we had a chance to win the Cup that night. But I wasn't upset or angry because I knew we had a long flight home to Jersey for Game 7, and I was happy that Schwab had a chance to play. By that point in my career, most of the time I would pull myself rather than have the coach give me the yank.

That wasn't quite the case earlier in my career, of course, and it was often a frustrating, irritating thing. Of all the coaches I had, Lemaire was the one who pulled me most frequently, and left me the most exasperated. Of course, I was a young goalie at the time, but it was tough to take at times when he would pull me, for example, when we were losing 2–1 or 1–0. At a neutral site game in Halifax once against the Rangers, we were down 2–1 after two periods and he pulled me in favor of Chris Terreri.

Another time, we were playing Tampa Bay at home and I got scored on once in the first period. Two minutes before going back out for the second, Lemaire walked past and didn't even look at me as he said to Terreri, "You're in for the second." He didn't say a word to me. The next day, we traveled to Ottawa for a game, and at the morning workout on the day of the game he skated over and said, "Do you know why I pulled you?" I told him I had no idea. He said that between periods of the Tampa game he was told that I had shot a puck at one of my teammates, Valery Zelepukin, in the pre-game skate that day, which was true. Zelepukin was a good guy, but he had a bad eye and couldn't see that well. He had shot one puck over my head, had hit me once in the mask and then shot a hard one off my shoulder. So I got angry and shot the puck at him. Bill Guerin started yapping at me and cursed at me, but I was angry with my own teammate for shooting like that on me in a morning skate. Lemaire wasn't even on the ice when it happened, but he found out and pulled me in the Tampa game as a result.

On another occasion, we had traveled to Montreal for a game, and at breakfast on the day of the game Caron told me the pre-game practice was optional and asked if I planned to go. I was tired, so I told him I wasn't going to go. No problem, he said, and I went back to bed for a few hours. When I arrived at the Forum for the game, I found out I wasn't playing and Mike Dunham was getting ready to face the Habs. Apparently, because the game was in my hometown, Lemaire figured I had gone out the night before and partied too hard, and so I was tired. As punishment, he didn't play me. It was the only time after I became a full-time NHL goalie that I didn't play a game in Montreal. As well, since breaking in, I had played every game against the Rangers that was on our schedule, except for the times I was injured. I was pulled six times in games against them, however, every time by Lemaire. I came to understand that if I was taken out, it wasn't necessarily my fault or because I was playing badly. Sometimes it was about strategy, sometimes it was about getting a rest for the next game. As a goalie, it's hard not to take it as criticism, but you have to learn to do that.

After all, it wasn't as though I ever had reason to be uncertain about my position with the team, or to lose my confidence. From the 1993–94 season through the 2005–06 season, I started 85 per cent of New Jersey's regular season games, including playing 70 games or more in a season nine times. By the end of the '06 play-offs, I had started an NHL record 142 consecutive playoff games, all for the Devils. I always felt that the organization wanted me to be in net for as many games as possible. The only time I really ever felt a challenge was from Dunham for the two seasons he was with the Devils, the 1996–97 season and the '97–98 season, and when I reflect back upon it I think it was as much the creation of the media as a real challenge. I think people wanted to see me challenged, and Lemaire helped create the perception that Dunham was closing the gap by pulling me so often. In the 1996–97 season, I played in 67 games, but if you look at my minutes played you'll see I was about nine periods short of actually playing 67 full games. Dunham, on the other hand, played in 26 games, but his minutes played added up to only about 17 full games. Part of the issue was that the team needed to make sure he had 25 or more appearances that season to avoid losing him to free agency under the terms of the existing collective bargaining agreement. It was a strange season in that way, but after that, I never played fewer than 70 games in a season again. Dunham was a very talented goalie, but he kept getting hurt. He would get hurt just practicing, which made it difficult for him to really try to grab the No. 1 job.

Any goalie's confidence is built around understanding his game, experience and being able to rebound when things don't go well. I'm no exception, and a big part of that is understanding what is a bad goal and what isn't. To me, a bad goal is when the puck is in the corner, it's shot towards the net, hits you and bounces in. I believe that's a goal I can't let happen. Or a long shot on which you have a clear view. Wraparounds can be very difficult, but aren't necessarily a bad goal. Any time a player creates something, you have to give that player some credit if it results in a goal. When there is a crowd of players around you, people don't understand how difficult it can be. The puck is going 100 miles per hour, there are 200-pound players blocking your vision and, quite frankly, a lot of the time you don't find the puck—it finds you. Sometimes, players are bumping into you, jostling your stick or even knocking you down. At different times in my career, the rules for contacting goalies have varied widely. At one point, if a player was caught with even a toe in the crease, it was no goal. At other times, a great deal of contact has been allowed, even to the point that three or four players have their skates in the crease. Goalies have to just deal with the changing conditions.

It's often assumed that a "five hole" goal—one that goes between the goalie's legs—is a bad goal that should be stopped. In truth, it's one of the hardest shots to stop if you understand how goalies position themselves. Simply put, unless you stand straight and force your legs together, there's going to be a hole there whenever a goaltender moves into a crouch position. If a shooter hits the spot, it's going to go in. A goalie simply can't control that, and if you can take control away from a goalie, that's how you get to him and shake his confidence.

My mindset has always been to take responsibility for my game and my teammates, but at the same time I have to put my part of the game in perspective. I've always found it interesting that fans will blame a goalie for a certain goal, but if a shooter fans on an open net, that's not viewed as a similarly serious error. That's how I overcome bad goals. I realize I can't put it all on my shoulders. If possible, I want to put myself in a position where I can make the save that makes the difference, because I'm not going to stop them all. The worst thing I can ever do is start doubting myself, or stop believing in what I'm doing. Even in the worst circumstances, I try not to do that.

—⁂—

There's a method I have developed for getting ready to play, and I don't like to deviate from it very much. Before any game, it starts with sitting down and viewing a DVD of the last game I played against the team I'm facing that night. I used to watch it at the arena, but now I usually watch it at home or at the team hotel before I go to the rink. The DVD will show me every shot, every save, every goal and every time I handled the puck. I analyze myself, my positioning, my mistakes and my decision-making, and I also look at my defensemen, their tendencies, mistakes that were made and ways to improve our performance together. For example, I never want my defensemen in the blue paint with me. I want our guys, as much as they can, to stay on their feet and buy time rather than make desperate, risky plays. When we get a new player, there's usually an adjustment. It was difficult, for example, for a player like Richard Matvichuk when he came to the Devils because he was used to blocking shots in Dallas in a variety of ways. He learned under one of the game's best shot blockers, Craig Ludwig, and naturally he wanted to play the same way when he came to New Jersey. But we don't do that. We don't sprawl and throw our bodies around. We buy time.

My routine also includes the pre-game meal, and my favorite is spaghetti with tomato sauce, sometimes with grilled chicken. My preference is to arrive at 5 o'clock for a 7:30 game, although the frustrating traffic patterns of northern New Jersey sometimes make that difficult. I play with a new stick every game, so the first thing I do at the rink is get my sticks ready. I'll use one for warmup, one to play and have three new ones on the bench. Some of the sticks I may use later for practice. I mark the ones I use in games on the knob with the date and the opponent, so if I give them away to friends, family or charity, that information is there on the stick. I give away more than a hundred sticks every season. My teammates always want them, but I often laugh when I see them everywhere for sale. In my first year, I used Sherwood sticks, but since then I have used CCM or Heaton. I haven't changed my stick pattern in a decade.

Dressed in shorts, a T-shirt and flipflops, I like to sit on the couch and hang out with my teammates, just shooting the breeze and talking about just about anything until the team meeting with the coaches 90 minutes before game time. That meeting is usually short and to the point, just going over some basic information about our opponent. When that's over, I'm the first one on the massage table. We've had different people over the years, but my favorite was Tom Plasko, who joined the Devils for the '05–06 season. While he works, he talks to you positively, makes sure you feel loose. I first used him with the 2004 World Cup when I was struggling with a stress hernia problem. After that tournament, I felt better than I had in years. He releases the muscles, cracks my back, and does a little work on my hamstring or shoulder, whatever might be bothering me. He knows exactly what needs to be done to my stomach and abdominal muscles, and the whole treatment takes about five minutes. After that, I go into the trainer's room, talk to the trainer, make sure my teammates have been able to organize the tickets they need for that game and little things like that. After that, I stretch for 10 minutes, nothing too fancy or elaborate, just enough to add to what has already been accomplished with the massage.

Now it's time to sit in my stall and focus on the game. I like to visualize the possibilities, and I look at the opposition's lineup to find the players I can see easily in my head. I don't keep a little black book on shooters. It's all in my head. I know from experience which way everybody shoots, their tendencies and what they like to do. Still, there are so many new guys all the time in a 30-team league, there are going to be unfamiliar players in many games. I start to get dressed, and I do everything left to right, more by habit than superstition. In every NHL dressing room, there is a pre-game clock that starts counting down from 40 minutes, and when it's down to zero that's the end of the 16-minute warmup. So at 35, I get dressed to the waist, and at 23 minutes I put on my shoulder pads and jersey. At 18 minutes and counting, I put on my gloves and helmet. The rule is, teams can't go on the ice until 16 minutes are left on the clock. If we're playing at home, I wait until 16:20 because I know that will have me stepping on the ice at exactly the 16-minute mark.

For the pre-game warmup itself, my routine changes, although I always like to take one shot on net, top shelf, before I skate off. That's the part of the evening when, particularly in New Jersey, fans get down close to the ice surface to get a look at their favorite NHL players. Sometimes it can be a bit dangerous for them. Before a game against Toronto in the 2005–06 season, one of my teammates took a slapshot from well out and the puck hit my stick, then bounced high in the air over the protective netting behind the goals. I watched it, and like a long, high punt it plummeted and hit an older lady right in the face. She went down hard, with her husband at her side. I knew it wasn't my fault, but it really left me feeling terrible. I skated to the bench and asked our trainer to send my stick to her and signed it. When I came back on the ice for the game, I looked for her and there she was, back up and ready to watch the game. She waved to me with the stick I had sent her. She was okay, and I sure felt a lot better. That kind of interaction with the fans is fun for me and great for them. One of the things I love to do is wink at people in the crowd during breaks in the game. It makes their day, and that connection with the fans is something I need to get out of the game.

After the warmup, I go into the dressing room, take my mask and gloves off, and drink three-quarters of a can of Sprite. That's my drink. Gatorade hurts my stomach, and water just doesn't give me enough of a lift. I'll drink three cans of Sprite a night; one before the game, and one during each of the intermissions.

The clock in the dressing room then resets, with the countdown beginning at 15 minutes. At eight minutes, I put my body armor and jersey back on. At three minutes, I get fully dressed and ready to lead the team out onto the ice, something I've always done when I'm playing. I'm prepared and ready to play.

To be able to play goal is to be able to adjust, and sometimes you do that by stealing bits and pieces from other goalies. When I was young, I learned to lay the shaft, or "paddle," of my stick on the ice from Felix Potvin. In later years, I learned from Dominik Hasek the value of sometimes dropping your stick altogether in a desperate situation if you have to get across the net quickly.

For the 2005–06 season, being adaptable took on a whole new meaning, starting with getting used to shootouts to decide games. The format was set at three shooters for each team, but there were frequent changes in preparing for the shootout. At first they wanted to clean the middle of the ice with Zambonis, reasonable enough after 25 straight minutes of play. Then they went to using workers with shovels to scrape the crease and goal area. Then they went back to Zambonis. After the Olympics, they started measuring sticks for illegal curves, and I remember in one of the first games after Turin we went to a shootout against Philadelphia, and at the last moment before he was to shoot I saw Petr Nedved grab a stick from one of his teammates. Guess he didn't want to get caught. But he didn't score, either. In all, we were involved in 13 shootouts, and I was the goalie for 11 of them, winning eight times. I don't like the shootout, mostly because it takes the team concept out of the game. But I understand that it's good for the game and the fans, and it happens to be something that plays to my strengths.

I had to make another major adjustment, with the new restrictions for goaltenders playing the puck. These were instituted along with the shootout. Previously, the only restriction was that goalies couldn't skate across center with the puck. But for the 2005–06 season, two lines were drawn in the ice from the goalline back to the boards on an angle, creating a trapezoid in which goalies were permitted to play the puck with their stick. Anything on the other side of the goal line in the offensive zone was still okay, but the corners of the rink were now a no man's land for netminders. The idea was to create more opportunities for attacking teams to forecheck and gain possession in the offensive zone without a goalie getting to the puck first and clearing it to safety. If a goalie violated this rule, it was a two-minute penalty. I'm sure I took it personally, but I really felt the rule was directly aimed at me, as no goalie had handled the puck as frequently and consistently as I had over the previous decade. It had become a very important part of our team's game, to the point that our defensemen didn't even skate back to retrieve the puck on some occasions, but simply made themselves available for a pass. Most hockey people believed the Devils were affected by this rule more than any other NHL club.

I was only caught for a penalty once in the season, during a game against Ottawa, but the trapezoid really spooked me for a while and shut down a great deal of my ability to use my stick to help my team. It became so much easier for opposing teams to keep the puck away from me. With those lines in place, it's going to be more difficult for any goalie to score again because it will have to happen only when the puck can be controlled right in front of the net, and in those instances the other team's forwards are usually on you too quick to make a play. But it's not over. I'll score at least one more goal before I retire.

—◊◊◊—

As well as instituting new rules, the NHL decided to crack down on goaltending equipment before the '05–06 season, to essentially "shrink" the size of the goalies to help increase scoring. For some netminders, this was a significant problem, for some had gone to larger pads, enormous catching gloves and bulky body armor that had gone far beyond the need for protection. But it wasn't a problem for me. I didn't have to change my equipment at all. Not my gloves, or my pads or my body armor. Even under the new regulations, it was all still legal.

For years, I have worn CCM equipment. By 2006 it almost seemed old-fashioned, and certainly by modern standards it was among the heaviest any NHL goaltender wore. You couldn't find my gear in a store because I hadn't changed technology in 10 years. With the increasing popularity of the butterfly style, pads in particular had evolved to fit the needs of goalies who spent more of their time down on the knees. For example, manufacturers developed "boards," extra flaps on the pads that helped cover the five-hole area more effectively when a goalie was in the butterfly. But the same stuff had always worked for me.

As a rule, I have usually used three pairs of pads per season, and five pairs of gloves. When it starts feeling as though the pads are breaking down, I start practicing with new ones until I feel comfortable making a switch. I still have the three sets of pads I used to win the Cup in 1995, 2000 and 2003, and the '95 and '00 sets sit atop a shelf in my office at home. I have a variety of memorabilia, including my four Team Canada masks, dozens of commemorative pucks, baseballs signed by Manny Ramirez, David Ortiz and Derek Jeter and a basketball signed by Michael Jordan. I also have pictures taken with two U.S. presidents, Bill Clinton and George Bush, and another with Wayne Gretzky after we won Olympic gold in Salt Lake City. There are three mini-Stanley Cups and various medals and diplomas from international hockey. But my most prized possession—and you may find this strange—is a golf ball. It's the one I used in 2001 to make a hole in one from 150 yards out with a pitching wedge at the Essex Falls country club.

Getting the pads the way I like them has always been easy. But when CCM closed its plant in Windsor and moved the operation to Quebec, they had to start making equipment from scratch and soon found they couldn't get the pattern of my catching glove quite right. I took a dozen of my old gloves to the manufacturer so they could try to just copy them, and I still didn't like what they were able to make. It's crucial to me because when I move my hands to play the puck, I need to have just the right feel of my catching mitt on the bottom part of my stick. It was a strange problem that the people at CCM worked diligently to fix, but it almost cost me a chance to play in the gold medal game at the 2004 World Cup. The glove I was using in that tournament was 18 months old, and when I tried to stop a shot in the quarterfinals I suffered a hand and wrist injury that was initially feared to be a fracture. Luongo had to play the semifinal game against the Czech Republic, and while I played and won the final against Finland, you'll notice in any of the celebratory pictures that my hand was heavily bandaged.

—⚓—

As the NHL and the NHL Players' Association emerged from the lockout that erased the entire 2004–05 season, the new collective bargaining agreement called for the formation of a new competition committee, with representatives from ownership, players and management. In the fall of '05 I was asked to be the sole goaltender on the committee, which already included Rob Blake of the Los Angeles Kings, Brendan Shanahan of Detroit, Trevor Linden of the Vancouver Canucks and Calgary's Jarome Iginla. Also on the committee were four general managers: Kevin Lowe of Edmonton, Don Waddell of Atlanta, David Poile of Nashville and Bob Gainey of the Montreal Canadiens. Ed Snider, the longtime chairman of the Philadelphia Flyers, represented the league's 30 owners. It was a nice compliment to be included on the committee, to be the first goaltender. That meant they saw me as having something to add, and I believed this was something I could do to help the other players.

Unfortunately, I didn't have much input during my first season on the committee. The only formal "meeting" we had was during a conference call in December when I had only 40 minutes before I had to catch a flight to Columbus. We went through the rule changes and some of the concerns that had been raised. They asked me about the new rules restricting the ability of goalies to play the puck, as well as complaints that the practice of "crashing the crease" was on the increase. Just before the conference call, Vancouver goalie Dan Cloutier had suffered a season-ending knee injury after a collision with Rob Niedermayer of the Anaheim Mighty Ducks. I told them that I felt that was a growing problem. I also said that when I played the puck, I felt it would be fair if I was able to skate with the puck in the corner and outside of the trapezoid as long as I first gained control of the puck behind the net. My plan going in was that I would organize a conference call once a year with all the league's goalies, and then take their ideas and recommendations to the competition committee. Given that players had never had input before, it seemed to be the start of something positive. I looked forward to more meetings with the committee in July 2006 and the chance to make my thoughts on our game known.

—ᴖᴖ—

When my career is over, I'll have had the opportunity to approach, and possibly break, some of the greatest goaltending records in the history of the game. In fact, by the end of my 13th season, I already had a few records to my name, including the most consecutive playoff starts by an NHL goalie and the most consecutive seasons with 30 or more victories.

But there's one record I really want, that I would really treasure, and that's the most regular season victories by a goaltender, a mark set by Patrick Roy with 551 victories over 19 outstanding seasons. Why is it so special? I just believe winning is what it's all about. Winning is the ultimate. You win and everybody's happy. You don't win, and the game's not much fun. All players want to be associated with success, and that's why that is the record I would most like to break.

The other significant record would be Terry Sawchuk's all-time record of 103 career shutouts during regular season play. By the end of the 2005–06 season, at the age of 34, I had 80 shutouts in the regular season. But with the NHL switching from the low-scoring hockey of the late 1990s to a more offensive style, that will be an extremely difficult record to break. For years, it was thought of as virtually unapproachable. Sawchuk died in 1970, two years before I was born. To chase that record will be like chasing a ghost, something a seven-year-old boy never considered many years ago when asked by his hockey coach if he'd like to be a goalie.

The Toughest Shooters

(and how many times they beat me)

JOE SAKIC

28 games, 14 goals*

Sakic has the quickest wrist shot you're ever going to see. He plays with a stick that has a lot of flex in it, which makes it hard to read: the puck just seems to fly off his stick. He's not a physical player, and he's never been a player you can hit easily or for whom you can make life miserable. He darts, and finds openings. He was one of the few players Scott Stevens couldn't get to. In Game 7 of the 2001 Stanley Cup final, after scoring a number of goals low on the blocker side, he beat me with a wrist shot high to the glove side. Pretty important game to throw me a changeup.

---

*Source: Elias Sports Bureau. Statistics combine regular season and playoffs and are current as of conclusion of 2005–06 season.

chapter 4
Father to Son

A DISTANCE CAN BE MEASURED IN MILES. Or, sometimes, it can be better measured in years.

For three generations of Brodeur goalkeepers, the distance from the Italian ski resort of Cortina d'Ampezzo, high in the Dolomite mountain range, to the industrial city of Turin measures precisely 50 years.

It was in Cortina at the 1956 Winter Olympics that my father, Denis, won a bronze medal in men's hockey representing Canada, and it was to Turin a half century later that I traveled with my three sons, two of them young goalies, to try to duplicate my father's feat. Actually, the plan was to do even better, to capture a gold medal for Canada at the 2006 Olympics.

From the moment NHL players stepped back onto the ice to begin training for the 2005–06 season, the looming presence of the '06 Olympics meant it was going to be a very different season. The lockout was over, but bad feelings were left on both sides. Inside the players' union, in some ways the fight was just starting with a messy disagreement over the leadership of the new executive director, Ted Saskin. A new economic structure was in place for the league and, quite frankly, there was a lot of confusion throughout management and among players as to how the new system was to work and what the rules were. Players had taken a 24 per cent cut in pay and there was going to be an escrow tax through which thousands of dollars would be taken off our pay checks every week to make sure the players' take of league revenues did not exceed the agreed-upon 54 per cent. The concept of a salary cap was now part of our daily conversation.

Another part of the new collective bargaining agreement was that the NHL and the NHL Players' Association agreed to participate in both the 2006 Winter Olympics in Turin, Italy, and the 2010 Olympics in Vancouver. Going into Turin, Canada was the reigning Olympic champion, having beaten the United States to win gold in Salt Lake City in 2002. For Canada, that victory ended a 50-year drought without winning the Olympic tournament. Given that the Americans had won twice in the interim, at Squaw Valley in 1960 and, of course, Lake Placid in 1980, the Canadian victory was a long, long time coming.

Starting with the 1972 Summit Series, it had become tradition in Canada that for every major tournament the selection of the players who would play for Canada generated an extraordinary amount of speculation and controversy, more than in any other major hockey-playing country. In '72, the first time Canada's top professionals had played in a major international event, top players such as Bobby Hull were excluded from consideration for the team because they had jumped to the new World Hockey Association. Others, like high-scoring New York Rangers winger Vic Hadfield, chafed at not being given enough opportunities to play, and left the team partway through the competition. Player selection had been enormously controversial, and it would continue to be that way for other major international hockey events in the coming years. Being rich in players was sometimes a burden for Team Canada organizers to bear.

The run-up to the 2006 Games was really no different. But for me it came with added emphasis. It was the opportunity to

The earliest years. At this point, closing the five-hole was the least of young Martin's worries.

Home street advantage. Shutting the door in a road hockey game on Mauriac Street.

A flair for the dramatic. Martin has always caught with his left hand. Here, the catching glove is on his right hand, the result of inheriting equipment from his dad, who also played the position, but caught with the opposite hand.

A quarter-century later. Still flexible at the 2006 Turin Olympics.

Small enough to fit under big brother Claude's legs. Thirteen years separate the brothers, two of the five Brodeur children.

By winning the 1955 Allen Cup, the Kitchener-Waterloo Dutchmen also won the right to represent Canada at the 1956 Winter Olympics in Cortina d'Ampezzo, Italy. With Denis Brodeur (bottom left) sharing the goaltending duties, the "Dutchies" captured the bronze.

When your dad is the team's official photographer, you get a little special access. A young Martin (in the foreground with No. 30 on his sleeve) hovers near Chris Nilan and Mats Naslund at a Montreal Canadiens' morning skate.

A talented family. Oldest brother, Claude, pitched in the Montreal Expos chain.

Denis Jr., meanwhile, had his eye on BMX stunt riding.

A family's Olympic legacy. Martin compares his 2002 gold with Denis' 1956 bronze.

Displaying his early butterfly technique with the St. Hyacinthe Laser of the Quebec junior league. No. 20 in white is a future NHL opponent, Martin Lapointe.

At Vladislav Tretiak's goaltending school, where Brodeur (right) was first a student and later an instructor. Martin admired the Russian goalie's flexible approach to different techniques, rather than being married to only the butterfly.

try to complete my family's Olympic legacy, which had begun 50 years earlier in Cortina.

For my dad, the Olympics defined his life in sports. Growing up, I didn't have the usual backdrop of the NHL—it was always the Olympics. In the 1956 Olympics, my dad had played against a member of the Christian family of Warroad, Minnesota, and for years after, right up until Dave Christian represented the United States at Lake Placid, that family was typical of many American hockey families in that the Olympics was the primary objective. But most Canadian kids didn't get that. For them, the pinnacle of hockey was the NHL, the highest level to which a player could climb. So the Brodeur household of St. Léonard, Quebec, was a bit of an exception. We saw the Olympics as something special, something that meant a lot to my father. His Olympic medal was always there in the house, and as the years passed until I finally had the chance to play in the Olympics myself, it gradually became more and more significant to me. To have a father and son play in the Olympics in the same country, 50 years apart, was an amazing opportunity for our family. The odds are you'll never have a father-son combination playing goal in the Olympics again, let alone for the same country, in the same country, a half-century later.

Our Olympic stories were similar, but not exactly the same. Cortina was, and is, a very different place from Turin, which is a large, historic city with an industrial past. Turin has long been home to the giant Fiat car company and the powerful Juventus of European soccer fame. Cortina, on the other hand, is a small town northeast of Turin, a winter playground that is actually closer to Venice than to Turin. For decades, it has been one of Europe's most popular ski destinations, 1,224 meters above sea level in the southern Alps, so famous that it was featured in the original 1964 film version of *The Pink Panther*, starring Peter

Sellers. Overlooking the town are the towering Dolomite peaks of Lagazuoi, Tofana, Forcella Staunies and Faloria, which give it a natural beauty that gritty, hardworking Turin does not have. Cortina's hockey history lives in the presence of the Olympic Ice Stadium, which was built to host hockey, figure skating and the opening and closing ceremonies of the 7th Winter Olympics. It's still there today, one of only two artificial rinks in the town, but it has been renovated, with a roof installed after decades of being an open-air facility. An Italian Serie-A club team, SG Cortina, calls the arena home these days. Two players from the Cortina team were part of the Italian national squad that competed at the 2006 Games, and NHLer Matt Cullen starred for Cortina during the NHL lockout.

Back in 1956, it had been only 11 years since the American army had marched into Cortina and other Italian towns and cities, as the country's participation in the Second World War concluded. In fact, Cortina was originally supposed to host the 1944 Olympics, but Italy was occupied by Germany at the time and the Games were cancelled. Cortina had been used mainly as a hospital town by Italy and Germany during the final years of the war. In 1949, however, the Olympics were again awarded to Cortina, and buildings that had been hospitals and military head-quarters for three different armies were converted into hotels in anticipation of the event, which was to involve 32 nations and 923 athletes. For Turin 50 years later, there would be 87 countries involved and 2,500 athletes, and today most believe the time of small towns such as Cortina hosting the Olympics is gone. In 2010, Vancouver will be the largest city ever to host the Winter Olympics.

So Cortina, in terms of time and place and history, was certainly a different stage than Turin. But even back in '56, the pressure on Canada to win the men's hockey competition—there would be no women's hockey at the Olympics for another 42 years—was as intense as it is today. In Cortina, it was simply expected that Canada would win hockey gold again, just as Brazil is expected to win soccer's World Cup every four years and the United States were heavily favored to capture the first World Baseball Classic when it was played in the spring of 2006.

In '56, Canada was the defending Olympic hockey champion, with the Edmonton Mercurys club team having won gold four years earlier in Oslo, Norway. The Olympics were more than 40 years away from having NHL players participate, and the teams that had won for Canada before the Mercurys were club squads like the RCAF Flyers (1948), The Winnipegs (1932), the University of Toronto (1928) and the Toronto Granites (1924). Using these club teams, Canada had won every Winter Olympics tournament except in 1936 when Great Britain took the gold, and that was using mostly Canadian military personnel stationed overseas.

Other than that British team, Canada had always won. So in Cortina, there was the expectation that my dad, then 25 years old (the same age I was at my first Olympics in 1998), and his team, the Kitchener-Waterloo Dutchmen, who had qualified to represent Canada by winning the 1955 Allan Cup, would continue the tradition. But there was an ominous new Olympic hockey presence on the scene for the first time in Cortina: the Soviet Union. The Soviets had stunned the hockey world two years earlier by winning the world championships on their first try, defeating the Toronto East York Lyndhursts en route to the title. The next year, the Penticton V's, representing Canada, avenged that defeat at the worlds with a resounding 5–0 win, but it had become clear the Soviets were the greatest threat to Canada's dominance in international hockey. Cortina was to be the first Olympics broadcast on television, although in Italy only, and big-name Canadian sportswriters like Milt Dunnell, Red Fisher, Dink Carroll, Baz O'Meara and Andy O'Brien had been sent to cover the hockey tournament and carefully measure the shift in the tectonic plates of global hockey.

—⁓—

My dad was born in the east end of Montreal in 1930, the only child of René and Simone Brodeur. His father did a little bit of everything, from being a butcher to a barber, and even owned a couple of restaurants that had pool tables. My father learned how to play pool on the top of an empty Coca-Cola box and didn't start playing organized hockey as we know it today until he was 16 years old.

He started out as a forward, but by his late teens had started to play goal for a team sponsored by a local church, St. Victor. His team did well, getting to the Montreal juvenile final, and after that game Georges Mantha, who had played in the NHL for 13 seasons along with his brother, Sylvio, approached my father and asked if he wanted to play Junior B hockey in Champêtre, just north of Montreal. He did, and the next season, his third as a goalie, he attended a junior A game at the Montreal Forum with his father. Jean Béliveau scored three goals that night for Victoriaville. That was the same night, after they had gone home, that my father received a call from the Victoriaville coach inviting him to join their team. He did, and he had to leave that night, arriving in Victoriaville at about 3 a.m. It was then immediately on to Quebec City to play the Citadels, who had won 16 straight games with a young goaltender named Jacques Plante. With my dad in goal, Victoriaville won the game 4–2, and he stayed with the team.

The next summer, he played baseball as a shortstop with Béliveau, a first baseman. While hockey was his first love, baseball was a close second, and his pursuit of the game would take him all over North America to play, including North and South Dakota, where he played against future major league star Frank Howard and was once traded from Williston, North Dakota, to Huron, South Dakota, for second baseman Jerry Adair, who went on to a solid big-league career.

A small goalie at 5-foot-5, 160 pounds, my dad never did get the big break to play in the NHL. In those days of the Original Six, with NHL teams carrying only one goalie apiece, there were only six big-league jobs. At one point, the New York Rovers, an affiliate of the Rangers, were looking for an emergency goalie after their starter had been injured, and they called to ask Victoriaville about my dad. That night, however, he had decided to go to a movie with friends and couldn't be found, so instead the Rovers called the Verdun Cyclones and arranged for their young goaltender, Lorne (Gump) Worsley, to be the fill-in. Worsley had a lot of ups and downs in the following years before he made it big and became one of the game's greatest and most colorful netminders, but that call from the Rovers was the start for him, the break my dad never did get.

Over the years, my dad moved around to pursue hockey opportunities in the winter, acquiring 113 stitches in his face playing mostly without a mask for teams in Saint John, New Brunswick, and Charlottetown, Prince Edward Island, moving back to Jonquière of the Quebec senior league, and then briefly to a team in Rivière-du-Loup, where he first met my mother, Mireille. The next year, he turned down an offer to play in Fort Wayne, Indiana, and instead decided to play with Windsor in the Ontario senior league. Soon after, that team traded him to the Kitchener-Waterloo Dutchmen during the 1954–55 season, a team coached by Bobby Bauer, a famous player in his own right from his days with the Boston Bruins on the famous Kraut Line with Milt Schmidt and Woody Dumart. That spring, with my dad as the starting goalie, the Flying Dutchmen won the Allan Cup over the Fort William Beavers and the right to represent Canada at the Olympics the following year.

—⚉—

For the '56 Games, the Dutchmen flew to Innsbruck, then drove to Cortina in a blinding snowstorm. The Soviets had already been there for two weeks getting acclimatized to the altitude, an indication of how serious they were about being successful at their first Winter Games. The captain of the Soviet team was Vsevolod Bobrov, who would later be the Soviet coach against Canada in the famous '72 Summit Series. In the Cortina opening ceremonies, a skater carrying the Olympic flame tripped and fell over a microphone cord, but managed not to drop the precious torch. The Dutchmen were there to watch, a very different situation than Nagano, Salt Lake City and Turin, when NHL players, including me, arrived after the opening ceremonies had already taken place because of our professional commitments. For Cortina, a young movie star named Sophia Loren was there, and the big Italian hero was a local bobsledder named Eugenio Monti.

Wearing thick, white wool jerseys for the outdoor competition with green trim and an emblem featuring a green Maple Leaf and a red Olympic crest, the Dutchmen were placed in a preliminary pool with Italy, Austria and West Germany. The Dutchies started the tournament with a 4–0 victory over the West Germans with my dad in goal, then beat the weak Austrians 23–0 with backup goalie Keith Woodall. Canada beat the Italians 3–1 with my dad back in net, and he was in goal again for a 6–3 victory over Czechoslovakia. At 4–0, the Dutchmen looked solid heading into a game with the United States, which had hastily organized a team of mostly college students coached by Johnny Mariucci, one of the first Americans to play in the NHL.

It turned out to be one of the biggest upsets in Olympic hockey, although the Americans had actually tied Canada at the Olympics four years earlier in Norway. The game was played in a snowstorm, with players wearing toques—this was long before helmets became common. The Americans received dazzling performances from two players in a stunning 4–1 victory. Forward Johnny Mayasich scored three goals, and goalie Willard (Wee Willie) Ikola, an Air Force navigator, stopped 39 of 40 Canadian shots. It was only the second loss ever for Canada at the Olympics, with the previous defeat a 2–1 loss for the Port Arthur Bearcats to Great Britain at the '36 Games. Canadians back home took the loss hard, and my dad, having allowed a flukey goal off a shot he lost in the snow and lights at the outdoor rink, was replaced by Woodall for the next game. He never did regain his No. 1 status and the confidence of Bauer.

After easy wins over the West Germans again and then Sweden, it was time to face the Soviets, with CBC radio broadcasting the game with the immortal Foster Hewitt doing the play-by-play back to Canada. The anticipation was enormous, given the results of the previous two world championships, but the Dutchmen faced the extra pressure of having to win by three goals or more to still have a shot at the gold. "The Dutchies Can Do It in Russia Showdown," read the headline in the *Toronto Telegram* on February 4, 1956, the day of the big game. In front of a packed crowd of 12,700 at the ice stadium, and with my father watching from the bench as Woodall played, Canada outshot the Soviets 23–11. But with Soviet goalie Nikolai Puchkov putting on a show, the Soviets produced a 2–0 victory. Combined with the Americans' victory over Czechoslovakia, the loss dropped the Dutchmen to third and the bronze medal.

After the game, everyone was crying in the Canadian dressing room. They knew what the defeat meant. My father, interestingly, had worn a converted first baseman's glove throughout the tournament, and following the Soviet win there was a knock on the dressing room door. It was the Soviet interpreter, saying Puchkov wanted to meet my dad. As it turned out, he admired the catching glove, and asked if he could have it. My father gave him an older, worn model he had as a spare, and in that way the catching glove was introduced to Russian hockey. Later, at the medal ceremony, Puchkov gave my father a gorgeous, hand-crafted wallet as a gift. In the days after the game, the Cleveland Barons of the American Hockey League cabled a $10,000-a-year offer to Puchkov, who turned it down. More than three decades would pass before Soviet and Russian players would start arriving in substantial numbers to play pro hockey in North America.

As is the case today when a Canadian team loses in international hockey, the reaction in Canada to the defeat of the mighty Dutchmen was strong. It was similar to the reaction in the United States after the American basketball team was upset by the Soviets for the gold medal at the '72 Munich Olympics. All Canadians had expected to win the Olympic hockey gold in Cortina. "Boys Sent on a Man's Errand," screamed one headline. Hewitt said: "It is also a warning that no longer can we think of European clubs as pushovers. They aren't. They're good." Some suggested Canada should start sending all-star teams to the Olympics. It was similar to the reaction that would follow every major Canadian defeat in international hockey over the next 50 years.

In '56, with the Cold War just starting to move into deep freeze, Canadians were beginning to understand that Russian "amateurs" were a different breed, players paid by the government to train

together 11 months of the year in a country that used sports
for political reasons. Art Hurst, a member of the Dutchmen, explained the difference in a newspaper interview: "I am a carpenter
by profession. I love my job, my hockey as a sideline, my family and my way of life. I would want no part of the Russian approach to hockey. It shouldn't be that important." These were two
hockey cultures that wouldn't understand each other for decades.
After the Dutchmen lost, NHL president Clarence Campbell said
it was the "greatest thing that could have happened" to promote
the international game. He also said, "But let's face it, there are
at least 25 teams in North America that could probably beat (the
Soviets)." It was the beginning, really, of a rivalry that would
reach a climax in the '72 Summit Series and is still a major feature
of international hockey today.

The Olympics were a big thrill for my dad. I think his only
disappointment was that he didn't play the big game against the
Soviets. I always felt that. I know in Nagano, Japan, at the 1998
Winter Olympics he felt disappointed that, in his mind, Team
Canada didn't even try to win the bronze medal game against
Finland after losing the shootout semifinal to the Czechs. My
dad's life has been about winning that bronze medal, and he felt
the NHL players on that '98 team couldn't have cared less about
it. He knew it was different because we were professionals, but it
was still an Olympic medal. He stopped playing in 1959 because
of stomach problems, but toured during the sixties with the Montreal Canadiens Oldtimers when Rocket Richard called. It was as
close to the NHL as he ever got.

—∞—

Given our family's history, the 2006 Olympics were going to be
a very big deal, both for me and my dad. Sure, the gold medal I
had won with Canada at the 2002 Salt Lake City Olympics was

an enormous achievement, but going back to Italy to deal with unfinished family business made '06 special. Just as the '05–06 season got underway, Canada submitted a list of 81 names to the International Ice Hockey Federation. Only players on this list were eligible to be picked for Turin, and there was some controversy even at that stage as talented players like Rod Brind'Amour of the Carolina Hurricanes and Anaheim Mighty Ducks goalie Jean-Sébastien Giguère were left off. Giguère, who had won MVP honors in the 2003 Stanley Cup final, despite the fact the Devils had beaten the Ducks, was really annoyed. "Cam Who?" he told reporters after he learned Carolina rookie goalie Cam Ward had made the big list and he hadn't. By the end of the '06 Stanley Cup playoffs, when the Hurricanes won the Cup, nobody in the hockey world would have any questions about who Ward was any longer.

Having played in the 1998 Olympics in Nagano, the 2002 Olympics in Salt Lake City, the 2004 World Cup and the 2005 IIHF World Championships, and having been the starting goalie in all of those tournaments except Nagano, I felt pretty sure I was going to be on the team this time around. I thought I would have my spot, particularly since with the '02 Olympics and '04 World Cup, the team had been organized by Wayne Gretzky and coached by Pat Quinn, and Gretzky and Quinn were again in charge for Turin. I felt confident they believed in me. But when I didn't get off to a great start in the '05–06 season, and then when I suffered a right knee sprain in late October and missed six games, I figured that I was going to have to earn the No. 1 job again.

The way it looked was that I could probably count on starting the first game in Turin, but there was no guarantee I would keep playing. Curtis Joseph had actually been the starter in Salt Lake City, but when Canada lost to Sweden right out of the gate

I got the chance to play after sitting and watching four years earlier. We didn't lose another game. At the '04 World Cup, Roberto Luongo of Florida played some of the games, and when I sprained my catching hand in a game against Slovakia while recording my first shutout (5–0) in international hockey, he had to play the semifinal game against the Czechs. Despite being outshot 40–24, we won 4–3 on Vincent Lecavalier's overtime goal. Luongo played very well and made a game-saving stop on Milan Hedjuk in OT, but with my hand heavily wrapped I was back in net for the final against Finland, which we won to capture the World Cup for the first time.

So, even with Luongo establishing himself at both the NHL and international level, I felt I would be the starting goalie for Turin, at least for the first game. I figured it would be me, Luongo and probably José Théodore. Maybe Marty Turco, who had been No. 3 with Luongo and me at the world championships in Austria the previous spring. Everybody, at least among the Canadian players, craved a chance to play. It seemed even more that way for Turin, as though the lockout and then coming back to a league with very different rules had made players hungrier than ever to be part of the Olympics, to be part of a great hockey experience.

It was the same for other countries. Early in the 2005–06 season, the Devils were losing to Boston 2–1 after two periods and Scott Gomez, who loves to talk, came into the dressing room and said, "C'mon, guys, we gotta go U.S. style and win this one." I just rolled my eyes, thinking, oh boy, we're in trouble. I guess it was the natural reaction of a player from a rival country. But you know what? We won the game. Gomez is a player who is really into U.S. hockey, and a lot of players feel that way. It's an accomplishment to represent your country. It's a select few that get to do that and everybody wants to be there.

Some people wonder why, when we get paid so much money to play for NHL teams, we would want to travel to a distant country and play in the Olympics for free. Well, it's your sport. Let's say you love playing tennis, and let's say somebody would pay you to play tennis. You'd say that was excellent. Exactly. We didn't have to get paid. We would have played hockey anyway. But there's a league, and the best players get picked to play and get paid. But the love of the game is still there. With the Olympics, you're in the middle of the greatest sports event in the world, part of something bigger than just hockey. The world doesn't revolve just around you and your sport. You go into the athletes' village and meet the other athletes, see the way they live and understand the way they sacrifice themselves. It's so rewarding to be part of that. You never know when the next time might come, and it also makes you so happy that people like Gretzky believe you can help them win.

For Canada, the team selection process was complicated by the fact the entire 2004–05 season had been wiped out by the lockout and because a group of young, talented stars made huge splashes when they arrived with their new teams in the fall of 2005. To many, that meant Team Canada was going to have to be filled with young players and totally changed from the 2004 World Cup team. I didn't see it quite that way. To build a team, you need a consistent approach. More important, the focus has to be on building the best team, not gathering the best individual players. That sounds simple, but people get mesmerized by talent and lose track of the idea that it's a team. For example, let's say there's an excellent player used to playing 22 minutes a night with his NHL club. Is he going to be able to handle playing only 15 minutes a game with Team Canada? Can he be effective with less work, or does he need that extra ice time to stay warm and loose and sharp?

Every major competition provides new information and new lessons. To me, the lesson of Nagano, an Olympic tournament in which Canada lost in the semifinals to the Czech Republic and then lost the bronze to Finland as well, was that there was no clear-cut leader, or even group of leaders. There were so many big names on that team—from Wayne Gretzky to Patrick Roy to Eric Lindros to Steve Yzerman to Ray Bourque to Scott Stevens—that it was difficult to sort out leaders and roles. There were so many stars that if that plane to Japan had gone down, they would have had to shut down the entire league. Lindros was named captain, but asking him at 24 years of age to take charge on a team with that many veteran standouts was a very, very difficult challenge.

We learned from that experience, and by Salt Lake City, Mario Lemieux was both the captain and clearly "the guy." Other players were strong leaders, as well. Brendan Shanahan, for example, was the one who stood up in the dressing room in between the second and third periods of a game we barely won over Germany and said some strong words. But Lemieux was the captain. He just had that presence, and everybody surrounded him and did their thing. It was the same with the World Cup two years later. There was Mario, then players like myself and Joe Sakic, and a lot of the rest of the guys were just happy to be there and play. It's interesting that in the end, a youngster like Lecavalier prospered so much he was named the tournament MVP, while arguably the team's most effective line had Joe Thornton and Shane Doan, two more young guys. On any team, you can't have too many leaders. You have to pick and choose who's going to lead the team. If you have too many leaders, nobody wants to step on anybody's toes and that makes it tough to be successful. As it turned out, that leadership issue would pop up again for Turin.

Of the 81 players on the Canadian master list, only 35, in
my estimation, were really contenders for Olympic roster posi-
tions. There were obvious guarantees, players that would be there
for sure. Simon Gagné? For sure. Thornton, a player excluded
in 2002? This time around, for sure. Mario, of course, was a
shoe-in if he wanted to play. Sakic was in. Jarome Iginla, too.
Kris Draper, for sure. If you don't have a guy like that, a player
committed to defensive hockey and sacrificing his offensive statistics for the good of the team, you won't win. Adam Foote, I
was pretty sure, would be on the team. Chris Pronger. Rob Blake.
Scott Niedermayer. Lecavalier, for sure, and his Tampa teammate
Brad Richards as well. So 12 to 15 guys, when the process began,
seemed like locks. Players like Ed Jovanovski, Scott Hannan and
Robyn Regehr had each gotten a foot in the door at other competitions, so they would be a very good bet for Turin. Really, then, it
was going to be a tough lineup for anybody new to crack. At least
that's the way I looked at it. I believed from the start that Gretzky
and his coaching team wouldn't make very many changes.

But the player everybody wanted to talk about was Sidney
Crosby of the Pittsburgh Penguins, who in the first half of his
first season was looking like a sure-fire star. I thought he deserved
to be looked at, but as I said, in the grand scheme of things, you
have to build a team. People are always going to be talking about
the players who are flashiest at the time. That's normal. But that's
not necessarily the way to build a team.

I remember when my general manager in New Jersey, Lou
Lamoriello, came up to me after our top rivals, the New York
Rangers, acquired Pavel Bure in a trade. He said, "You know
what's the difference between us and the Rangers right now? The
difference is the Rangers will get the best player available. We're
going to get the best player for our team." That always stayed
in my mind. You make a personnel decision by considering the

implications for the entire team. The best player may not be right for you. Everybody has a personality, and the people creating a team have to do their homework as to the type of person a player is. If you're in the locker room and you don't talk to anybody and you don't blend in and you're going to be unhappy because you're playing only 10 minutes—well, Team Canada doesn't have time to babysit anybody. Crosby seemed like a terrific kid with great talent, but he had received a certain status without playing a single professional game, and that's hard on those who feel that status should be earned. The NHL, coming out of the lockout, needed to promote players like Crosby to sell the game. But when it came to picking an Olympic team for 2006, I sure didn't think we needed that to sell Team Canada.

If Crosby was the player people were talking about the most during the months leading up to the December 21 deadline for selecting the final roster, the second-most-discussed player was Todd Bertuzzi of the Vancouver Canucks. Bertuzzi, of course, was suspended by the league in March 2004 after he jumped Steve Moore of the Colorado Avalanche during a game, and seriously injured him. The incident was in retaliation for a hit by Moore on one of Vancouver's top players, Markus Naslund, a few weeks earlier. Bertuzzi's hit was ugly, and it was controversial. Bertuzzi was suspended indefinitely, and when the lockout came, his suspension just kept going. He couldn't play at the '04 World Cup, he couldn't play overseas that season and he wasn't eligible to play at the 2005 world championships. He was reinstated by the NHL just before the Kelowna camp, and of course he was the focus of a lot of media attention.

Everybody had a different opinion on what happened between Bertuzzi and Moore. One of my Devils teammates, Darren Langdon, is a close of friend of Bertuzzi's, and I remember listening to Langdon and Sergei Brylin have a long discussion over the entire incident. To Langdon, Bertuzzi paid a huge price and was made a scapegoat by the league. To Brylin, Moore was just a player trying to work his way into the league, just a player doing his job, and he ended up being victimized by a star player. From my perspective, I felt some sympathy for Bertuzzi. The shot he laid on Moore was vicious and nasty, but the truth is, I had seen many, many hits like that over the course of my career. The difference was Moore was hurt badly: His neck was broken. If I felt badly for Bertuzzi, it was because the price he paid was too high, not in terms of money or a suspension, but in terms of his reputation. He's going to be marked by that single incident his entire career.

The truth is that similar things happen all the time. It's not right, but it's true. Early in the '05–06 season, I saw Zach Parise from our team crosscheck Cory Sarich of the Lightning in the face, and Sarich retaliated by suckering Parise from behind, but didn't hurt him badly. Bertuzzi paid the price because Moore's neck was broken. But that punch was no harder than punches I've seen many times. In fact, I've seen worse.

To me, that entire mess could have been avoided if the league had taken a stronger stand when Moore hit Naslund. I thought that was a dirty hit. That's just the way it looked to me. I don't want to be the guy who says that if you play a certain way, bad things can happen. But I wouldn't want my kids to play that way, running around and being agitators. I also understand that some players need to play that way, and it certainly doesn't give anybody the right to hurt them. I just believe the NHL should protect its best players at all costs. If Moore had been suspended for the hit on Naslund, perhaps Vancouver would have been satisfied. But I really worry about the league's judgment when it comes to things like this.

During the 2005–06 season, Erik Cole of the Carolina Hurricanes was injured pretty badly, suffering a cracked vertebrae in his neck when Brooks Orpik of the Pittsburgh Penguins took him into the boards from behind. That, in my estimation, was an average player taking out one of the best players on the other team. Orpik received a three-game suspension, but it didn't seem to be enough. Cole didn't play again for almost three months until returning dramatically for Game 6 of the '06 Stanley Cup final. I just believe the league has to be stronger in protecting its top players. I felt the same earlier in the '05–06 season when, during a game against the Toronto Maple Leafs, Darcy Tucker hit me with his stick across the back of my neck like a lumberjack chopping wood. Later in the game, he came up to me and said, "Sorry about that. I didn't mean to do it. We're going to need you [at the Olympics] in a couple of months." I looked at him kind of funny, thinking, "Does he think he's going to be on Team Canada?" But he wasn't suspended. Nothing. That just didn't make any sense to me at all.

When it came to Team Canada, I didn't think Bertuzzi's past would work against him. He is a player with all the tools, just the type of player we would need for Turin. I never asked him about all that had happened. I've been through my own personal problems, and I really don't feel the need to know anybody else's private life. If I was supportive of Bertuzzi, maybe it was selfish because he is Canadian and he looked like a player who could help us at the Olympics. Maybe, if he had been American, I would have felt differently.

Just before the final team was selected, both Yzerman and Lemieux pulled out. They were big losses. From the start, I didn't think Yzerman would play. He had an eye injury in the 2004 playoffs and didn't play in the 2004 World Cup. He struggled to get back for the Detroit Red Wings, and early in the 2005–06 season he was only playing about seven minutes per game. It just seemed it would be too hard for him to get ready for the Olympics. I felt that if Canada was going to take Steve Yzerman, it wasn't going to take him as a checker or a role player. If he was going to Turin, it was because he would be a threat to the other teams. I wasn't surprised at all when he pulled out about two weeks before the team was named, and I thought it was a good decision for him. He had been there in Salt Lake City, of course, but he was quiet, and I didn't feel I had the chance to get to know him too much. He didn't dominate games, but he was there all the time, just making one good play after another. He was in a lot of pain because of a knee injury, and the training staff gave him a combination of painkillers and anti-inflammatories that afterwards they referred to as "Stevie Ys." Watching him in Salt Lake made me understand the value of faceoffs, really understand for the first time. With Yzerman and Sakic, it just seemed like we started with the puck after every faceoff. I came back from that tournament and told our management that was something we were missing. A little later, the Devils acquired Joe Nieuwendyk, and Nieuwendyk was a significant player the next season when the Devils won the Stanley Cup.

Lemieux, in the end, really didn't have much choice. In early December, he found himself in hospital with what was diagnosed as an irregular heartbeat. After having battled cancer and back problems in his amazing career, it was incredible that he had another major health issue to deal with. Two days later, he announced that he was withdrawing his name from consideration for Team Canada, which only made sense to everyone involved. He had struggled to find his game that season and he was facing all kinds of pressures as an owner with the financially challenged Penguins. To lose Mario was more than just losing a player. When you lose somebody like that, you lose a little bit of respect from other teams. Sometimes a battle can be won just by the other team looking at your lineup. Mario was something we had that no other country had.

Both Lemieux and Yzerman had been outstanding NHL players. But before the season was over, Lemieux retired, and Yzerman retired as well later that summer.

It seemed like the problems were just starting for Team Canada. On the weekend of December 10, my father had a minor stroke and ended up in hospital for a few days. It was worrisome on its own, and even more so because I was hoping he would be able to travel to Turin for the Olympics. Just over a week later, with the final announcement of Team Canada a few days away, Gretzky suffered a terrible loss when his mother, Phyllis, died of lung cancer. His mother's health had been a concern for months, and it was the reason he didn't run Team Canada at the '05 world championships. Her death forced him to leave his position as head coach of the Phoenix Coyotes temporarily, and it must have made it seem as though Team Canada wasn't very important at all anymore.

My father turned out to be okay. What really bothered me was that he was in a bed in the hallway of a Montreal hospital for three days waiting for a room to open up. I started calling my friends to see if they could get something done, but just as I was considering a call to the hospital he finally got a room. It's hard for some people to understand, when they look at NHL players and see the wealth and all the advantages, but money doesn't fix everything. It doesn't ensure your kid won't get in trouble, and it doesn't ensure your family members won't get sick.

On December 21, after all the speculation and all the unusual developments, Team Canada '06 was finally named. The goalies were me, Luongo and Turco. Théodore just hadn't had the kind of first half he had hoped for, which is why Turco was picked instead.

As it turned out, Théodore wouldn't have been eligible to play anyway. Just before the Olympics, it was announced he had tested positive the previous fall for a steroid-masking agent. Théodore, whom I had known since he was a teenager, said it was a substance contained in a hair restoration product he had been taking for eight years. Eventually he decided not to appeal the ruling, and he was banned from international competition for two years. An American player, Bryan Berard, had also tested positive for a banned substance, norandrosterone, in the fall Olympic testing, and he voluntarily accepted a two-year ban from international hockey. His suspension was announced during the first week of NHL drug testing in early January, a program that the league and players had agreed to as part of the new collective bargaining agreement from the previous summer.

Having Berard and Théodore test positive, unfortunately, fueled the arguments of Dick Pound, the World Anti-Doping Agency boss, who in November 2005 had said publicly he believed 30 per cent of NHL players were probably using performance-enhancing substances. I was shocked and disappointed. In his position, Pound should have been more careful about what he said because he can really damage reputations. Thirty per cent—that would have meant eight guys on my team were taking drugs. I had played the game for 13 years and had never seen anybody take anything illegal. I had seen guys get painkilling shots in the playoffs, but that wasn't illegal. I had seen players take Sudafed cold medication, but that's not illegal. I had always been crazy careful about what I put in my body. I don't take recovery drinks, for example. I'd rather have two beers, which does the same thing for me. I want to be safe and not risk ingesting a substance that I may not even be aware I'm putting in my body. If I'm sick, I go to the doctor and tell him to be careful what he gives me. I take Advil sinus medication before games, because I don't like to be stuffed up, and I take Tums. That's about it.

It seemed that Pound, who had been locked in a long fight with famed cyclist Lance Armstrong, was just taking a free shot. In the NHL we had decided to take the initiative on drug-testing through our new collective bargaining agreement; there was no commission or anybody else asking us to do it. We weren't forced to do it, and we didn't decide to do it because somebody died. So why would a person like Pound come out with this when he didn't have hard evidence? It's not like dozens of NHL players had tested positive at world championships or Olympics in previous years. Look, I'm sure somebody in the league is doing something, and I'm sure somebody will eventually get caught. People will try to beat the system. It's human nature, which is why I'm for drug testing. But 30 per cent? That just blew my mind. At the end of the 2005–06 season, the NHL's anti-doping program showed that out of 1,406 tests done on players, there were no positive tests.

Kevin Lowe, Gretzky's key assistant, called me at the Garden City Hotel in Long Island to give me the news that I'd been picked for Team Canada '06. Gretzky, my roommate in Nagano, had called me four years earlier for the Salt Lake City team, and it's always special to get a call like that. Lowe told me they'd have a really good defense in front of me. In Montreal a few weeks earlier, Gretzky had joked that he wasn't too worried about my status since he figured Canada would have a stronger blueline than the Devils.

It was a pretty strong looking team everywhere. Bertuzzi made it, while Crosby didn't. Two of the young forwards everybody had been talking about, Eric Staal and Jason Spezza, were named to the three-man taxi squad along with Bryan McCabe, a defense-man with the Maple Leafs. There were no big surprises, although, to be honest, I didn't even notice that Eric Brewer, who had been on the '02 Olympic team and '04 World Cup team, didn't make it for Turin until a few days after the formal announcement.

I really believed it was a terrific team. Gretzky had decided to go with the horses he knew best, the players who had won before.

Unfortunately, the team that was originally chosen wasn't the team that went to Turin. In late January, Jovanovski announced he was going to have abdominal surgery and wouldn't be able to play. Niedermayer announced the week before the Games that he had decided to have arthroscopic surgery on his knee instead of going to the Olympics. Niedermayer said the knee had been bothering him for weeks, and that he wanted to make sure he was healthy enough to play for the Ducks after the Olympics. Interestingly, Niedermayer had consulted with the Devils' trainer, Bill Murray, even though he was now with the Ducks. I thought it was very disappointing he decided not to go to Turin, because he hadn't even missed a game with Anaheim. It was a question of playing through pain, just as Yzerman had done in Salt Lake City. But you can't judge people. They have to make their own decisions, and for Niedermayer, there was an awful lot of money on the table in Anaheim after he had signed a four-year, $27-million contract the previous summer.

Losing Niedermayer hurt us a lot. He can play 23 to 25 minutes a game so easily without any fatigue, and is so skilled, so fast. He's about the best package you can get in terms of a defenseman with both offense and defense. In place of him and Jovanovski, Team Canada moved McCabe from the taxi squad to the main roster, and brought in Jay Bouwmeester. Dan Boyle was added to the taxi squad. I liked Bouwmeester, who had played at the World Cup in '04. He is a good skater who gets in people's faces, and he has the ability to recover. With his reach, he can really control players in the corners. McCabe I didn't know as well. The first few games in Turin would tell us a lot, would give us a chance to see what he could do at a level of competition he had never been part of before. He was like Jovanovski, a high-risk, high-reward type of player, the kind I usually don't play with on the Devils. The changes on the blueline were a concern, but then again, we hadn't had Chris Pronger and Rob Blake at the World Cup, and Wade Redden had been hurt early in that tournament. For Turin, we had those players.

So we were set to go. My father was healthy enough to come, and my boys were with me as well. For the Brodeur family, it was a date with history.

The Toughest Shooters

(and how many times they beat me)

ALEXEY MOROZOV

38 games, 14 goals*

They called him the Devil Killer. I wasn't sad to see him go home to Russia during the lockout and not come back. He played for Pittsburgh from 1997 to 2004, and every time he touched the puck against us he seemed to turn it into goal. He never scored more than 20 goals in an NHL season, but he was like a 50-goal shooter against me. He knew it, too. When I played in a farewell game for Slava Fetisov in Moscow, he lit me up there as well.

---

*Source: Elias Sports Bureau. Statistics combine regular season and playoffs and are current as of conclusion of 2005–06 season.

chapter 5
Turin

IN THE FINAL DAYS BEFORE TURIN, two storms broke.

The first was "Operation Slapshot." New Jersey police announced they had busted an alleged illegal gambling ring, and former NHL player Rick Tocchet was named in the investigation. At the time, Tocchet was working as an assistant coach with the Phoenix Coyotes under head coach Wayne Gretzky, and so the entire mess immediately implicated Gretzky. Even worse, Gretzky's wife, Janet, was linked to the alleged bookmaking operation as a person who may have made bets. It didn't matter whether any of it was true, it was in the news, and because Gretzky was executive director of Canada's Olympic team, it became part of our story as well.

Within a day or so, Tocchet met with NHL commissioner Gary Bettman and took a leave of absence from his job. It was clear right away that the investigation was going to take months, and the media raised the question: Should Gretzky even go to Turin with Team Canada? From my point of view, he needed to be there. He was in charge of Team Canada, and I expected him to be there. I believed it would have been more of a distraction had he decided not to go. Ultimately, he did make the trip, but he never really said a word about it to us.

The second storm was more literal, and more personal. As my girlfriend Geneviève and I made our final preparations to leave for Toronto for a one-day stop before flying on to Turin with the rest of Team Canada, forecasts suggested some really bad weather was coming in. I woke up the next day and there was a foot and a half of snow on the ground. Flights out of Newark were cancelled, including our morning flight. Soon the phone was ringing off the hook with calls from worried Team Canada officials who wanted me in Toronto for a scheduled practice the next day, the only team workout we would have before flying overseas. We went through a variety of possible plans, including driving to the Philadelphia airport or one in upstate New York, or even taking the train, which would have been impossible with Gen, as well as Anthony, Jeremy and William, who were coming to the Olympics with us. I said I would just go in the next day, but they desperately wanted me in Toronto that night. Finally, I said, "Well, then get me a charter if you want."

As it turned out, a wealthy Toronto businessman and former owner of the NBA Toronto Raptors, John Bitove, was flying back to Toronto from Florida that day. Team Canada officials contacted him, and a few hours later, at about 10 p.m., we were aboard Bitove's private plane with his father and his mother. The kids, of course, loved it, and we met up the next morning with my father at a hotel in Toronto. Between Operation Slapshot and the weather, it had been a crazy, unsettling start to my third Olympic journey.

—⚉—

Aside from the Tocchet story, there was a great deal going on in the final days before the Olympics. For starters, teams were losing players, just as Scott Niedermayer and Ed Jovanovski had been lost to Team Canada. Germany, our second opponent in the tournament, found out at the last moment it wouldn't have Jochen

Hecht of the Buffalo Sabres or Marco Sturm of Boston, probably that country's two best forwards. Markus Naslund announced he wouldn't play for Sweden, and Philadelphia Flyers president Ed Snider said publicly he didn't want Peter Forsberg to play for the Swedes either because of all the injuries he'd already had that season. Snider, in fact, also said he didn't want goalie Robert Esche to play for the United States or defenseman Joni Pitkanen to dress for Team Finland, basically for the same reasons.

For the Devils, it seemed likely the Olympics would have an impact, as almost one-third of our team was participating. I was playing for Canada, and Patrik Elias, who had played only 18 games before the Olympic break after recovering from hepatitis, had been named at the last minute to the Czech team to replace Petr Prucha of the Rangers. Viktor Kozlov was playing for Russia, while Brian Gionta, Scott Gomez and Brian Rafalski were playing for Team USA and Paul Martin was going over as a spare for the Americans. Kozlov was kind of interesting, because he had been playing very little for us, playing a bit of five-on-five and a little on the power play. His most important role was in the shootout, where he had become our most dangerous weapon. In the weeks before the Olympics, he started riding the bike at practice and after games more frequently, explaining that he wanted to be in good enough shape to play a regular shift in Turin.

For me, this was going to be different from my other two Olympic experiences right from the start. Eight years earlier in Nagano, Japan, Team Canada's head coach, Marc Crawford, informed me on the long flight to Asia that his goaltender with the Colorado Avalanche, Patrick Roy, was going to start all the games regardless of the scores or how he played. It was devastating news to absorb, if only because my brothers, my sisters, my father, my wife and my children were all coming to Japan to watch, and already I had been told I wasn't going to play a single minute unless Roy was hurt.

Don't get me wrong. I was thrilled to be there because it was the first time NHL players had agreed to play in the Olympics, and I had spent more than $30,000 to fly my family from Montreal to Japan and take care of them while they were there. But, based on a brief conversation, I was supposed to accept that Roy would play every game. It really bummed me out, even though at least I would be on the bench while Curtis Joseph, the No. 3 goalie, was in street clothes in the stands. In retrospect, it wasn't right at all to be told on the plane, and I didn't think it was fair to the team. What if there had been an injury? How could Crawford have possibly hoped that either I or Joseph would be ready to play since we had been told not to expect that opportunity? Every goalie's approach is different from the next guy's. Roy's approach, right or wrong, was that he felt he had to know he wouldn't be challenged and didn't have to worry about another goalie taking over. That's what he felt he needed to prepare himself properly. I can say that I would never demand that.

Ultimately, with Roy playing every second of every game, we finished out of the medals in Nagano. Four years later in Salt Lake City, Roy didn't end up being in the picture at all. The rules that year were that every team would initially name eight players, and when Roy wasn't one of Canada's first eight, he withdrew his name from consideration. The '02 Games were Gretzky's first opportunity to run the Olympic program. He had been my roommate in Nagano, and he had suffered his own disappointment when Crawford didn't select him for the shootout in our semifinal loss to the Czech Republic, an enormous controversy, far greater than the fact I hadn't played.

Before Salt Lake, I told Gretzky that I would like to have the opportunity to play at least one game. He never did say yes or no, but when we lost the opening game of the tournament to Sweden with Joseph in net, head coach Pat Quinn put me in for the next game against Germany for my first ever Olympic start. We barely won, 3–2, and we tied our next game against the Czechs, 3–3. It was after that game that Gretzky held a press conference and said he felt the entire world wanted Canada to lose, and that "American propaganda" was trying to undermine our team. His words made headlines around the world, and some speculated he was simply trying to take the heat off the players. As players, however, we knew nothing about his press conference, and didn't know what he had said until hours later or even the next day.

In the quarterfinals, we beat Finland, and then defeated Belarus, which had upset Sweden. In the final we played the host Americans, and it seemed that history wasn't exactly on our side. Herb Brooks, the architect of the 1980 Miracle On Ice victory at the Lake Placid Olympics, was again the U.S. coach, and he had never lost an Olympic game. The Americans had not lost an Olympic men's game on U.S. soil since 1932, including unbeaten gold medal performances in Squaw Valley (1960) and Lake Placid.

Tony Amonte scored in the first period to put the Americans ahead 1–0, but Jarome Iginla and Paul Kariya put Canada ahead later in the period. Rafalski, my New Jersey teammate, beat me in the second to tie the game 2–2, but it was our day. Three straight goals made it a 5–2 Canadian win at the E Center in West Valley City, just outside Salt Lake City, and Canada had won gold in men's hockey at the Olympics for the first time in 50 years.

Of all the memories, what I remember most was the celebration on the ice, and then in the dressing room, with the people who had made it happen. No media, no family, no floaters—just players, coaches and staff, drinking champagne and drinking in the moment. Some of the guys were drunk for the first time in their lives, I think, and it was a wonderful thing watching teammates of two weeks feel so close.

—m—

Our flight to Italy on February 13, 2006, was a quiet one, and I traveled with the knowledge that, unlike my previous two Olympic experiences, I would be the starter going into the competition. All the players sat at the front of the plane, with family members and everybody else at the back. Well, almost everybody. Gretzky actually sat in the back with his son Ty, while Janet and one of her relatives sat in front. The idea was that the players would be able to get some sleep so we would be able to hit the ground in Turin the next morning, practice and then be ready to play the following day. I sat with Shane Doan, talked a little bit about his team and my team, and other players we knew around the league. Quinn, who had been asked by Gretzky to be the head coach again, sat in the seats beside us with one of his assistants, Jacques Martin. We had dinner, I went back to see Gen and the kids, then popped a sleeping pill and got three or four hours' sleep.

After we arrived on the morning of the 14th, the players went straight to the athletes' village. I shared a unit with Wade Redden and Rob Blake, and by the second day Blake had dragged his bed out into the common room to get more room. My family was staying at a spacious apartment on the other side of the city, on a small street called Via Santa Giulia overlooking the Po River, and on nights before games I wasn't scheduled to play, or days off, I had permission to stay at the apartment. Once we worked out how to get a cab when we needed it, it was perfect and gave me time to spend with the boys and my dad. I only spent as much time in the village as I had to.

The evening of our arrival we had a 6 p.m. practice at the Palasport Olimpico, the main rink for the hockey competition, and the next day we had the early game at 1 p.m. against the host Italians. It was a good warmup-type game, very different from four years earlier when we had faced Sweden right out of the box. Jason Muzzati, who had played in the NHL and had even played a few games for the Canadian national team, was in goal for Italy, and their two goals were scored by Giulio Scandella and John Parco, who had either been born in Canada or played major junior hockey there. On Parco's goal, the Italians had flipped the puck high down the ice and one of our defensemen, Bryan Mc-Cabe, had batted it down with a high-stick, right onto the stick of one of the Italian players. One pass later, Parco slapped a low shot past me. Later, I told McCabe just to let the puck go on a play like that. It would have been an icing call, and if it hadn't, my experience told me that playing on the larger international ice surface was less about races for the puck and more about giving up ground and buying time while your team gets into defensive position. Those little details are part of how a team learns to play together in a non-NHL environment, and I felt it was part of my role to pass on that information to other players. Jarome Iginla scored twice, Todd Bertuzzi had two nice assists, and I stopped 18 shots, giving us a final score of 7–2. All in all it was a good start as we were getting used to playing as a team.

For that game, I wore my new Olympic mask for the first time. On the chin, it had "Turin/Torino, 2006." Behind the left ear, in bronze, was written "Cortina d'Ampezzo, 1956," the year my dad played in the Olympics. Behind the right ear, in gold, was "Salt Lake City, 2002." With red Olympic flames, it was a gorgeous mask, but every mask takes time before it feels comfortable. In New Jersey, team rules forbid facial hair. So for international tournaments, I usually try to grow something, and in Turin I went with a goatee. I'm not used to playing with facial hair, so that made my mask feel a little different, as well. I was thinking that when I returned to North America I would maybe wear the goatee at practice before shaving it off. A little bit of rebellion, you know.

After the game, Quinn announced that Roberto Luongo would start the second game. They asked me whether I wanted to be on the bench or if Turco could dress instead. I said my preference was to be on the bench so I could talk to the guys and get to know the team better, but that the final decision was up to the coaching staff. The strange part was that when Quinn told us of the goalie change, he turned to Luongo and said, "Carlo, you're in." We laughed and wondered if it was just a mistake, but he called him "Carlo" again later on when he was talking to Jason Spezza and Eric Staal about practicing the next day.

As far as when I would play and when I wouldn't, I was trying to "play the game" with the coaching staff, let them know that I wasn't trying to dictate the lineup. I wanted the coaching staff to make the decisions, and the more I put the ball in their court, the more I felt they wanted me to be in there. I felt their confidence, which meant there was no issue at all. I had been in the position that Luongo and Turco were in, just waiting for a chance to play. Both are outstanding starting NHL goalies, and suddenly they had to adjust to being backups, something I had been forced to do in the past.

I wanted to feel part of the team, and more important, I wanted the team to challenge me with the way they practiced and played. I needed to be at a certain level when we got to the big games, not to have just floated through the earlier games feeling as though it didn't matter how I had played. At the same time, I would have to get my rest during the tournament, which would be difficult given the number of games we were scheduled to play in a short time. Team Canada had four games in the first five days, and it was possible we would be required to play eight games in 12 days. That's a tougher schedule than in the NHL, where no team can play more than three games in four days. It was important that the other goalies would shoulder some of the load. And based on my own experience in Nagano, I felt it was important that the two other goalies had the hope, at least, that they might play.

On the same day that we beat Italy, goalie Dominik Hasek suffered a groin injury in the first period of the Czech Republic's first game against Germany. He went home the next day, and while nobody knew it at the time, he wouldn't play again that season for the Ottawa Senators. Serious injuries, of course, had been the concern of Snider, the Flyers owner, at the start of the Olympics, explaining his reluctance concerning Forsberg, Pit-kanen and Esche.

Patrik Elias, my New Jersey teammate, hurt his ribs in the same game, and after a short trip to Prague to see his girl-friend, he too went back to North America. While injuries are a concern, I believe you can't prevent athletes from trying to experience something special like the Olympics, something that might, in the end, feed back into that athlete's success. Sure, the Turin schedule was tough. Unlike athletes in some of the other Olympic sports, we had responsibilities to our profes-sional teams back home after the Games were over, and I really felt that the Turin organizers should have been making it as easy as possible on us while still organizing a competitive, legitimate tournament. But that didn't seem to be the case. For example, after the Italy game at 1 p.m. local time, we were scheduled to play Germany the next evening at 9 p.m., after three other games had been played on that ice surface that day. That's just not taking care of the players.

Some have suggested that the NHL should adjust to the demands of the Olympics by shortening its regular season sched-ule in an Olympic year. I wouldn't support that, although maybe I would have before we—the players—became "partners" with the NHL as part of the 2005 collective bargaining agreement, with our salaries linked to league revenues. Now the players need overall revenues to increase if our share is to increase, which makes it counterproductive to play fewer games in a shortened schedule.

There were players, such as Calgary goalie Mikka Kiprusoff, who decided well in advance of the Games that it was better for them to stay home and rest. Niedermayer had made a similar choice. Would it have been better for me and for the Devils to be at home? I didn't see it that way. As a goalie who likes to play a lot, I certainly didn't feel that resting for two weeks would give me a big benefit. To live the Olympic experience was a greater benefit. As well, if I'm healthy and in good enough shape, I feel it's my responsibility to play for my country, if asked. It's also so good for our sport to be at center stage in the world, and I feel it's imperative that players participate as much as they can.

Losing Elias in Turin, needless to say, was worrisome even though when you go to the Olympics you almost stop thinking about your NHL team for the duration. In the first days in Turin, I received a text message from Darren Langdon that made me think about my teammates. None had stayed in Jersey during the Olympic break. A few, such as Langdon and Mad Dog Madden, went to Disneyworld in Florida. Zach Parise, one of our rookies, went to Minnesota and took his hockey equipment with him. Richard Matvichuk flew to the Bahamas, then to Jamaica. Colin White and his buddy from Nova Scotia, Jon Sim, went to the Turks and Caicos. I figured Lou Lamoriello was using the time to catch up on his general manager's work after spending so much time coaching.

—⁂—

After the Italian game, I went out to dinner with my family and Simon Gagné and his family at a restaurant on Via Santo

Agostino in central Turin, enjoyed a veal T-bone steak and some terrific wine. It was a nice way to relax. Even though we had a game the next day, I wasn't playing, which was an unusual feeling for me.

Bertuzzi had played well in the opener, but back in Canada it was announced that Steve Moore had launched a new lawsuit in Ontario against Bertuzzi in connection with the March 9, 2004, incident in which Moore had been injured and Bertuzzi had been suspended for the remainder of the season and playoffs. An earlier lawsuit launched by Moore in Colorado had been thrown out. The timing of the new suit was lousy. I don't know the reason it had to happen then, but, to me, it really showed some vindictiveness on Moore's part. It reminded me of when my ex-wife served me divorce papers in the middle of the 2003 Stanley Cup playoffs. I don't think you generate much sympathy for your position by doing things like that. The media reaction seemed restrained, almost as if the story was getting old and this was just another lawsuit. Bertuzzi seemed to handle it fine. If you didn't know the history, you wouldn't have been able to tell there was anything unusual going on with him. His demeanor never changed.

The Slovaks beat the Russians on opening night, and the next day the Swiss beat the Czechs 3–2. Those results meant the tournament was already getting interesting by the time Canada, dressed head to toe in black, took on Germany the next day, our fourth day in Turin. I wasn't playing, so I spent the morning at Canada House, then went shopping with the boys for running shoes. All they had were boots, and there wasn't even a snowflake on the ground in the city. The boys went to play street hockey in front of the spectacular log cabin at B.C. House at the Piazza Valdo Fusi while I went back to the village for a team meeting and some sleep. The Germans had been tough on us in Salt Lake City, but without Sturm and Hecht, they were a little easier to handle and we won 5–1, with Luongo playing well in net.

From my vantage point on the bench, it was a quiet game. I watched the coaching staff, but there wasn't much coaching going on as we basically rolled the lines and got ice time for all 13 forwards and seven defensemen. Ken Hitchcock, one of Quinn's assistants, was by far the most vocal member of the staff. Quinn usually did his talking before the games, always short and right to the point. As head coach of Team Canada for the '02 Olympics, '04 World Cup and the Turin Olympics, he usually reviewed the game plan designed by Hitchcock and Jacques Martin, his key assistants for all three events. Quinn reminded me of a football coach, not afraid to rely on his assistants. But he had this presence. He is a big man and people listen to him. When you walk on skates beside him, he's as big as you are.

The day after the Germany game was our first day off as a team, and I spent it with the family wandering around central Turin. At the time, Anthony was 10 years old while the twins, William and Jeremy, were nine. It was already proving to be a challenge to find activities for them in a strange European city. They played a little more street hockey, then we wandered to the sponsors' village where a temporary curling rink and skating rink had been set up, with an enormous bronze sculpture of a famous Italian figure on a rearing horse in the middle. We stopped in a café for espresso and sandwiches and Gretzky walked in. "Hey, the Brodeur family!" he said.

—ᴡᴡ—

When you're a hockey Goliath, every once in a while a new David comes along. For my father and the Kitchener-Waterloo Dutchmen in 1956, there was the shocking loss to the U.S. that left Canada reeling with hockey embarrassment. In 1998, the Canadian national junior team lost a game at the world junior championships in Finland to the former Soviet republic of Kazakhstan. Our 2–0 loss to Switzerland at the XX Winter Olympics in Turin, it's fair to say, ranks right up there, a defeat that left the players silent and disbelieving in the dressing room afterwards.

Instead of giving us energy, the day off between the Germany game and the meeting with the Swiss seemed to sap our strength. The real stunner was that we didn't score a goal. Martin Gerber of the Carolina Hurricanes was superb with 49 saves, although photos later seemed to prove that a shot by Rick Nash was actually over the goal line at the time Gerber reached back to grab it. The game was played in mid-afternoon at the much smaller Torino Esposizioni, before fewer than 5,000 fans, but the Swiss supporters in attendance made it a noisy and colorful atmosphere that just got louder as their national team skated to its greatest victory ever in international hockey.

Like the Italians, the Swiss had a significant Canadian element to their team. Paul DiPietro, who grew up in Sault Ste. Marie, Ontario, played junior hockey in Sudbury and was part of the Montreal Stanley Cup team in '93, scored both goals for the Swiss. After years playing in the Swiss league, he had received his Swiss passport in 2004 and earned his way on to their national team. The head coach was Ralph Krueger, a native of Winnipeg, and Peter Lee, formerly a big scorer in Canadian junior hockey with the Ottawa 67s, was one of their assistant coaches.

After the loss, there was shock and the realization that it didn't matter how much talent we had, we weren't invincible. We had already learned in '98 that the Olympics can come down to one game. This time, it seemed we had been beaten by an individual performance, by a terrific game from a goalie. We had outshot them 24–1 in the third period, so why would we feel embarrassed? They played hard and were in our faces the entire game, and we ended up taking more penalties—12 in all—than we should have, which left some of our players sitting on the bench for a long time. I think Vincent Lecavalier played about one shift every five minutes.

It was one of those games in which everything about playing in a European rink far from our usual NHL environment seemed a little different, a little uncomfortable. The rink is wider, the bluelines are closer to the nets and the spacing everywhere on the ice is different. Instead of counting down from 20 minutes to zero, the clock counts upwards, and instead of having a single clock hanging over center ice, the clocks are placed on the walls at either end. The lighting is slightly different, and the boards are a little higher, which means shots deflect off them in different ways. The posts are smaller and make a tinny sound when hit by pucks, and because of the different rink dimensions the net seems to be in a different place. Marty St. Louis told me about making one of his usual spin moves and shooting, but missing the net by four feet. A player like McCabe had found great success in the NHL before we left, with the bluelines having been moved several feet further away from the net for the 2005–06 season. In Turin, the distance between the blueline and net were different, and he struggled to find his shot. The coaching staff stressed the importance of not being mesmerized by the space that appears to be available on the larger ice surface, but it's not easy. This is all part of the challenge, part of finding a way to succeed in an environment that seems familiar but yet not quite the same.

The Swiss game also showed how players on our team were still trying to figure out each other's tendencies and abilities. On a power play, I noticed Bertuzzi parked himself in front of the net, shielding his stick from the defenseman, and tapped his stick, begging Joe Sakic to give him the puck. In Vancouver, that's where Markus Naslund would give him the puck, but Sakic didn't see him and was thinking about creating something different elsewhere on the ice. These are the subtle ways in which the unfamiliarity of players is expressed. It just takes time, but in a tournament like this, your time is very limited. The Swiss team had played together many times, and you could see that familiarity on the ice for them.

Sakic was hit late in the game and suffered a nasty cut and a fractured cheekbone. It didn't force him out of the lineup, but he did have to wear a full face mask for the rest of the tournament. As team captain, he was the primary leader, but it was definitely different for him and the team not having Mario Lemieux and Steve Yzerman around. Not because of what they do, but because of what they have done. Their absence put more weight on Sakic to lead the way, and that job became a little tougher with his injury.

Gretzky dropped by the room after the loss. He just said hi, and hung out with the coaches. His role was to sit back, relax and hope his horses came in. He had done his job in picking the team, and now it was a matter of making it gel. Still, it was important that he was around. People wanted to see him. He looked a little more tired than usual, not surprising with all the things that had happened to him, from starting out as a rookie NHL head coach to the death of his mother several months earlier to the Tocchet gambling story. He was a person I didn't really know, but I felt as though I knew him. I felt fortunate to be part of his life. When he finishes his career in hockey, a big part of what he will have accomplished will be with Team Canada, and it meant a lot to be part of that with him.

The next day, a cold, hard rain made Turin seem gray and unfriendly. There wasn't a speck of snow anywhere and the mountains seemed only a rumor, covered in fog and mist. It finally snowed heavy flakes late in the day, a nice change. I had started to worry that my dad was getting tired. He had, after all, suffered that stroke two months earlier, and now he was staying up very late watching television, and getting up early in the morning, ready to take more pictures of the city. I asked the boys about their homework, made sure they were getting something done, then around noon took a cab back to the athletes' village for a 1 p.m. team meeting to get ready for a game against the tough Finns that night.

The village was made up of rows and rows of eight-story apartment buildings that stretched for about six city blocks, buildings brightly painted in yellows and reds but still drab and somber on a rainy day. The athletes from all the different countries tried to bring a little home with them to Turin, and national flags hung from the balconies and walls. The security was heavy, a reminder that during the 1972 Summer Olympics in Munich terrorists broke into the athletes' village and killed several Israeli athletes. It's hard to believe, with today's security levels, that such a thing could ever happen again.

Our village was located in south central Turin, near the Lingotto train station and the speed-skating oval, far from the other athletes' villages. When Italian police raided the mountain hamlets of San Sacario and Pragelato on the ninth day of the Games, looking for evidence of doping on the Austrian cross-country and biathalon teams, we were nowhere close. It was a big deal, especially since, in Italy, athletes caught with illegal performance-enhancing drugs can be jailed, a policy the country refused to change for the Olympics.

We expected to play a lot better against Finland. Instead, we lost again 2–0, leaving us without a goal since the final minute of the Germany game, more than six periods of scoreless hockey. After four games, we were 2–2 and struggling. Rick Nash, who wasn't producing offence like he had in the previous year's world championships, was benched in the third period, and that became a big news story. Like the Swiss, the Finns played us hard, and it almost seemed to surprise us. Hitchcock pointed out that this wasn't the World Cup or the NHL, and that a Finn at the Olympics in Europe may be a very different type of player from the Finn we see regularly in the NHL, more aggressive and emotional. These players have a lot of pride in their countries and bring a lot of intensity to this competition. Finland had never won a gold medal in Olympic hockey, and the biggest hockey victory in the country's history had been in upsetting the host Swedes in Stockholm in the gold medal at the 1995 world championships. They had that focus, and maybe it was time to wonder about ours. We seemed to lack the sense of purpose that our opponents had.

On the final day of the round robin portion of the tournament, we faced the Czechs, who had lost Hasek and Elias with injuries. We knew they would play tough anyway. At the world championships the previous spring in Vienna, they had played a very physical game and beaten us in the gold medal game, and they'd almost beaten us at the '04 World Cup in the semifinals. The previous day, after practice, Gretzky had held a press conference and told reporters that our younger players needed to step up their play. In front of 9,126 fans at the Palasport Olimpico, Brad Richards scored before the game was eight minutes old, ending more than 128 minutes of scoreless hockey for Team Canada. Before the period was over, Martin St. Louis and Chris Pronger had also scored to give us a 3–0 lead. Finally, we were able to start feeling better about ourselves, at least temporarily.

In the middle of the second period, however, Czech forward Petr Cajanek fell on me in the crease, and I tweaked my left knee in the same way I had done three weeks earlier in New Jersey against the Islanders. The right knee had been the one I'd injured in October that had knocked me out of the lineup for two weeks. After Cajanek got off me, I barely managed to get to my feet, and the play kept going until I snagged a bullet off the stick of Jaromir Jagr to draw a whistle. After 10 seconds, I knew I just needed time to shake it off and that I would be able to stay in the game even though I was sore. Between the second and third periods, with Canada still leading 3–1 after Czech defenceman Pavel Kubina had scored partway through the second, Gretzky came down to the dressing room to see if I was all right.

At 2:41 of the third, Cajanek beat me on a wrist shot from the right circle that I should have had. I got that one back a minute later when he faked me out of position, but I was able to reach back with the stick and stop his shot before it went into the net.

The Czechs stormed our net for the final half of the third period but we held on to win 3–2 despite being outshot 33–16, including 12–2 in the third. I felt I'd played really well, and afterwards the guys had some nice things to say in the media. Ryan Smyth, known as "Captain Canada" for the many times he had led Canada into the world championships, said I was the "backbone of Hockey Canada," and Quinn said I was a captain without a "C" on my jersey. With a huge quarterfinal match against Russia the next day, I iced my newly injured knee before I went to bed and took a couple of painkillers just to take the edge off.

With three wins and two losses, Canada had finished third in its pool behind the Finns and Swiss, but ahead of the Czechs, which meant we would play the Russians at the Esposizioni. Sweden, interestingly, had ended up missing a matchup with us and playing Switzerland instead after the Swedish head coach, a former NHL player named Bengt Ake Gustafsson, had said in an interview before their final round robin game against the Slovaks that he wasn't sure if his team should try to win. A loss, Gustafsson knew, would mean facing the Swiss in the quarters, while a win would put his country against Team Canada.

Not surprisingly, I suppose, the Swedes lost 3–0 to the Slovaks in a game in which observers felt Sweden barely tried to score and didn't get a shot with a five-on-three advantage in the second period. I don't know if they threw the game, but even talking about it was something I didn't understand. I would never agree to play in a game if I felt my team was not trying to win. We had played our game against the Czechs hoping that it would help us to be playing as well as possible going into the quarterfinals, not trying to figure out which result would give us the best strategic advantage. Now, we knew we couldn't afford to lose another game.

Incredibly, for the first Olympic meeting between Canada and Russia in more than a decade, with only 5,000 seats in the temporary rink, there were still tickets available at the box office for 100 euros just a few hours before game time. The atmosphere was electric nonetheless. This was to be a collision between two proud, strong hockey cultures, and there were more blue-red-white Russian flags and banners in the arena than Canadian ones. There was a sense of hockey history in the building. Alan Eagleson, the architect of the '72 Summit Series, was there, as was Alexander Yakushev, a star forward on the Soviet team in that famous encounter. Canada hadn't beaten the Russians at the Olympics since 1960 in Squaw Valley, and growing up I'd always heard how the Russians had beaten my dad and the Kitchener-Waterloo Dutchmen in Cortina. A half century later, I was getting the opportunity to be part of something truly special.

Pavel Bure, the former NHL superstar, had organized the Russian team, just as Gretzky had picked our squad, and the Russians were very strong. The first period was played in a very careful, deliberate way as the Russian fans beat their drums and blew their noisemakers. Both teams had three power plays but neither could score. Near the end of the period, Gagné was hit hard by a Darius Kasparaitis hip check—a clean hit—just to the side of the Russian net. Gagné left the ice in obvious pain. He came back but wasn't the same, and that took an important weapon away from us.

The second period stayed scoreless. As the clock ticked and the play became more intense, the tension in the building began to rise. It wasn't hard to get the feeling that one moment might well make the difference as a scoreless tie between two great hockey powers churned into the third period.

In the first minute of the third, on a fresh sheet of ice, Bertuzzi went behind the net to try to run a pick for Joe Thornton. Instead of just getting in the way, Bertuzzi accidentally flattened Russian defenseman Sergei Gonchar, and was sent to the penalty box for interference at 55 seconds. The Russians, sensing opportunity, came down into our zone, and we knocked the puck loose from behind the net. For an instant, it looked like either Doan or Pronger was going to grab the puck and clear it to safety, but Alexander Ovechkin poked it loose to Kozlov. Kozlov backed away from the net beside the left post, then flipped a pass back to Ovechkin, who had circled and come back looking for a pass. He put a perfect shot high to give the Russians a 1–0 lead.

It happened in one of those moments that passes by quickly but contains telling information. When I saw the puck on the stick of a Russian player getting ready to shoot, I didn't realize it was Ovechkin. For an instant, I mistakenly thought it was a left-handed defenseman, and from that position on the ice it would have been almost impossible for that player to roof the puck. So I covered the lower part of the net. If I had realized it was Ovechkin, I would have stayed up because a right-handed shooter has a greater ability to get the puck up from that angle, and in his first NHL season with the Washington Capitals, Ovechkin had already demonstrated that was his preferred shot. A momentary case of mistaken identity, then, made all the difference.

We had been shut out by the Swiss and Finns, and in beating the Czechs we had scored all three of our goals in the first period. So we hadn't scored a goal in 10 of the 11 previous periods, and now we were down 1–0. In the next four minutes, we got two power plays, but really couldn't generate much in the way of really good scoring chances as the Russians started to check harder. The play seemed to get faster and nastier. All over the ice, players were furiously hacking and chopping at each other, fighting for pucks, with sticks breaking everywhere.

With 1:20 left and the teams playing with four skaters aside, Russian goalie Evgeny Nabokov made a great save lying on his side, reaching out with his left arm and stopping Dany Heatley from tying the game. With the faceoff in the Russian zone to the left of Nabokov, Quinn indicated it was time for me to come out and allow an extra skater to go in, which would at least give us a five-on-four advantage. Standing between Adam Foote and Jay Bouwmeester on the bench at the Esposizioni, I felt helpless, hoping we could get just one goal and keep the game going. But it wasn't meant to be. Instead, moments later, Pronger was forced to take a penalty, and soon after Alexei Kovalev scored another goal for the Russians.

Maybe the final 2–0 score was symbolic. It was the same score as 50 years earlier when the K-W Dutchmen, with my father on the bench, had lost to the Russians to end their gold medal dream.

As the final buzzer sounded, I took one long, final drink on my water bottle, and dropped it back on top of the net. As we lined up to shake hands, I was the last in line. I had a quick word for Kozlov, my Jersey teammate, gave Nabokov a hug at center ice and skated slowly off the ice. Our dream was over.

We were going home without a medal, and it was difficult to pinpoint what had gone so wrong for a team that seemed to have so much talent but ended up being unable to score in the world's most important hockey tournament. Some of it was, of course, our opponents. Rob Blake called the Russian team the

best he'd ever seen from that country. We had been shut out by
Gerber, Antero Niittymaki and Nabokov, and all had played very,
very well. A lot of it was discipline. The second Swiss goal in that
shocking defeat had been on a five-on-three power play, and we
had seen many of our own power plays erased by taking penalties
of our own. Nash took a lot of criticism, and so much had been
expected of him because he had been such a big star at the world
championships the year before. But I think he wasn't in the same
shape I'd seen in Austria the previous spring, and that was almost
certainly because he'd had so much trouble with injuries during
the NHL season.

We missed Niedermayer's presence for sure, and many of our
players had not played at all during the NHL lockout and still
had not been able to lift their games to the same height they'd
been at before the lockout. Most of the European players, on
the other hand, had gone back to their native countries when the
NHL was shut down, and maybe that made a difference in Turin.
I really believed our team had a lot of qualities. Nothing went
terribly wrong, but nothing went terribly right, either.

Sakic gave an emotional speech after the game, and said he
didn't think our younger players had understood what it was going to take to defend the Olympic title. He urged them to use the
experience to win the gold back in Vancouver in 2010. He spoke
in a quiet voice sitting down in his stall, knowing that, at 37 years
of age, he probably wouldn't be back in 2010.

Canada had dominated the hockey world from 2002 to 2006,
winning the Olympics, the World Cup and two world championships. In the modern world of international hockey, four years is a
long time. Losing in Turin was a setback, but not a major setback.
Hopefully, it would be a learning experience, even for players
such as Sidney Crosby who had remained at home, probably believing in their hearts they should have been with us and could

have made a difference. It was hard to be happy with the result, but I felt able to look at myself and feel I played well. I felt I had given us a chance to win, and that's how I've evaluated my performance throughout my career. Gretzky talked to us next day at a team meeting and said he was proud of us and felt we had worked really hard. I certainly hope that he'll be there in Vancouver in some capacity, and if he wants me to be there, I will. Hopefully, the loss to the Russians wasn't my last moment to shine in the spotlight of international hockey.

The 26th of February was the last day of the Turin Olympics. It was sunny and warm, probably the best weather of the entire time we had been in Italy. The Swedes, a team that had lost twice during the competition and had in the eyes of many "thrown" a game, won the gold against Finland. Canada finished seventh behind the Slovaks and Swiss, a huge fall from the glory of Salt Lake City four years earlier.

Partway through the last day, I went to the athletes' village one last time to meet with a 14-year-old boy from New Brunswick named James Bateman. He was suffering from a brain tumor and was in Turin courtesy of the Children's Wish Foundation. His wish had been to go to the Olympics and see his hero—me—play a game. He was also a goalie for his team back home. To have someone want to meet you that much, and to be that person's hero, is something I find hard to understand. I never had a hero in that way, never felt that way towards an athlete. But I see the pleasure in people when they meet me. Sometimes they're shaking and can barely talk. It makes me pretty proud of what I've accomplished, and that I can be in a position to meet people like James, just say hello and meet his parents. His family is going through the toughest time of their lives, and they wanted me to be a small part of dealing with it.

That night, Team Canada officially flew home, although some team members—Smyth, Pronger, Lecavalier, Richards, McCabe, Thornton and Gagné—had all gone home earlier. Team Canada 2006 was gone forever, and we were heading back to our NHL lives.

Leaving for home empty-handed meant that despite all my accomplishments as a professional goaltender, my father still has something on me, something I'll never be able to match.

He has an Olympic medal won in Italy.

The Toughest Shooters

(and how many times they beat me)

ZIGMUND PALFFY

25 games, 13 goals*

If you knew how Ziggy made life difficult for me over the years, you'd know why it was so rewarding for me to stop him on a penalty shot at the 2005 world championships in Austria. When he was with the Islanders, what was most impressive was how he was able to get all alone for a scoring chance. It seems he had more breakaways against me than any other player. He often beat me with a low shot to the blocker. Once, on a breakaway, I guessed right and stopped that shot. Then he put in the rebound.

**Source: Elias Sports Bureau. Statistics combine regular season and playoffs and are current as of conclusion of 2005–06 season.*

chapter 6
North of the Lamp Post

ST. LÉONARD IS A COMMUNITY IN MONTREAL.

But to me, my street, Mauriac Street, *was* St. Léonard.

If you look at a map of the island of Montreal, imagine it as a foot, with the foot tilted back on its heel. St. Léonard, home to about 70,000 people, sits on the top of the foot just above where the toes begin, a community in northeast Montreal far from downtown, a place more Italian than French in many ways. Typical to Montreal neighborhoods, the white brick homes on Mauriac Street featured "tempos" in the winter, temporary plastic and tarp garages designed to keep snow off the driveways and cars. Mauriac Street was where my life was centered as the youngest of five children, and although we attended school and played outdoor hockey at nearby Parc Ferland, and skated indoors at the St. Léonard Arena a few blocks away, everything I needed was on my street.

It was a long, L-shaped street that would get heavy with snow by mid-December, so it was perfect for road hockey. It was wide enough that we could play diagonally across the street with nets on either side, so we didn't have to move the nets and interrupt the games for the cars that did come through. Our house was just before the bend in the street, and the games generally took place close to our front lawn. Across the street was a lady who would sometimes leave her garage door open, and when the ball from our game would bounce in she'd quickly shut the door and keep our ball. The snow would pile high on the curbs, and we could use them as boards, knocking our opponents into the snow.

Montreal is a diverse city with lots of different types of people and ethnic groups. Our street was mostly French-speaking, but there were many Italian-speaking families on nearby streets. Roberto Luongo, who later became my backup on Team Canada for the World Cup in 2004, the 2005 world championships and the 2006 Olympics, grew up just a couple of streets away. His father, Antonio, was born in Naples, and Roberto grew up fluent in Italian, French and English. He was typical of St. Léonard, although some of the families in our community could speak Italian but no French. My friend Guy Martin once dated a girl who he would speak to in French, and she would speak to him in English. Our street was mostly French, and if there was an Italian kid that I or my brothers knew from school, we might challenge that kid's street to a game of street hockey at the school. It got really competitive, but our street was mostly just for us, families that knew each other with about two waves of age groups, one for my older brothers, Claude and Denis, and one for younger kids like Guy and me.

Looking back, I think we had it pretty easy. Everybody had a nice bike, we always had nets for road hockey and everybody always had a stick. I had the reputation for being the fastest eater. My mother would call us in for dinner, and five minutes later I'd be back out picking up my stick and playing again. And I ate well!

My parents never entertained us, never took us on "play dates." I remember when I got to New Jersey and eventually had my own kids and people would talk about setting up play dates for their children. I thought because I was French I didn't understand what they were talking about. Growing up, my neighborhood was fun, a place where we could play hide-and-seek until midnight or one o'clock in the morning. The lamp post at the end of our driveway was "home" for hide-and-seek, and it was the dividing line for our games. North of the lamp post, you were with the Brodeurs. South of the lamp post, well, there was Guy and his four brothers: Ivan, Denis, Robert and Bruno, whoever might be around. For years, that lamp post and that street defined the boundaries of my world. When we organized a road hockey game there as part of the celebration after I won the Stanley Cup with the Devils in 1995, the dividing line remained the same. Mauriac Street was where my parents, Denis and Mireille, bought a house when they were married in 1956, and it was still their home a half century later when they celebrated their 50th wedding anniversary.

These days, you often hear of athletes who were driven to succeed in sports by their parents. Every athlete, I guess, has a story that explains how he or she came to be who they are. Walter Gretzky is the most famous hockey father in the world, and there are lots of stories out there about parents who gave up their jobs to follow their children around the world in pursuit of a career in sports. Even though my father had played goal in the Olympics, he didn't drive us to play hockey or spend hours with us teaching us the finer points of hockey. In fact, only once when I was a boy did he ever put his skates on and try to teach me something about goaltending. But to this day, he never thinks I let in a bad goal. He'll blame the defense or the forwards, but never me. That's the way it should be between father and son.

As an adult and father, I now know it's often not easy to watch your children play a sport. I learned that during the NHL lockout of 2004–05 when I took Anthony, William and Jeremy to a tournament in Lake Placid, New York. Anyone who has played the game at a high level knows what to do to be successful. But when your children are playing on a team, you feel as though you have all this information inside that you can't give them, and it kind of kills you. I had a hard time watching them play in Lake Placid, just being nervous and wanting them to do well.

I think I learned this part of being a parent very well, and I learned it from my father. Children should have fun and enjoy what they do. If they want it badly enough, they'll have an opportunity to play a sport. They need to be pushed in the right direction, and for educational purposes, I really believe team sports are the way to go. It's important that they have other people in their lives to push them, not just their parents. They need structure and discipline and accountability towards other people. That's what you gain through team sports. It's not just about what you want. You get good habits from that.

Today, my father lives and dies with every game I play, imagining the saves in his mind as he watches me make them on television or when he comes to the games in person. But it wasn't like he pushed me to play. Ever. I think I played more outdoor hockey than organized hockey growing up, sometimes 20-on-20 over at Parc Ferland. Since I was a goalie I wore goalie skates, and that gave me an advantage when the puck became frozen and would hurt other kids when it hit their skates. My mother was always around, with all these kids going in different directions, making it happen for everybody, including my older sisters, Line and Sylvie. One of my sisters, or my brother Claude, would drive me to my games. When I wanted to quit hockey at 14 because the coach wouldn't play me after I came home from a Florida vacation with my family, it was Claude who convinced me to return to the team. I was into skiing at the time, as were a lot of my school friends. Unlike in hockey, nobody told me what to do when I was on the hill, and that appealed to me. So I quit hockey, but it didn't last long. I don't know what Claude said. All I remember is that my big brother told me to go back, so I went back.

My father didn't make me go to hockey school or anything like that. He was so busy working all the time as a professional photographer for various Montreal newspapers, and later he was the official photographer of the Montreal Canadiens and the Montreal Expos. He would come to see me play, but afterwards we would never really talk about hockey. I always appreciated it, and now that I have kids of my own and see how other parents conduct themselves when their children are playing sports, I don't see my parents in those parents at all.

When I grew up, being an athlete wasn't about being rich. We never heard about how much Guy Lafleur made or Patrick Roy made. Now it's the first thing you know about a player. Salary disclosure has been great for driving salaries up, but now players are judged on the basis of their salaries. From my father, I learned about having a passion for something and not just doing it for money. A brilliant photographer, he has published many books, but it was never about making money. He just wanted to make sure as many of his pictures as possible were published. The passion he has had for photography all his life has just been amazing.

His darkroom in our basement, which pretty much looks the same today as it always did, was a big part of our daily lives. We all helped my dad with his photography work at different times, and I remember wondering why our garage was so small. Well, it was that size because he had built a darkroom that took up half the space where the garage should have been. Both Claude and Denis Jr. learned about photography, and there are thousands and thousands of pictures on the walls and in dusty binders on shelves and in a huge safe on the floor. There are countless pictures of hockey players from Bobby Orr to Gordie Howe to Bobby Hull to Jacques Plante, and, of course, some of my father and some of me. There are also photographs of baseball stars like Mike Schmidt, Hank Aaron and Gary Carter, and thick binders of slides from events like the famous 1972 Summit Series between Team Canada and the Soviet Union. My father was working for *Montréal-Matin* and covered the entire eight-game series. The first four games were in Montreal, Toronto, Winnipeg and Vancouver, and the final four games were in Moscow. In the eighth and final game, Paul Henderson scored the winning goal late in the third period for Canada, and my father was one of two Canadian photographers who snapped the famous photo of that historic goal. Along with the shot of an airborne Bobby Orr an instant after scoring the goal that won the Stanley Cup for the Boston Bruins in 1970, my father's photo of the Henderson goal is one of the most famous in the history of hockey.

Elsewhere in my father's workshop, there are pictures of small children with thick mops of blond hair on the shoulders of famous athletes, and these are photos of my brothers and sisters and me when we were used as extras for television commercials made by people my father knew. They needed kids for the commercials and he had lots of kids. My sister Line made more than a hundred, and Denis Jr. figures he made about 75.

Upstairs, in the room that was mine growing up, there are more pictures and memorabilia, including three dusty champagne bottles sitting on top of a bookshelf, one from each of the Stanley Cup celebrations when the Devils won it all. Our home is a museum filled with hockey history, and of the history of the Brodeur family in hockey.

—⚝—

To look at our family is to understand that so much of what happens in sports, whether it's to a team or to an individual, is based on circumstances and luck, often more than talent or training or planning. My father might have been good enough to play in the NHL, but he never got the chance. Of his three sons, all had abilities in sports, but only one made it to the big leagues. My brother Claude, 13 years older than me, was a classic two-sport athlete who played at a very high level in both baseball and hockey. He was a good defenseman, big and strong with a heavy shot, and he played in the Quebec Major Junior Hockey League with the Chicoutimi Saguenéens for two seasons in the late 1970s. His teammates were players like Guy Carbonneau, Alain Côté, Louis Sleigher, Alan Haworth and goalie Sam St. Laurent, all of whom made it to the NHL, and he played against stars like Mike Bossy of Laval, who went on to a Hall of Fame career with the New York Islanders.

Baseball, however, was really Claude's game, and he quit hockey to pursue it. My father had also played a lot of baseball, so there was a love for that sport in our family as well. Claude was a left-handed pitcher who threw hard, around 91 to 92 miles per hour, and he graduated from the Saint Léonard Cougars junior team and landed a professional contract with the Montreal Expos when he was 18. He played a year of rookie ball in Calgary with future major leaguers like Andres Galaragga and Randy St. Claire, and then moved up to A-ball in Jamestown, New York. My brother Denis and I went to see him play there, and with Woody Fryman getting on in years as the top left-handed reliever with the Expos, it looked like Claude might one day be a rarity, a French-Canadian player who made it to the top in baseball with the Expos. But during that year in Jamestown, he tore the rotator cuff in his pitching arm, and his career was over. Just like that. No hockey. No baseball. My big brother wasn't going to get his chance.

It never seemed that Claude was bitter about what had happened to his dream of being a professional athlete, although he says the hard part about losing his career to injury is that he'll never know if he could have made it to the majors. But he also says that seeing me make it to the NHL "eases the pain" a bit.

Denis Jr. played hockey as a boy, like the rest of us, but then he took a different path. He fell in love with BMX bike riding, spinning and jumping off ramps and basically being a daredevil on a bike. He loved it, and was very good at it. He competed in Long Island, New Jersey and Chicago, and was rated as one of the top BMX riders in Canada. But at that Chicago event, he fell awkwardly, hitting his head on a ramp and splitting his helmet in two. He recovered from the head injury, but he never got his nerve back. After that, he just couldn't get himself to do it again.

When I was named to Team Canada for the 1998 Winter Olympics in Nagano, Japan, my whole family came, except for my mother, who is claustrophobic and afraid of flying. In fact, she has never seen me play in person, as a pro. She just can't stand the crowds or the feeling of being in an arena, so she doesn't come to see me play in the NHL and didn't make the trip to Nagano. But everyone else did. Claude missed two weeks of work, and so did Denis. They saw 13 events in 14 days, everything from figure skating to hockey to the closing ceremonies, and it was a wonderful family experience. The only bad part was that I didn't play a single game in those Olympics.

I've never felt any disappointment or any resentment from my brothers because I made it in professional sports and they didn't. If anybody tries to compare me with another goalie, even Patrick Roy, Claude just lets them have it. My brothers really believe in me. I know it must be hard for Claude, and Denis Jr. too, because everybody has dreams. But because we had the opportunity to be close to that life through my dad's work as a photographer, we were never overwhelmed by it. We would go down to the Forum with my father when he was photographing players. I met Guy Lafleur many times, and other players, but being at the Forum isn't what inspired me to be a player. We would skate there when they had Christmas parties for the families of photographers and writers who covered the Canadiens, but I never played a game there until 1993, after I'd made it to the NHL with the Devils.

To be honest, I always preferred playing hockey to watching the Canadiens play. I remember when they were close to winning the Stanley Cup in 1986, my mom said if they won she would order a pizza. When they did win and held a parade downtown, we all skipped school and rode our bikes to watch. We stood there, at Peel and Ste. Catherine, and watched the parade, but boy, did we ever get in trouble for skipping school.

In my competitive minor hockey years, I played at the St. Léonard Arena, which today is called the Martin Brodeur Arena. Of course, I still can't call it that, and when I drive past I still feel surprised that it has my name on it. It happened after we won the Stanley Cup in 2000, and in a city where there are many arenas named after NHL players—the Maurice Richard Arena, Mike Bossy Arena, Martin Lapointe Arena, Gilles Lupien Arena in Bronsberg, Quebec—it's a special honor. The arena was built in 1969, and has a gorgeous, half-oval ceiling with heavy wooden beams, dozens of banners hanging from the walls and ceiling, and four rows of seats on either side. My boyhood pal, Guy Martin, still skates there with his four brothers every Thursday, and they have a big international midget tournament in the arena every year. My first goalie coach, Mario Baril, still runs the arena.

I played at that rink until I was 15 years old, then moved on to the Montreal Bourassa AAA midget team where my hockey career began to get serious. My jersey from that season is in a display case in the arena they named after me, along with a Team Canada jersey, some photos, a hat from the 2004 NHL All-Star game in Minnesota and a commemorative puck. Montreal Bourassa was, and is, an enormously successful program that draws players from

St. Léonard, Anjou and Montreal North, players such as Stéphane Fiset, Felix Potvin, Mike Ribeiro and Vincent Damphousse.

In May 1989, the Quebec Major Junior Hockey League draft was conducted at the Maurice Richard Arena. I was 17 years old, 5-foot-11 and 168 pounds, and I was drafted by the Montreal Junior Canadiens, a team that had Jacques Lemaire as its general manager, my future coach in New Jersey. But before I could even begin my junior career, the team moved 45 minutes east of Montreal to St. Hyacinthe and became known as the St. Hyacinthe Laser. I came home for the summers, but Mauriac Street was no longer my full-time home.

Today, St. Léonard is where my parents live. In the off-season, I spend my time at my cottage in St. Adolphe d'Howard in the Laurentian mountains north of Montreal, but most of the year I live in the United States, in Morristown, New Jersey. My parents are French-Canadian, while my children are American and all their friends are American. My children are bilingual, and that's really important to me. I would be cheating them if I didn't make sure they spoke French, and make a point of teaching them where they're from.

Me? I'm from parts unknown, I guess. I'm French, I'm from Canada and I live in the States and have since 1993. So what does that make me? I suppose I'm French-Canadian first. If I know somebody is French and he speaks to me in English, I have no respect for him. I understand that when there are non-French-speaking people around, English may be more polite. I know it's not very nice when we have Europeans around and they speak to each other in their native language and nobody else can understand. But when I say hello to somebody who I know is French, I expect an answer in French. That's who we are. That's the liaison we have with each other. The NHL referees and linesmen who are French-Canadian, they speak to me in French. But certain older players will come to me and start speaking in English, and I always make a point of speaking in French back to them. I just think that it's about respect. We're from there; we should talk to each other in the language we share.

If somebody asks me where I'm from, I say Canada. But I think the national pride I have for Canada I got through playing hockey and representing the country in international competitions. In Canada, the first of July is Canada Day, but that date was nothing for us growing up. The most significant holiday in Quebec was and is June 24, the feast day of St. Jean Baptiste, the patron saint of French Canada. All my life I grew up thinking that way. I was not very often exposed to the idea of Canada, until I started playing for Canada. Sure, my dad had played hockey for Canada at the Olympics, but when you're young you don't think about it; you don't understand or appreciate it.

The first time I played for Canada was at the world championships in 1996 at the age of 23. I had never played at the world junior championships. When I was still a junior, Trevor Kidd was seen as the top junior goalie in the country, and I guess they didn't want competition for him, or didn't want him to feel pressured by that competition. He and I had been through the draft together, and maybe it was too close for comfort to have us both on the same team. I went to the world junior tryouts twice. They picked Mike Fountain instead of me. Rick Cornacchia was the head coach, and he told me, "Don't worry too much. Patrick Roy never made it either." That always stayed with me. Kidd was really successful with Canada as a junior. He put his foot in there and kept it there, just like I would do later with Team Canada in the Olympics.

In 1996, the world championships were in Austria. The Devils had missed the playoffs after winning the Stanley Cup the previous season, a huge disappointment, and as usual Hockey Canada was inviting players from non-playoff teams to participate in the worlds. I had pretty good information I was going to be part of the '96 World Cup team, so I figured I had better get used to playing these international games. I don't know if it changed my way of thinking about being Canadian. I had just never experienced it before. It wasn't that big a deal until I saw the pride of the people of Hockey Canada, saw how much guys like Bob Nicholson and Johnny Misley and Brad Pascall care, how well they take care of you and how much they want Canada to be successful as a hockey nation.

To be from Quebec, of course, is to be asked about separatism. It's just something in which I have no interest. My preference is for Canada to stay together, but it's not unusual for Quebec-born athletes to get dragged into the endless debate over the province's future in Canada. For example, when a federal election was called in Canada in November 2005, Gilles Duceppe of the Parti Québécois, the party dedicated to Quebec's separation from the other nine Canadian provinces, said publicly he wanted one day to see a Team Québec in hockey at the Olympics. He mentioned my name as one of the players that would be on his team, although I have never met Duceppe or discussed the matter with him.

Would I ever play for Team Québec? Only if I had no choice. If I had to play for Quebec in order to play at all, I would play for Quebec. But if there was a choice between playing for Canada or Quebec, I wouldn't change anything. I would play for Canada, although inside I would be divided. In Quebec, we take a lot of pride in our small population and the unique history of our province. In the brief lockout of 1994–95, there was a four-on-four challenge organized for NHL players in Hamilton, Ontario. There was a Team Québec, a Team Western Canada, and a Team United States. Even though I had barely played in the NHL to that point, Claude Lemieux asked me to come and be a backup to Patrick Roy. It was great fun, and today I think I'd love to see how Quebec could compete against the rest of Canada. It would be interesting to see where we're at compared to the other provinces. But on the world stage, I play for Canada.

To be from Canada, to be from Quebec, and to have lived in the United States most of my adult life, leaves me feeling as though I'm a part of all those places. Maybe it's the way it's always been for me, growing up in St. Léonard, knowing as many Italian-speaking people as Francophones and Anglophones. Maybe it's understanding that home can be about more than one thing, about more than just one type of people. It can be a street, or it can be the connection between two countries and two languages for a hockey player who remembers those games of road hockey on snowy streets as affectionately as the first time he lifted the Stanley Cup over his head in the shadow of the Manhattan skyline.

The Toughest Shooters

(and how many times they beat me)

MARIO LEMIEUX

25 games, 11 goals*

Mario had tons of moves, and was really nifty on his skates for a big man. His reach made such a difference. I always found it amazing how he could get the puck from point A to point B and then shoot it. He could do anything. He even had a one-timer backhand. To practice with him for the 2002 Olympics and 2004 World Cup was to sit back and watch his skill every day. He could shoot hard, but more important, he knew where to shoot.

---

*Source: *Elias Sports Bureau*. Statistics combine regular season and playoffs and are current as of conclusion of 2005–06 season.

chapter 7
Every Boy's Dream

IT'S A PIECE OUT of every child's sporting imagination, just like being at bat in the bottom of the ninth in the World Series with two out, or having the basketball in your hands with time running out in the NBA final, or running for a touchdown in the fourth quarter of the Super Bowl.

Game 7 of the Stanley Cup final. If you're a hockey player or a hockey fan, other than being in the gold medal game at the Olympics, this is the ultimate.

So close to the legendary silver trophy that so many NHLers, from Howie Morenz to Gordie Howe to Bobby Orr to Steve Yzerman, have won.

Sixty minutes away from lifting the Cup over your head. Or watching 20 players on the other team do the same.

Game 7 of the Stanley Cup final. It has only happened 14 times in the history of the NHL. By luck or circumstance, I am one of only three goaltenders in NHL history to have started in Game 7 of a Cup final more than once. The other men to do so were Hall of Fame netminders Terry Sawchuk and Harry Lumley, and both did it while playing for the Detroit Red Wings. Lumley lost Game 7 of the 1945 final to Toronto, then beat the New York Rangers in the '50 final in the seventh and deciding contest. Sawchuk, who replaced Lumley as the starting goalie with the

Wings, played in three Game 7 matches, winning twice, in 1953 and 1954, and losing once, in 1964.

Sawchuk, Lumley and me. That's a pretty exclusive group. That said, I have to admit I was also partly to blame on both occasions when the series in which I was involved went seven games. Against Colorado in the 2001 Cup final, and against Anaheim two years later, the Devils, with me in net, were ahead 3–2 in both series with a chance to clinch the title in Game 6. Both times, the first time in New Jersey and the second time at the Arrowhead Pond in Anaheim, we failed to do so, and both times it happened because I didn't have a particularly strong game. By that point in my career, I had already won two Cups, one in 1995 and one in 2000, so being unable to close the deal twice wasn't about nerves or inexperience. It was about how very difficult it is to win it all, or even get close to winning it all. So much has to go right for a young hockey player to even make it to the NHL, and so much more has to go right for such a player to end up on a team that comes that close to capturing the Cup.

My first trip to Game 7 of the Cup final, in 2001, was, in part, an attempt to overcome the dream of a hockey legend.

The second trip, in 2003, had more to do with finding a way to conquer the problems of real life while playing the sport at its highest level.

—⚓—

Looking back, it's hard to believe we were considered the underdogs in the 2001 Stanley Cup final against the Colorado Avalanche. After all, we were the defending champions with the same head coach, the same goaltender and the same elite players on defense and up front. Moreover, the Devils had enjoyed another terrific year with 111 points during the regular season, first in the Eastern Conference and third overall, two points ahead of a young and improved Ottawa team that had emerged from years of losing to become one of the league's top teams. In many ways, we were better than ever.

The Avs, to give them their due, were an awfully good team as well. With 118 points during the season, they had finished first overall, led by center Joe Sakic, who had finished behind only Jaromir Jagr in league scoring and would go on to win the Hart, Lester Pearson and Lady Byng trophies that year. Patrick Roy, who had won Stanley Cups with Montreal in 1986 and 1993, and with Colorado in 1996, was their goaltender, making this a terrific one-on-one collision between two all-star French-Canadian goalies.

But the leading man for the Avs wasn't Sakic or Roy. It was Raymond Bourque, the classy defenseman who had played 20 years for the Boston Bruins before being traded to the Avalanche the previous season. Bourque, then 40 years of age, had never won a Stanley Cup ring in all those years of competition, despite getting to the final twice with the Bruins. In his first year in Denver, the Avs had reached the 2000 Western Conference final, but had lost to Eddie Belfour and the Dallas Stars.

For the 2001 final, it was almost like the entire hockey world was against us because so many people wanted Bourque to win a Cup. It didn't matter that John Vanbiesbrouck, the backup goalie on our club, had never won a Cup himself after 19 years in the league. The sentiment of the hockey world was concentrated on Bourque. For some reason, everybody felt badly for him that he hadn't won, which put us in the position of being the bad guys in this hockey drama. Even the referees were telling him they wanted him to win. The atmosphere surrounding the final, which would have been heightened anyway because of the quality of the teams and the number of outstanding players involved, was unbelievable. It was all about Bourque, a great storyline for everybody. And we were in their building for Game 7.

We had beaten Carolina in the first round that season, then knocked off Toronto in seven games. In Game 4 of a very emotional series, the Leafs won 3–1 at the Air Canada Centre to tie the series 2-2, but in the final seconds of that fourth game Tie Domi coldcocked Scott Niedermayer with a vicious elbow. It happened at the other end of the ice, which meant I saw it clearly, unlike many hits that happen in my end that I don't see because I'm following the puck. For example, when Scott Stevens crushed Eric Lindros with a violent open-ice bodycheck the year before in Game 7 of the Eastern Conference final, I hadn't seen it. I just heard it. Lindros had come back for that game after missing a long period with a concussion. When Stevens delivered the hit, I was off in the corner playing the puck. I just heard the hit, and I said to myself, "Oh no, did he hit him again?"

In the case of Domi and Niedermayer, Domi was Toronto's enforcer, and he had been threatening Niedermayer the entire game, trying to intimidate him. Niedermayer had kept responding by telling Domi that if he came after him, he was going to "get the Easton," meaning get a taste of Niedermayer's stick. In the final seconds of the game with the result no longer in question, Domi skated past, lifted his elbow and hit Niedermayer with a glancing blow on the chin, knocking him out. Stevens was in the penalty box at the time, and I remember him going crazy, like a caged animal, smashing his stick on the glass because he was so enraged at what Domi had done. Niedermayer was carried off on a stretcher, and the soap opera that followed was even crazier than the incident.

The Leafs and their fans suggested that Niedermayer wasn't hurt that badly, that he was seen out at a bar after the game, while Domi insisted Niedermayer had provoked him with a dirty play earlier in the game. Well, Niedermayer wasn't faking, as he missed the remainder of the series. Domi was tossed out of the series, the rest of the playoffs and the first eight games of the next season. It took away the attention from the hockey, and the fact they were very close to beating us. The Leafs won Game 5 in Jersey, but we came back to take the next two and win the series to advance to the Eastern Conference final against the Pittsburgh Penguins.

The Pittsburgh series was, by comparison, rather uneventful, and we advanced in five games to face Colorado. The Avs had swept Vancouver in the first round, received a scare from Los Angeles, going seven hard games with the Kings before emerging victorious, then knocked off St. Louis quickly in the Western Conference final. Niedermayer came back for us, but by the time the final arrived, the Avs had lost a key player. Colorado center Peter Forsberg had been forced to undergo an emergency splenectomy after the seventh game of the series against L.A. and couldn't return for the Cup final.

If that gave us an advantage, it sure didn't show in Game 1, as the Avs romped to an easy 5–0 win at home. But we won three of the next four, including Game 5 in Denver, which set us up for the perfect chance to end the series on home ice. After winning the Cup in Dallas the year before, it would have been a nice treat for our home fans. Instead, after my teammate Colin White accidentally hit me in the head with a shot during the pre-game warmup, I played indifferently and we lost 4–0, looking as flat as a hockey team could look. But we didn't feel like we had blown our chance to win the Cup and end Bourque's dream, mostly because we knew we had another chance to win it and we'd done it before in the other team's building.

We followed a crazy travel schedule after winning Game 5 in Denver, and I believe it influenced our play for the next game.

The Game 5 victory had been uplifting, but instead of leaving right after the game and getting home by 2 or 3 a.m., and then sleeping in our own beds, we decided to stay over in Denver. We took a flight back east the next day and arrived in time for an enormous traffic jam outside Newark Airport. As had long been our habit, the team was staying at an area hotel, so we had time to go home to change and say hello to our families, then drive back to the hotel. It was chaotic, and we had spent the first of two off-days between games traveling, essentially wasting our advantage. When it came to travel, it seemed as though the Avs were ahead of us the whole series.

It means a lot to players that team management does everything possible around the games so they don't have to worry about small details. I'll never understand why we stayed that extra night in Denver. I guess it was just a mistake, but it made it seem like we were overwhelmed by everything, worried about the altitude, getting there early, getting there late—it was like we did too much to prevent the worst instead of doing our usual thing and preparing as we normally would to win games. The altitude of Denver alone—5,280 feet—became a distraction because our organization was so consumed by it. In these crucial playoff games, your head is half the battle, and our approach to Game 6 and the chance to win the Cup on home ice showed a team that had lost that battle.

So back to Denver we went for Game 7 with a planeload full of family members, including my wife, Mélanie, my dad and my kids. Before I left, I was playing with the boys at home, and one of them hit me hard on the foot with a hockey stick, hard enough that my foot became swollen and I couldn't put my shoe on. I was scared the whole way out to Colorado, worried that it would affect my game.

One of the strange things that happened before Game 7 was that Vanbiesbrouck asked to make a pre-game speech to stir up the troops. He had only been with us since March of that year, but he was really emotional about the opportunity to win the Cup in what he felt would be the last game of his career, so our coach, Larry Robinson, told him to go ahead. It was unusual that a relatively new player would be the one to deliver such a speech before a big game. Vanbiesbrouck's heart was definitely in the right place. He talked about playing so many years in the league, and how difficult it was not to be a regular with the Devils but that it would be as meaningful to be part of a Cup winner as if he had been playing himself. He stood in the middle of the room, talked about getting to the final with Florida in '96 and losing to Colorado, and just told us how he felt.

It was a very emotional speech that seemed to pump the players up, but then Stevens totally deflated the mood. "Let's just go out there and play," he said. Stevens was our captain and a strong leader, and it was his way of expressing how anxious he was to get out on the ice. He didn't mean to spoil Vanbiesbrouck's speech, but it created an awkward moment. Vanbiesbrouck had joined us at the trade deadline that year in a deal for Chris Terreri, and he really helped me out. He was a really solid, solid man, and I had tons of respect for him. (The following year we were switching backups back and forth, J.F. Damphouse and a couple of other goalies. Beezer was retired and came to see me before a game in Long Island just before the Olympic break. Lamoriello saw him, and told him to come and talk to him afterwards. "Do you want to play a few more games after the break?" Lamoriello asked Vanbiesbrouck, and eventually offered him $500,000 for the rest of the year. He took the Olympic break to get back in shape, and was my backup the rest of the season. So just because he wanted to drop by and say hi to me, he ended up making an extra half-million.)

The crowd in Denver for Game 7 was amazing, such a difference from the low-key gathering in our building the game before. Of course, we hadn't given our fans much to cheer for. The pre-game hype was all about Bourque, about his "Mission 16W"—16 wins—to capture his first Cup. It was a zoo inside the Pepsi Center, really great fun and the kind of atmosphere any athlete should want to be in. It's such a grind to play four rounds in the Stanley Cup playoffs, with the number of games, the traveling, the emotional ups and downs and the physical demands. You get to Game 7, and you just want it to end, really. Your body is "saying uncle." An athlete in that situation knows that it will end that night, and there will be a winner and a loser. It becomes a gold medal game, and all the players involved are pushed to the limit. It raises the stakes—there are no more chances to come back in the next game.

The Avs scored early, just before the eight-minute mark of the first, when Alex Tanguay went high with a wraparound attempt. We couldn't get much going, managing only nine shots on Roy in the first period. In between periods, it was all focus. In big games with an experienced, veteran team, not much is said in the dressing room. Everybody has his own responsibilities, and everybody respects the space of other players. We had lost the momentum in the series by losing Game 6, and falling behind early in Game 7 just narrowed our allowable margin of error even further.

They played the heck out of three defensemen—Rob Blake, Adam Foote and Bourque—and they did a great job wasting time between whistles to give those three defensemen extra breathers. If the league had been using the hurry-up faceoff rule back then, Colorado would never have beaten us because they would have had to use their other defensemen more. Every faceoff, it seemed, took about two minutes, with their players talking to the referees and generally taking their time. It was like the old days with Wayne Gretzky and Mark Messier talking to the referees forever about everything just to slow things down. The Avs used that strategy effectively, and it got frustrating for us. By the end of the game, Bourque had played 29 minutes and 35 seconds, Foote 29:44 and Blake 24:34. The rest of the Colorado blueline corps—Greg deVries, Jon Klemm and Martin Skoula—played a combined 36:37, and there was rarely a time when two of those three defensemen were out together.

Tanguay scored again at 4:57 of the second, and then Sakic scored a pretty goal just over a minute later on a power play with Sean O'Donnell off for high-sticking. We had used Bobby Holik and Stevens against Sakic most of the series pretty effectively, but on his goal, Sakic faked Stevens down to the ice and then put a high shot past me to make it 3–0 for Colorado. Petr Sykora scored to cut the lead to 3–1 three minutes after that, but the Avs checked very well the rest of the way, particularly in the third period when we got only five shots.

The final score was 3–1, and Roy was named winner of the Conn Smythe Trophy as playoff MVP. After the game, I bolted out of the dressing room, feeling so bad for my kids having to watch that game and watch us lose. They had seen me win games and lose games many times, of course, but for some reason at that moment I felt like a very protective father, as though rushing to their side would somehow ease their vulnerability in a hostile arena far from home. Of course, when I walked into the room where they were waiting, they were playing ball hockey like nothing had happened, but it worried me so much at the time. That was one of the few times I didn't stop to speak to the media after a game, any game, and I regret that still. That's part of my job, and it's my responsibility to do it every night.

We had blown two shots at winning our second straight Stanley Cup, and we were enormously disappointed. For me, there was also disappointment to lose to Roy. There were memories of Nagano, when he had insisted on playing every game and I hadn't played a minute. I took the 2001 final personally because it was a chance to go toe-to-toe with a goalie who had so many records, a goalie who was supposed to be "The Man," a real playoff warrior. We had him on the ropes but couldn't finish him off. Bourque, in his 22nd and final season, finally had his Stanley Cup ring, and perhaps his presence had given the Avalanche the central rallying point that allowed them to win that championship.

A few years later, I heard an interview with Tom Brady, quarterback of the New England Patriots, and he was asked which of his Super Bowl championships was sweeter. "The next one," he said. He's right. Even if you've won before, you feel so small when you don't win. It's like you can't win anymore. People outside the game, and sometimes people inside the game, don't understand how much commitment is required, but also how much luck is involved by coaches, players, the referees. The stars have to be perfectly aligned, no matter how good you are, no matter how good your team is—it's still amazing to me the breaks you need to be successful.

—m—

When you hurt people, they can react in different ways, ways you might never have expected or anticipated.

That was a lesson I learned in the spring of 2003 when my wife, Mélanie, filed for divorce. The story of our marital split had been public knowledge ever since a Quebec-based tabloid called *Photo Police* had published a story the previous month filled with all kinds of allegations and untrue statements, and a few weeks after that I had been interviewed by Bertrand Raymond of *Le Journal de Montréal* to tell my side of the story. Mélanie and I had been apart since the final days of December 2002, and it was a very difficult time for both of us and our four children. I had hoped to keep the matter private, knowing, of course, that would be difficult to do.

When the story became public, it was a painful time for my family and for me, and the timing for an NHL player could not have been worse, the beginning of the Stanley Cup playoffs. During the Devils' first-round series against Boston, and in the second round against Tampa Bay, fans in both cities had taunted me with chants and signs, some of which were vicious and some of which were pretty creative, I had to admit. They focused to a large degree on the fact that, by that time, I was in a serious relationship with Geneviève Nault, who at an earlier time had been married to Mélanie's half-brother. It was the type of unpleasant situation I had never had to deal with before as a professional athlete, where everybody knew something about my private life and I was being closely scrutinized.

The whispers were so loud that partway through the Tampa series, I realized I had to face the music with the New Jersey and New York media, many members of which I had been dealing with for years. After one of the games, I brought everybody over and confirmed to them that I had separated from my wife, and that we weren't going to be together anymore. It wasn't easy. I just realized it was something that had to be done. I know my responsibilities as a professional athlete, and that sometimes one's personal life can get in the way of fulfilling those responsibilities. And, rightly or wrongly, people believe they have the right to know what's going on in your life. Most of the time, the interest of fans and the media is simply that: interest, or curiosity. But when people are trying to hurt you by going further and further with the story, it's different.

There was one New Jersey hockey writer who I felt went too far, and since then we haven't spoken. I don't believe he needed to do what he did just to keep the story going. I realize, of course, that it's not always a simple issue for the media to decide how far to pursue a story. But I felt my situation was different, for example, from that of my teammate Ken Daneyko. In November 1997, Daneyko became the first NHL player to voluntarily enter the league's new substance abuse program. He missed 45 games, returning in February 1998. It was a courageous decision he made, and there was a lot of media interest. But my situation was different in that I didn't miss a practice or a game. There was no indication my marriage problems were affecting my game at all.

By the end of the Tampa series, for example, I was 8–2 with three shutouts. At one point during the regular season, after our initial breakup, Mélanie had wanted me to leave the team while we were in Ottawa to go back to New Jersey and discuss our problems, and she called team officials to make her concerns known. I told her I would be back as scheduled, the next day by noon, and we could talk about it then. People in my job count on me. It wasn't life-threatening, the kids weren't sick, she wasn't sick—it was something we had to deal with on our own time. There was absolutely no evidence that my personal life was affecting my play or the results of the team.

As hard as things were, and as messy as they got publicly, it was easier to compete in the playoffs through all of this than if I had sat at home. That would have been excruciating. For me, the rink became my safe haven, the place where I could go and not have to deal with the stress of my failed marriage. Those hours at practice or a game were precious to me at a time when my personal life was in disarray.

The news that Mélanie had filed for divorce hit the headlines on May 20, the day after we had lost Game 5 to the Ottawa Senators in the Eastern Conference final, a defeat that cut our lead to three games to two. When I was asked about the divorce petition after the game, it was the first I had heard about it, but it wasn't difficult to figure out the timing had been deliberate. As I said, when you hurt people, you don't know how they're going to react. And I had hurt her. I had made mistakes, and at times had acted like a model idiot.

The challenge for me, however, was to focus on my job. I couldn't just fall apart, or leave the team. I had to play, and try to play well, knowing that if my performance was sub-par the story would be that I had been unable to handle the pressure of my personal problems, and those problems had cost the Devils. When we lost Game 6 at home on an overtime goal by Ottawa defenseman Chris Phillips, the situation went from bad to worse. How did I hold it together? My closest friends still say they don't know how I did it. To be honest, *I* don't really know. I suppose the simplest explanation is that hockey is a game in which there are always distractions and you have to learn how to block them out. When a slapshot is coming at me at 100 miles per hour, am I going to think about something else?

Maybe the Senators saw the Anaheim Mighty Ducks waiting for them in the Stanley Cup final, and took their eye off us for just a moment. Maybe the moment got to them as Canada waited for its first Stanley Cup finalist since 1994. They had home ice for Game 7, and luck seemed to have turned against us. Our team bus broke down on the way to the rink, and we were forced to use a school bus. Our trainers got in a car accident on the way to the game. We had scored only two goals in the previous two games and blown a 3–1 series lead. But a fairly dull game tied 2–2 late in the third period looked to be headed for overtime until Grant Marshall slipped a pass through the feet of Ottawa defenseman Wade Redden to Jeff Friesen, who beat Sens goalie Patrick Lalime with a pretty forehand move to give the Devils a 3–2 lead.

For the final 2:14, Ottawa couldn't even manage a shot on me, and we were through to our third Stanley Cup final in four years. Despite all the controversy about my divorce, I had won 12 of 17 playoff games and allowed only 27 goals. And my best hockey was yet to come. Getting to the final made me think back to the eve of the playoffs when my nephew, Philippe Gendron, had told me that we were going to win the Cup. Maybe he was going to be proven correct.

—⁂—

The final against Anaheim would involve at least one trip to California for Games 3 and 4, and possibly a second trip for Game 5. It had become increasingly difficult for me to see my children, both because of the demands of the playoffs and because I was living most of the time in either a hotel room or an apartment, places that are difficult to share with four children under the age of seven. Geneviève had basically made herself into a ghost, because we both knew it wasn't the right time for her to be around the kids. The first time she really came out with me in public was for a dinner after the final. For one of the trips to the west coast, my dad and my brothers came along so that my children could come, and another family friend, Mark DiGiacomo, made the effort to fly to California as well to help me manage the children.

The Ducks weren't a storied team like Montreal or Detroit, but they had done a lot of surprising damage in the playoffs, riding the excellent goalkeeping of Jean-Sébastien Giguère. They had swept the Red Wings in the first round, knocked off Dallas in six games in the second round and then swept Minnesota in the Western Conference final, allowing only 21 goals in the 14 games. Against the Wild, Giguère had registered three shutouts in four games. I really didn't know Giguère well as a goalie, but we had to respect what he had accomplished, that he had been almost unbeatable in the playoffs. He was a goalie who had managed to really get in the heads of the other teams.

In Games 1 and 2, I picked up two shutouts as we won both by identical 3–0 scores. Anaheim had been resting and waiting for us for 10 days while we fought it out with the Senators, and they weren't that sharp to start the series. But they won the next two at home in overtime, and suddenly we had a battle on our hands. In Game 3, I allowed one of the weirdest goals in my goaltending career. Sandis Ozolinsh, an Anaheim defenseman, dumped the puck into our zone with the game tied 1–1 in the second period, and I left my crease to play the puck. By accident, I dropped my stick as I tried to slide my blocker hand up the shaft. Usually, I catch the taped knob before I play the puck, but I somehow missed it and dropped the stick. The puck was rolling really slowly, but somehow it hit my stick, bounced through my legs and went into the net. It was worse than peewee hockey and it was embarrassing, but at the same time all I could really do was laugh at myself. Maybe a goalie is supposed to be crushed by a misplay like that, but I really did find it funny. We tied the game later anyway, but then lost in overtime. Of course, I also knew that if we lost the Cup, everybody would go back and point to that mistake and that goal.

Back in Jersey for Game 5, the offenses opened up and we won 6–3, by far the most goals any team had scored on Giguère in the playoffs. Just as in '01, that gave us the opportunity to take the Cup in Game 6, although this time the potential clinching game was on the road.

Again, we failed to put our opponent away. The Ducks scored three times on me in the first period and were leading 3–1 when Scott Stevens delivered another one of his spectacular hits, this time absolutely decking Paul Kariya of the Ducks. Like Lindros in 2000, Kariya was a player who had suffered through concussion problems before, and he lay on the ice like there was no way he'd be playing again in the series. Instead, he got to his feet, returned to the Anaheim bench and 11 minutes later skated down the left wing and beat me with a rising slapshot. It was like he had come back from the dead, and it was a hugely emotional moment for the Ducks.

Knowing that we had to fly back east for Game 7 two days later, head coach Pat Burns pulled me in favor of Corey Schwab with 11 minutes left and we lost 5–2. As in 2001, Game 6 had been a lopsided loss for the Devils, and the objective going home was to make sure the conclusion was different this time around. For the Ducks, it was a double victory to have won the game and to have knocked me out of the net. It gave them the false impression that they had got to me.

Going into Game 7, I really wasn't reliving 2001 at all, although in an interview with Larry Brooks of the *New York Post* I said the pain of that defeat "never completely goes away." As well, there was a similar element to the series compared to '01, as both Adam Oates and Steve Thomas of the Ducks were classy, veteran players who were looking for their first Cup ring in the same way Bourque had been searching for that opportunity two years earlier. Still, I felt far more confident against the Mighty Ducks than the Avalanche, particularly since we had already shut them out twice in our building. In general, I didn't see any important parallels between '01 and this Game 7. It felt totally different, and part of it was the feeling of being home. As well, the Ducks just didn't have an intimidating presence as a team. I don't know if it was their duck logo, or the fact that in our building they hadn't really shown us anything in three games, all of which we had won by three-goal margins. In Anaheim, they had been much better. But this game was in East Rutherford, New Jersey.

Many athletes have special routines before big games, and many prefer to be left undisturbed so they can focus on the challenge ahead. Not me. While some goalies can't even talk to the media on the day of a game, it's never bothered me, and on the afternoon of Game 7 against the Ducks, June 9, 2003, I spent the time booking a trip to the Caribbean. Usually I sleep for two hours on the day of a game, but this time I booked a trip to the Grace Point resort in the Turks and Caicos in the first hour, then slept the second. I knew the playoffs were going to be over that night, and the chaos in my life and the pressure of chasing the Cup left me knowing I wanted to get out of town as soon as possible after the series was over.

We had won it all in 2000 and lost to the Avs in '01 with Larry Robinson as coach, and for this trip to the Cup final we were coached by Burns, who was in his first year with the Devils. He had joined us that season after the playoff disaster of the previous spring in which we had been shocked by Carolina in six games. Kevin Constantine had coached us in that series after replacing Robinson during the season, just as Robinson had replaced Robbie Ftorek two years earlier. Constantine was a big departure for the Devils. His system of defensive points was a little peculiar, a little over the top, even for us, a team that was very focused on defense. A blocked shot, for example, was worth two points, and he wanted everybody diving to block pucks. At one point, we had to practice with foam rubber pucks because he wanted us to work on blocking shots so much. Robinson hadn't wanted anybody leaving their feet to block shots, so Constantine's approach was a drastic change. Even before we lost to Carolina, we had a pretty good idea Constantine wouldn't be sticking around.

Burns' hiring came out of the blue, just as had been the case when Lemaire was hired a decade earlier. Burns had coached the Canadiens and the Maple Leafs, and he had been fired by Boston eight games into the 2000–01 season and then had kind of disappeared after that. Nobody expected his hiring, but it turned out to be a good fit. Burns used the kind of strong defensive system we were used to and added the grit we needed. He made players accountable. One look from Burns could scare the hell out of a player, and he could get the best out of players who went soft on other coaches. He was very conscious of the defensive part of the game, and as a goalie that's what you want. It can make the difference between playing 65 or 70 games for a goalie, or a lot fewer, and that year I had played 73 regular season games and another 23 playoff games heading into Game 7.

One of the very difficult decisions Burns made in the '03 playoffs was to sit out Daneyko, a very close friend of mine. Daneyko broke in with the Devils in 1983 and, despite his substance abuse issues, had played in every Devils playoff game going into that spring. Burns decided to scratch him for the fourth game of the first round, which snapped a 165-game consecutive playoff game streak for Daneyko. It really left Daneyko bummed out. He was an intense guy, and I loved playing with him, but Burns felt he didn't have that extra step anymore and we had Richard Smehlik, a more mobile defenseman. Daneyko was spotted over the next three rounds, playing 10 of the next 19 playoff games that spring. The night before Game 7 against the Ducks, Burns told him he was going to play instead of Oleg Tverdovsky, and for the next day Daneyko was like a kid in a candy store. He was a nervous player who sat on the bench and rocked back and forth, but he was funny and loved to talk, which made him a great player to be around. I can't say it made a big difference to the actual game that night, as big No. 3 only played 19 shifts, for 11:23 of ice time. But he brought something to the moment, maybe gave us a surge of emotion. For Burns, it was the right thing to do, and demonstrated the special feel of a special coach at the most crucial time.

The other new face for the final stages of the '03 Cup final was a young forward named Mike Rupp. Burns had put him into the lineup in Game 4, replacing Jiri Bicek. I don't think I'd even talked to Rupp before that, and certainly wouldn't have believed he was poised to be a hero. But hey, that's the playoffs. You have your big guys who are always there and so does the other team, and many times the difference in a series lies in the quality of your support players. If you keep guys believing and on their toes, the next thing you know you get the best out of them when it matters most.

Rupp, who had played 47 games in the minors during that season and only 26 for the Devils, scored once and assisted on two goals by Jeff Friesen as we beat the Ducks 3–0. It was our third Stanley Cup win in eight years. It was a strange game that had only three power plays, two of them for us, and all three of our goals were scored at even strength. I was only the third goalie ever to register a shutout in Game 7 of a final, and the 24-save win was my third shutout of the series. Still, Giguère was given the Conn Smythe Trophy as playoff MVP. The people in the building, mostly Devils fans, were shocked, and looking back, if I wasn't going to win, it should have been Niedermayer. Or some other member of the Devils. I don't think a player on the team that loses the Cup should win the Conn Smythe. I was disappointed, sure, but I had just won the Stanley Cup, and as Giguère received the trophy the fans chanted "Marty's Better!"

I've always looked at a career like a backpack. You put one experience in there, and then go looking for the next. That's the game.

—⁓—

The win capped what had been a tremendous 16 months for me, starting with winning gold for Canada at the 2002 Winter Olympics, followed by the 2003 Stanley Cup victory over Anaheim and, a few days later, my first Vezina Trophy as the NHL's best goaltender. In the middle of it all I had experienced the most difficult personal challenge of my life, dealing with the breakup of my marriage and the strain it put on my family and professional life. Looking back, I'm pretty proud of how I handled myself. Afterwards, I found it easier to deal with adversity because of what I had gone through. I made mistakes, and I paid the consequences in a variety of ways. A lot of my teammates didn't want to be seen socially with me for a while after all that happened that spring. They were worried their wives would think they were up to something because they were with me, which made me laugh. After all, I hadn't lost my marriage so I could be free and able to do whatever I wanted to do. I didn't do it to hurt my family. I did it for a relationship and the promise of a better future.

Just as 2001 had ended in disappointment, 2003 had delivered sweet success. They were two very different journeys to the top of the mountain, to the ultimate level of competition for any NHL player. Both seasons had ended in Game 7 of the Stanley Cup final, which had come after long, arduous campaigns filled with hard wins and sour defeats. The romance of Game 7, the charm of being in that special place that every little boy imagines with his friends while chasing a tennis ball in a game of street hockey, seemed to overshadow the reality that nine months of hard hockey labor had been reduced to a single game. No matter what had happened professionally or personally in the preceding months, it was all down to one game. Win that game, the season was a success. Lose it, and somebody else lifted the Cup. Such a fine line between joy and bitterness, between success and failure. But that's the game. That's the dream.

The Toughest Shooters

(and how many times they beat me)

BRETT HULL

22 games, 9 goals*

The goal I remember was a tic-tac-toe play while he was with the Blues. The pass went to him across the slot to the far circle, and I was on my back trying to get across. It was in the old rink in St. Louis, the first time I ever faced him. As I came across, he was lining up a one-timer and fired a rocket under the crossbar. I thought my life was over as I saw the shot coming. He was always hard to find out there. You'd turn around and he was somewhere else. And he always hit the net.

---

*Source: *Elias Sports Bureau. Statistics combine regular season and playoffs and are current as of conclusion of 2005–06 season.*

chapter 8
Shut Out

THE LOCKOUT THAT COST the hockey world the 2004–05 NHL season, and left the league without a Stanley Cup champion for the first time since 1919, was an opportunity for me to take a long look at life without the game.

No NHL schedule. No schedule at all. No planned or anticipated trips to familiar cities, arenas and hotels. No practices or workouts. No massage therapists or trainers. No contract. No income. No fans. No games involving other teams to watch. No counting down the minutes before warmup. No worrying about pads and equipment or tickets for friends and family. Instead of trade rumors, just endless speculation over the future of the league. No planes to catch. No curfews to watch, coaches to listen to, GMs to negotiate with or teammates to laugh with—or at. It was like an extended off-season, or a peek at retirement.

This lockout was very different from the one that NHL players had gone through 10 years earlier, a stoppage that reduced the 1994–95 season to 48 games. That year, there was uncertainty, but we always felt we'd be back playing. Some teams had new arenas, and there was a sense that the owners wouldn't be strong enough to cancel an entire season. Nobody believed there wouldn't be a Stanley Cup champion crowned in the spring of 1995, and we, the New Jersey Devils, ended up being that champion. So we were proved right. They didn't cancel the season.

But 2004 was different. As soon as the 2004 World Cup trophy was presented to Team Canada captain Mario Lemieux at the Air Canada Centre in Toronto by former Maple Leaf star defenseman Borje Salming, we knew there wasn't going to be hockey for a long, long time. The lockout was announced by NHL commissioner Gary Bettman on September 16, and just hours after being a teammate, Lemieux was now, as an owner with the Pittsburgh Penguins, on the other side of this labor fight. Wayne Gretzky, Team Canada's executive director, was also a part-owner of the Phoenix Coyotes, and therefore he was part of the opposition for the NHL Players' Association.

Joe Thornton had played incredibly well for Team Canada, but the day after the World Cup final victory over Finland he was on a jet to Switzerland to begin playing for the Davos club team. Eventually several hundred NHL players would head over to Europe to play in Russia, the Czech Republic, Slovakia, Sweden, Finland, Germany, Italy, Austria and even Hungary. The rest, including myself, decided to stay home and were left as hockey players without a team and a new life of inactivity and loose ends.

The most significant factor that triggered the lockout was that the NHL wanted "cost certainty," specifically in the form of a salary cap to limit payrolls, while the players' union vowed never to accept a salary cap, under any circumstances. With more than $2 billion of league revenues at stake, and with the league claiming enormous losses and the players earning an average of $1.8 million per season, it was clear from the start this was going to be a long, nasty fight between two committed opponents, the NHL and the players' association.

During the 1994–95 lockout, I was 22 years old, earning $140,000 per season and just getting established as a starting goalie in the NHL. By the fall of 2004, I was a 32-year-old divorced father of four making $8 million a season, had won three

Stanley Cups, two Vezina trophies (I had won Vezina again in 2004) and an Olympic gold medal. The stakes were a lot higher for me, for the union and for the league.

During the previous lockout, some of the players had skated together in anticipation of playing again, but that didn't happen this time. I spent a little time in New Jersey, a little time in St. Adolphe d'Howard at my summer home, and simply enjoyed the chance to be with my kids. A lot of mornings, there was this lingering, frustrating sense I had nowhere to go, especially since my children lived with my ex-wife and I didn't have them with me every day. My girlfriend Geneviève and I went to Florida in November with a couple of friends, François and Céline Jacobs. We rented motorcycles and basically just hung out. It was November, a time when my internal clock told me the NHL season would usually be starting to heat up. Instead, I was in Florida, working out every day, but not playing hockey anymore. There were no talks between the league and the union, and there was no optimism.

Later that month, a representative from IMG, the company that did some of my marketing work, approached me and asked if I was interested in participating in a European tour, something similar to that which Gretzky, then a member of the Los Angeles Kings, had organized 10 years earlier when the league had shut down. Right away, it seemed like a great idea to me, a chance to see Europe, to travel with some players I knew and liked and to have some fun. When you're a player and suddenly you're not playing, that's what you miss most, being with the guys. It almost becomes a game every day, finding a little dirt on teammates so you can make fun of them, kidding a guy who wears the same shirt two days in a row, anticipating funny lines teammates are going to use, going to a bar and laughing when something funny happens.

It's just a fun atmosphere to be on a team. Firemen get the
same feeling living in a firehall, and often police officers get that
same sense of camaraderie. For hockey players, it's an environment in which you can talk about anything you want and not have
to look over your shoulder and wonder what somebody outside of
the group will think. It's something you have to live and be part
of to understand. It's like you're a big kid, and in a lot of ways,
you're treated like children. How many men in their thirties do
you know who have somebody telling them what time to be in
bed or when they have to wear a tie? If you can't accept that, you
can't thrive in this environment. For professional hockey players, that sense of order is something we've been used to since we
were teenagers, or even younger. Other sports, like baseball and
basketball, are learned on the streets, sometimes in places where
they are played just to survive. In hockey, players are used to
buildings and structure and rules, used to being told what to do
and when to do it. We are told how to play the game. You can't
just freelance or do whatever you want on the ice, at least not on
a successful team. When that kind of order and organization is
taken away, as it was during the lockout, it's a very strange feeling,
and it's a feeling you yearn to have back. So when the IMG people
proposed the Primus Worldstars Tour, with some of the profits
going to charity and with the games broadcast on pay-per-view
back to North America, it was a welcome idea. It was a chance to
be part of a team.

The lineup for the tour was pretty impressive, and included
Dominik Hasek in goal, Rob Blake, Mattias Norstrom, John-
Michael Liles, Rhett Warrener, Stéphane Quintal, Barrett Jackman
and Robyn Regehr on defense and forwards like Sergei Fedorov,
Glen Murray, Kris Draper, Brendan Shanahan, Ian Laperrière,
Eric Bélanger, Luc Robitaille, Mats Sundin, Anson Carter, Ray
Whitney, Tie Domi and Tony Amonte. Players came and went

as the tour went along, almost like an elaborate pickup game of international shinny, or a traveling circus. Some players were supposed to show up but didn't. Daniel Brière was playing for a team in Bern, Switzerland, so he ended up playing one game with us in the Czech Republic, and one game against us two days later in Bern. Same with Sergei Gonchar.

For every game I played, I wore the "C" as team captain, just as Bill Durnan had done decades earlier with the Montreal Canadiens. We also usually had a forward or defenseman serving as captain, and although this was a friendly tour of exhibition games, it felt good to have that designation. I had always felt like a leader, increasingly so as I had gained experience and enjoyed success in the NHL. This was a chance to experience the feeling that others had, and I liked it.

The head coach was Marty McSorley, but this wasn't really a situation in which a team was going to be "coached" in the traditional sense. Marc Bergevin, one of the funniest people in hockey, was an assistant coach, and he ended up being the life of the party. While the tour was for fun, the schedule was extremely demanding, calling for 10 games in 14 days in seven countries. That didn't give us enough time to enjoy the cities—mostly just the restaurants and bars. We started in Toronto with 17 players at an open practice at the Ricoh Coliseum, and then, as speculation swirled about a new proposal from the NHLPA to the league, flew on December 8 to Riga, Latvia, which was a beautiful and historic place to start. Many of the local people spoke English, it was safe and secure compared to Russia (as we later found out), and the fans were unbelievably enthusiastic.

There was sadness there, too. Sergei Zholtok was a Latvian national who had played 10 years in the NHL for six different teams, including being part of the Minnesota Wild team that would have played against the Devils in the '03 Stanley

Cup final, but instead lost to Anaheim in the Western Conference final. Zholtok had played for the Nashville Predators in the 2003–04 season, and when the lockout started he joined a club team in his home country. During a tournament match in Minsk between his Riga 2000 team and Moscow Dynamo on November 3, he left the game with five minutes to play, made his way to the dressing room and then collapsed and died in the arms of Darby Hendrickson, a former Minnesota teammate who had also joined the Riga team. The official explanation was that Zholtok had died from a massive heart attack and it was later revealed that for several years he had suffered from a heart arrhythmia—similar to that which eventually forced Mario Lemieux into retirement a year later.

Zholtok was only 31 years old and was married with two children, and since he was a national sports figure in Latvia, his death was a major story. He was very popular among NHL players he had played with and, because of his age and his young children, his death touched many of us, particularly after we visited his grave and met his wife, Anna, his teenage son, Edgar, and infant daughter, Nikita. It was easy to feel it could have been any one of us.

Interestingly, in light of Zholtok's story, when we played the game against Riga, Blake really nailed one of their younger players with a thundering bodycheck, leaving him lying on the ice. After a few minutes, it was pretty clear their team didn't have a trainer, so we sent our trainers out to help the player. It certainly put things in perspective, and made you wonder what medical help had been available to Zholtok the day he died. It made me feel so fortunate for the people that are there for us in the NHL, and the importance of having qualified medical care nearby when you play a game as dangerous as hockey can be. We only had 15 skaters and two goalies, three fewer skaters than the NHL norm, but we won the game 4–2 over Riga 2000 in front of an announced crowd of 5,000 fans at the Sporta Pils arena, which was only supposed to hold 3,800.

All the countries we visited had put up money for us to be there, and every country wanted to entertain us as well, which made the tour very much like an unending party. There were nights when we wouldn't get back to our hotel until 4 or 5 in the morning, and then have to play a game at 5 p.m. that day. The generosity of our hosts was wonderful, but it made an already punishing schedule even more difficult. Hasek and I were the goalies, so even after a late night, for one or both of us, there was nowhere to hide. If you're a forward or a defenseman, you might be able to drift by in an exhibition game after a late night, but not if you're a goalie. Hasek, who I didn't know very well before the tour, is a different guy. He was a very accomplished athlete used to doing his own thing, often regardless of how it affected other people. Just as the Boston Red Sox would often deal with the antics of outfielder Manny Ramirez by shrugging and saying, "Manny is Manny," so too with Hasek. You had to be willing to say, "Dom is Dom." During the trip, we were often lucky if he arrived five minutes before game time. One game he didn't make it at all, and another day I expected him to play, but he was sound asleep on a massage table just before the game started, so I had to play.

From Riga, it was on to Russia for games in Moscow and then St. Petersburg, against all-star lineups of Russian players. In Moscow, the Russian team beat us 5–4 at the famous Luzhniki Arena, the rink at which Canada had won the Summit Series 32 years earlier with my father in attendance taking photographs. We fell behind 5–1, but fought back and almost won it. There was a skills competition before the game in which the goalies had to face three enemy shooters for one minute, with the forwards trying to score as many goals as possible. Hasek was playing so I had to do the skills drills. I had to face Pavel Datsyuk, Alexei Kovalev, Alexander Ovechkin and Ilya Kovalchuk—some of the shiftiest players on the planet, three at once. It was a challenging workout, especially when you're going in cold before a game. Sergei Fedorov and his brother, Fedor, played together for our team in that game, then Fedor joined another team of Russians for the game in St. Petersburg the next day. Our roster was changing almost every single day, even though we were at times playing teams that were in game shape and taking the games very seriously.

In St. Petersburg, it was my turn to play the entire game, and we won 5–4. The Russians, however, said that because each team had won a game, we had to play overtime for the Moscow Cup, which we hadn't even realized was at stake. The two teams argued back and forth, and finally it was decided we would have a shootout. I'd never played in a shootout, which at that point had not been used in the NHL. So I made sure I warmed up really well before it started. I sure didn't want to get hurt trying to twist my body into a pretzel. We won the shootout 2–1. Sadly, the game was marred by an idiot throwing bananas on the ice at Anson Carter, who is black, something that had happened previously to black players at European soccer games. To be honest, I didn't immediately put two and two together when I saw the banana on the ice. Carter handled it really well, but unfortunately the incident made headlines back in North America.

While the two games in Russia were interesting, the real intrigue was back home where, we learned to our surprise, the players' union had offered an across-the-board, 24 per cent salary rollback on existing contracts to the league on December 10, the day before our first game in Moscow. Just like that, the union had offered to turn a contract worth $1 million per season into a $760,000 deal. To say we were all stunned by this would be putting it mildly. None of the players on the tour had the slightest idea that the union had decided to do this, and I strongly disagreed with the entire concept. For players like me who were under contract and had made smart business decisions knowing a lockout was probably coming, it would be a hard price to pay. The players that gambled, or weren't smart, didn't have contracts anyway, so they didn't have the 24 per cent to give back.

Even more frustrating was that the NHL hadn't demanded this concession from the union. We had offered it out of the blue, and if it was a last attempt to make a deal, which is what some described it to be, it seemed very strange to do it in December—it was generally understood that a decision on canceling the season wouldn't have to be made until late January or early February. I just couldn't believe the union had done this. Still, we wondered if it would at least get the talks going. Five days later the NHL shot down the union's plan and offered one of its own at a 70-minute meeting in Toronto. The union quickly rejected it.

The league's proposal, which included the union's offer of a rollback for players making more than $800,000, also had a salary cap that would limit players to 54 per cent of revenues, with the cap ranging between $34.6 million and $38.6 million. The basic structure of that proposal was similar to the one we would accept seven months later, but at the time we as players didn't know how the fine print read on any of the offers. Even after a deal was struck—in fact, for months afterwards—we were still learning about the fine print. We relied on our union, NHLPA executive director Bob Goodenow and the executive committee to work out the best deal. Still, looking back, I feel certain there was no need for the season to be completely wiped out. Given what was being discussed in December, you can't tell me the two sides couldn't have reached an agreement in time to play some part of the season.

In Europe, after hearing the distressing news, we played on. Following St. Petersburg, the next Worldstars game was in Pilsen, Czech Republic. I didn't go there but instead went back to Moscow for a special event, Igor Larionov's final game. It was an incredible tribute to one of Russia's greatest hockey stars, and the reception for the game was equally extraordinary. The American rock star Kid Rock played at a party for "Iggy," who had been a teammate of mine with the Devils the previous NHL season. Larionov's daughters, who were professional singers, wrote and performed a song for their dad. Larionov, in the brief time I had played with him, had been an interesting teammate. They called him "The Professor" for the glasses he often wore and his scholarly approach to the sport. He was a nice guy and a creative player, but during his brief time in Jersey he was often in Pat Burns' doghouse. Still, Larionov was so poised, so in control, that it seemed nothing affected him. He had seen and accomplished so much in his 20-year career, from his days with the Red Army team to time spent playing in Switzerland and the NHL, he wasn't going to be fazed by what others thought of his game in his final year.

Meanwhile, Hasek was being received in Pilsen like a conquering hero in his first game back in his home country in more than a decade. Our team won 8–3 over HC Lasselsburger Pilsen, and he played half the game, while Nashville goalie Tomas Vokoun was recruited to play the rest while I was still in Moscow. It was our fourth game, and only 11 players had played in all four.

The next game was in Bern, Switzerland, two days later, and I rejoined the Worldstars team there. Hasek was supposed to split the game with me, but he said he wasn't feeling well and couldn't play, which meant I had to put the pads on after a three-hour trip from Russia. Ray Whitney's 51-year-old dad, Floyd, dressed as our backup goalie—he had been a practice goaltender with the Edmonton Oilers during a couple of their dynasty years. There was a very strange moment when an inebriated Swiss fan jumped onto the ice, collided with one of the Bern players and was knocked cold. Then the referee, skating backwards, tripped over him. Poor guy—they just dragged him off.

I was peppered with more than 40 shots and, in the very cold Bern arena, also pulled my groin, which ticked me off since I hadn't expected to play at all. The next day it was on to Karlstad, Sweden, to play Farjestad, the team my friend Sheldon Souray was playing for. I walked up to Hasek and said simply, "You're playing." He didn't say anything, but he played. We lost 6–1, and Floyd Whitney played the last four minutes.

Working with Hasek was unpredictable and a bit frustrating, but on the bright side, Bergevin turned out to be a joy every step of the way. In Moscow, he wore a big fur coat, huge fur hat, and walked around with a cigarette in his mouth. He developed a comic theme for every game. One game, he wore a toga like a Roman. For one of the games in Sweden, he showed up with a Viking helmet with two large penises coming out of the top instead of horns. He was hilarious. We went to a fashion show at the Café Opera in Stockholm in which male models wore body suits with masks. The next game, Bergevin came into the dressing room to make a pre-game speech dressed in the same outfit. It just went on and on. McSorley was more serious and did more of the technical stuff to get us decently prepared for the games, but Bergevin was like the class clown. Before one game, the trainers carried in a hockey bag and put it in middle of the dressing room floor. It was unzipped, and there was Bergevin lying inside the bag, stark naked. He said if we didn't start winning that was how he was going to have to go back to North America.

—◊◊◊—

By this point of the lockout, more than 300 NHL players were working in Europe, and not all of the stories were positive. When we arrived in Jonkoping, Sweden, after the Farjestad game, we found out that five days earlier Bryan McCabe of the Toronto Maple Leafs and Phoenix Coyotes goalie Brian Boucher had left the team and headed back to North America after struggling to adjust to the tough Swedish elite league. McCabe had been benched, and told his Swedish coach he had played too many games in the NHL to be sat out in Sweden. My Devils teammate John Madden had left his team in Finland, while players such as Mike Comrie, Marty Turco and Tyler Arnason had left other club teams in Sweden.

In some cases, the adjustment to the larger European ice surface and a different style of play was too difficult. Others just got homesick, or couldn't embrace a new lifestyle. Some European stories did have happy endings. Thornton and Rick Nash were lighting up the Swiss league in Davos, and that team eventually won the league championships and the prestigious Spengler Cup. A number of high-profile players were joining Ak Bars Kazan of the Russian league, including World Cup MVP Vincent Lecavalier.

—◊◊◊—

In Jonkoping, we beat the reigning Swedish league champs 5–1 and then got a good night's rest, largely because it was a small town without much of a night life. That was one of our best games on the tour. We spent the next evening in Stockholm, where Sundin treated us to a fabulous night on the town, then went to Linkoping. Feeling a little worse for wear, we were beaten 6–4 in one of our worst performances. They had an all-NHL line of Brendan Morrison, Mike Knuble and Kristian Huselius, while we had left most of our energy at the Café Opera in Stockholm. The rink wasn't very full for the game, and the president of the Linkoping team criticized our effort as "embarrassing." He probably didn't appreciate the way our players were laughing at each other as they tried to make plays after such a long night out in Stockholm. It could have also been that the president had paid good money to host the game, and was disappointed at the attendance.

After that game, we had only two left to play, and we were partied-out and pretty much ready to go home. During some games we'd had only 14 skaters, and the travel was really tiring. We flew from Linkoping to Oslo, and in our ninth game of the tour we defeated a Norwegian all-star team 7–6, after trailing 5–4 until the end of the second period. The next day, for our final game, we flew to Poland and a game in Katowice against a team of Polish all-stars, including NHLer Mariusz Czerkawski. Some of the players had been unsure about putting this game on the schedule, but it turned out to be a terrific experience. We won 4–3 in a shootout before an oversold crowd of 8,000 at the Spodek Arena, where the Poles had upset the Soviets in a famous game at the '76 world championships. The fans were incredibly enthusiastic, and the hotel and the food were much more like the North American style we were missing. Some of the players, including Rhett Warrener and Ray Whitney, went on a trip to the former Nazi concentration camp at Auschwitz. By then, I was just too tired to do any more sightseeing or learn any more history.

At the end of the tour, I was exhausted but glad I had decided to play. We had played 10 games, and won seven, an amazing performance given that most of our players weren't in serious hockey shape. Some parts of the trip were tough, the pay-per-view numbers back home were small, but the experience had been rewarding at a time when there was little to do back home. It was a chance to meet and get to know players I had never played with before, players such as Alexandre Daigle, who referred to himself as "The Daigle" and turned out to be a warm, funny guy who loved to live a fun life. I arrived home just before Christmas, happy to be back in North America.

—∞—

As the lockout stretched into January, there were new playing opportunities available, particularly with European teams starting to believe they could hire players for the entire season without having to worry that they would leave once the NHL resumed. Paul Theofanus, who was the agent for one of my Devils teammates, Sergei Brylin, contacted me and said there was a possible offer to play for a team in Omsk, Russia, for a salary of $2.5 million.

Omsk and Ak Bars Kazan were the two teams from the Russian league that were most aggressively pursuing NHL talent. I really didn't want to go, and certainly didn't want to leave my children for a long period of time to go to a country where few people spoke English and where I would probably need a translator and a bodyguard. With no end in sight to the lockout, I thought hard about it, and even went to a web site where they had a live webcam looking out onto the city. To me, it looked miserable, and finally I said I wasn't interested.

Another Czech team called me for the playoffs a few weeks later, but I declined that offer as well. I was interested in playing a little hockey just in case the NHL season started up again in late January, but nothing seemed to be a good fit.

We went back north to St. Adolphe in early January, then back to Florida with the same friends we had traveled with before. My Montreal buddy Andrea (Big Boy) Dell'Orefice, with whom I own a pizza business in Montreal called "La Pizzaria Etc," in which Montreal defenseman Sheldon Souray is also a partner, also came along. I spent a little bit of time helping out with my sons' hockey team, the Montclair Blues, and in March went with the team for a tournament in Lake Placid, New York. I hosted a charity black-jack tournament at a casino in Montreal, which raised $25,000 for an organization called MIRA that trains guide dogs for the blind. It's one of the organizations that have benefited from my annual summer golf tournament in Longueuil, Quebec, an event run by my brother Claude and my friend, Ronald "Bill" Belisle. Saku Koivu, Craig Rivet and Simon Gagné flew in for the black-jack tournament, as did my new friends from the Worldstars tour, Bergevin and "The Daigle."

Mostly, however, I waited and kept quiet. I had a lot to lose—about $10 million if the season was wiped out and the 24 per cent rollback kicked in for the next season—and I just didn't feel my input would have been the right input. It would have been selfish for me to push for a resolution that would have been good for me, but not for the association. The collective agreement we had signed in '95 after the first lockout had helped me make a lot of money, and even if I didn't necessarily agree with the strategies of the union this time, I felt the time wasn't right for me to speak out.

We weren't paid, of course, to go on the European tour, which was for charity. I made about $70,000 in union lockout pay, plus some other money from endorsements and business ventures in which I was involved. I wasn't worried sick about my financial future, but with lawyer fees from my divorce proceedings mount-ing, along with other costs, all I could see was my bank account shrinking. I cut back my lifestyle, eating more at home and things like that. I found it amazing how much I could save just by mak-ing simple changes. I moved to a new house in Morristown, which was a little further away from my ex-wife and the children, but was about $350,000 cheaper. It was a chance to change my life a bit, especially after all the upheaval in my life from the previous year, to move away from an area where many of my Devils teammates lived.

During the lockout, no one from the union ever called to ask for my opinion, which was another reason I kept my thoughts to myself. Brian Rafalski was my team's player rep, and the correct procedure was to get information either through him or from the union's secure web site. I hadn't been very active with the union in previous years, so I couldn't exactly start demanding answers from Goodenow or the union's president, Trevor Linden. More than just that, however, I really felt the entire mess was in the hands of two people, Bettman and Goodenow, and they were two people who had their own agendas. To me, nothing good was going to come of the lockout for the teams, the players, the fans or the sport. It really seemed to be a no-win situation for everyone, with all the damage being done to the game.

As a player, it was clear to me in January that the union was going to lose this fight. It was just a matter of how much we would lose, of how much of our previous gains we were willing to give back, or were going to be forced to give back. But unless you were one of the people in the meetings, it was impossible to judge which side was really trying to make a deal and which side was being stubborn.

The lockout began in mid-September, and one of the strangest facts about the entire process to me was that after exchanging those two proposals in mid-December, the two sides didn't get down to serious negotiations until mid-January. It made no sense that there were no discussions. How else could a deal be struck? At one point, NHLPA president Trevor Linden was meeting with Calgary Flames owner Harley Hotchkiss, the chairman of the NHL board of governors, with neither Bettman nor Goodenow present. There were two days of meetings on January 19 and 20, in Chicago and Toronto, when a proposal for an abbreviated 30-game season was floated. More meetings followed in New York and Toronto, and on February 9, the 147th day of the lockout, the league offered its first new proposal since December.

More shocking news for the players, again from their own union, was to come. In the third week of February, the union suddenly accepted the concept of a salary cap, and began to negotiate acceptable payroll figures. What had we been fighting for all along? The league, meanwhile, moved off the concept of linking a cap to revenues, and there was again optimism in the air. There was also rampant speculation that some prominent veteran players—news reports suggested Chris Pronger, Jeremy Roenick and Jarome Iginla—had quietly contacted NHL officials to try to help a deal come together. It was never clear what had happened, but even the suggestion that individual players had gone around their own union leadership to try and make a deal happen enraged many players. The league held fast to a $42-million cap number, while the players dropped their proposal from $52 million to $49 million. In the end, there was just not enough time to make a deal happen. On February 16, Bettman stepped to the microphone in New York City and officially canceled the 2004–05 season, an embarrassing moment for the 88-year-old NHL. When I heard, it didn't even make me upset. By then, I had been resigned to this conclusion for months. But there was more embarrassment still to come.

Almost as soon as Bettman canceled the season, there was speculation that it could be "uncanceled," possibly using Gretzky and Lemieux as dealmakers. I had gone to South Beach in Miami, and I was sitting in a bar watching the TV and having a beer when the news of Gretzky's involvement was reported. I almost pushed back my beer and ordered a Diet Coke, because for a brief moment it seemed Gretzky might be able to save the season after all and I had better start thinking about getting back into a competitive mindset. The rumor was that a $45-million salary cap might be the compromise.

Three days after Bettman's announcement, NHL officials, along with Gretzky and Lemieux, met with the union in New York, and it very quickly became apparent the season wasn't going to be miraculously saved. Neither side had a new proposal to offer. It was over, really over, with more than $1.1 billion in player salaries down the drain. The GM of the Devils, Lou Lamoriello, had been involved in the talks in January, and he said later a deal was never really close.

At least the cancelation of the season meant there would be no more playing around. They could finally start talking about a real deal, not just desperate attempts to "save the season." The most confusing part to me was why serious talks took so long to occur. I negotiate my own contracts, and I never wait until the last minute before training camp or into the season to make a deal. In fact, most of the time I've struck an arrangement in the season before my old contract expires. Of the three contracts I have negotiated, I have never been left playing the last year of the old deal. It never made sense to me for either the union or the league to have waited until the last possible second to agree on a new collective bargaining agreement. So much was at stake, and so many lives were affected. Ordinary working people who depend on NHL games for part- and full-time income were laid off. Referees and linesmen sacrificed an entire year's pay and were forced to find other income selling cars or making cabinets for homes. Some players even ultimately lost their NHL jobs.

As a member of the union, I hadn't known any other leader but Goodenow, who was leading the NHLPA when I played my first game in 1992. But given the deal he had helped us reach with the league in 1995, an agreement that made the players richer and richer over the years, how could we not have trusted him the second time around? He had helped NHL players make a lot of money, but in the end he didn't want to work with the NHL, and he ended up going toe-to-toe with an enemy that was unbeatable. I remember complaining to other players when I found out that he was making an annual salary of $2 million. I couldn't believe he was making more than the average player, and it made me wonder what else was going on at union headquarters. Still, as a player going into the lockout, I had no choice but to back him and trust him. Right to the end, Goodenow stuck to his guns, but in the final stages the players just didn't want to follow him right over the cliff. I was never a big fan of his or, really, of the union. I have always just wanted to go my own way and rely on my own instincts and skills. And I'd never really spoken to Goodenow about anything. We didn't have a personal relationship.

Bettman always seemed like a nice man to me, and like Goodenow, he was hired to do a job, regardless of whether I agreed with that job or not. I make business decisions, the owners make business decisions, and theirs was to have Bettman in charge. There was always talk that the players hated him, or that he was an obstacle to a deal getting done. Well, in my mind, to a large extent he made the decision for there not to be hockey in the 2004–05 season, so how could the players love him? So much money was lost by the players, how could they ever appreciate anything else he was able to do?

From the start, I knew there was nothing for me to gain from the lockout. My salary wasn't going to increase. I had something really good going, having won my third Stanley Cup with the Devils in 2003, and having won the Vezina Trophy in '03 and 2004. From an athletic point of view, there's no question the lockout hurt me at a time when I was on a roll, and by the end of my career it may cost me in terms of the records I'm able to break or set. Over the course of my career I have lost a season and a half of activity solely to lockouts and labor problems. Ultimately I will miss that more than the money I lost along the way. A career is so short, and those are games I'll never get to play. During the 2004–05 lockout, I just wanted to play hockey. We were never going to win that labor battle, and we should have figured that out earlier in the process and cut our losses.

Happily, there was at least a little more hockey to be played. I agreed to play in an outdoor game on April 2 at Ivor Wynne Stadium in Hamilton, Ontario. This exhibition game would be the second of its kind, designed to follow in the footsteps of the NHL regular season game from the previous season between the Edmonton Oilers and Montreal Canadiens that was held at Commonwealth Stadium in Edmonton. That was dubbed the "Heritage Classic," and the Hamilton game was promoted as "Our Game to Give," a way for NHLers to demonstrate their love for the sport and help some charitable causes at the same time.

Doug Gilmour, the former captain of the Maple Leafs and a New Jersey teammate at one time, was the chief organizer, and I played on his team. The game was broadcast on TSN, and I was "miked" for the whole game, which made it a unique experience. In all, 26 players participated, including Gilmour, Blake, McCabe, Todd Bertuzzi, Curtis Joseph and Joe Nieuwendyk. The weather was terrible, with high winds, frigid temperatures and rain that turned to sleet as the game wore on. The crowd was a little disappointing, with fewer than 20,000 fans in the 30,000-seat stadium, each paying $35 to watch the game. Given the horrible weather, however, I was amazed even that many came. The game was fairly entertaining, won 11–8 by Team Gilmour, and it was actually a bit of a lark. The ice was all pebbled by the rain and wind, and if I stood still in my crease, the wind would blow me back into the net. It was strange playing a game with raindrops on my mask, not breaking a sweat for 60 minutes.

The following month, it was back to serious hockey, with another chance to play for Canada. This time, it was the 2005 IIHF world championships in the Austrian cities of Innsbruck and Vienna, an opportunity for Team Canada to go for the "three-peat" after winning the competition the previous two years. It was only my second time at the world championships, and the previous time, in 1996, the tourney had been in Austria, as well. I was more than eager to play, and preparations under head coach Marc Habscheid began with a 10-day training camp followed by exhibitions in Halifax and Quebec City. Those warmup games were critical for our team because we had 14 players, including me, who hadn't played for any team during the lockout. It was a chance to get back to a team atmosphere, and the number of significant players who decided not to go, such as Iginla, Scott Niedermayer and Eric Brewer, surprised me. There were players who simply didn't want to get back into it, or didn't want to have to try to get back into shape or leave their families and go to Europe. Still, we had a strong team with a number of players who had been part of the 2004 World Cup winners. For me, it was a chance to see another part of Europe, the beautiful mountains of Innsbruck and the historic city of Vienna.

The tournament itself, however, was anything but a holiday. From the opening game, a 6–4 victory over Latvia that left me with a headache from the wall of noise created by Latvian drums and non-stop chanting, it was an enormous challenge. The fact was that most of our players hadn't been playing competitively that year. Nash scored three goals against the Latvians, and from the first game the line of Nash, Thornton and Gagné carried us as our No. 1 offensive line—not surprising, given that Nash and Thornton had played all season in Switzerland. With all our round robin games taking place in Innsbruck, we beat Slovenia and the United States, lost to Sweden, tied Finland and then barely got past Ukraine (2–1), to finish second in our pool with a 4–1–1 record.

We faced Slovakia in the quarterfinals, a terrific game in which I stopped the dangerous Ziggy Palffy on a penalty shot and then watched as the Slovak goalie, Jan Lasak, whiffed on a long shot by Thornton that turned out to be the game winner. That pushed us into the semifinals against Russia in Vienna, a spectacular game in a great atmosphere. We barely hung on to win 4–3 after almost blowing a four-goal lead. I made 39 saves and, despite a shoulder injury that was bothering me, felt ready to go for gold against the Czech Republic, the country that had almost upset us in Toronto at the World Cup nine months earlier.

The Czechs, however, beat us 3–0, a disappointment after all the disappointments of the season. They trapped us to death, which made for a pretty boring game, the same type of game the Devils have been criticized for over the years. We had spent nearly six weeks trying to win this tournament, and in the end we didn't play particularly well or particularly badly; the game just sort of took its course.

In the final minutes, there was some unfortunate ugliness after a confrontation between the Czech goalie, Vokoun, and Canadian forward Dany Heatley. Heatley had been charged with vehicular homicide and reckless driving after being behind the wheel in a tragic car crash on September 29, 2003, in suburban Atlanta in which Heatley's teammate with the Atlanta Thrashers, Dan Snyder, was killed. Heatley had been injured as well, but he returned to play the final portion of the 2003–04 season and then spent the lockout playing in Switzerland and Russia, sustaining a serious eye injury in the Swiss league along the way. In February, just before the NHL season had been canceled, Heatley pleaded guilty to four of the six charges against him and was sentenced to three years' probation. He had starred for Canada at the '03 worlds, but had struggled to find his game at the 2005 tournament going into the final against the Czechs. With the game no longer in doubt, Vokoun and Heatley became involved in the Czech crease, at which point Heatley thought he heard Vokoun say something derogatory relating to the tragic car accident. Heatley, understandably, went a little crazy, and when Vokoun tried to apologize in the post-game handshakes, Heatley refused to shake his hand. Many things are said out on a hockey rink, but some things are just uncalled for. If Vokoun did say something inappropriate, he shouldn't have. Such things should never be talked about on the ice, a place where, to some extent, hockey players are like family. It would be one thing if it were a fan, but not among brothers.

Still, Canada came away with silver, and that was the end of our hockey season. All that was left was for the union to find a way to strike a deal with the league, which had already won the fight. In June, the two sides began to meet, negotiating over ways to properly define league revenues, a process that should have happened a year earlier. Finally, on July 13, the union and league announced a tentative six-year agreement to end the 301-day lockout. Included were the 24 per cent rollback, linkage to league revenues that limited players' salaries to 54 per cent of the league's total revenues and a salary cap that, for the 2005–06 season, would be $39 million per team. There were some gains for players, such as lowering the free agency age gradually to 27 and raising the minimum salary. For me, the most tangible benefit was a clause that guaranteed veterans with 10 years in the league and 600 games played their own hotel rooms on the road, rather than having to share a room with teammates. For

14 years, I had always had a roommate, first Chris Terreri, then players from Stéphane Richer, Denis Pederson and Tommy Albelin to Jim McKenzie and Turner Stevenson. With this deal, I could finally have my own room, and I loved it. That was the lone benefit I could identify.

Within a few days, 87 per cent of the union's members approved the deal, one that seemed unimaginable when the lockout had started 11 months earlier. On July 29, Goodenow resigned, ending his 15-year run and opening a new era for the union, one that began with controversy about the hiring of a new executive director, Ted Saskin. As the first season after the lockout progressed, it was clear the wounds from the lockout were still deep, as players mounted challenges to Saskin's leadership, including attempts to have U.S. regulatory bodies force Saskin out. The way in which Saskin was immediately appointed to the top job after Goodenow departed certainly left players doubting the process, or at least left serious concerns as to whether the union's constitution had been adhered to. I think the players owed it to themselves to conduct a thorough internal investigation, but that didn't materialize.

Certainly, it seems unlikely the union will ever be as strong as it was before the lockout, if only because a salary cap is now involved in the relationship between teams and players. We'll have to live with that cap. We won't ever be able to take it out. As well as disputes over Saskin's leadership, there were also new debates over the details of the new collective agreement, including the level at which the salary cap should be set in successive seasons for players to avoid having to have "escrow payments" taken off their pay checks to ensure the union was taking no more than 54 per cent of the gross. The idea was that an escrow fund would be created, and if the players by the end of the season had collectively received more than 54 per cent, the owners would be reimbursed out of that fund. If the players had received less than 54 per cent, they would get the money back, which is exactly the way it worked out after the 2005–06 season. Still, it was hard for players to become accustomed to losing thousands of dollars off their pay checks every two weeks.

The process of the lockout hurt the union, and created a new set of problems at the leadership level that may take years to resolve. The union is now in a "partnership" with the league, with both sides sharing the mutual goal of growing league revenues to increase profits for owners and salaries for players. The owners got a pretty sweet deal, and it's now up to them to make it work and make the league more successful. I certainly didn't want a cap because I felt it would take away the individual player's freedom to negotiate his own deal. I had played all my career without specific financial limitations, so a cap was tough to accept. The biggest change will be that with free agency gradually being lowered to 27, players in their prime, from the ages of 26 to 31, will make the big money, whereas under the old system it was usually players over the age of 31 who were able to exploit unrestricted free agency and attract the largest salaries.

By the conclusion of the 2005–06 season, the league reported that revenues had actually been healthier than projected and the cap was raised to $44 million for the following season. It seemed the damage to the economics of the game had not been as extensive as feared.

For the Devils, there were ramifications that affected them more than other NHL clubs. Since the days of Jacques Lemaire, there had been a team bonus structure for a variety of achievements. With every shutout victory, for example, each player received $1,000. When we allowed one goal, the bonus was $500, and then $250 for surrendering two goals. It was a bonus structure designed to reward the two things the Devils valued most—wins and defense. Those bonuses drove the way we played. If we were winning a game 6–0, there was still $1,000 there for everybody to make sure we got the shutout. It helped the way the team played, and it certainly helped me as a goaltender. But the new collective bargaining agreement included a provision that such bonuses were now illegal. The new agreement had changed the landscape for every NHL player, and it had changed the terms of competition for my team. In the Devils' first season back, it took until January, after the resignation of head coach Larry Robinson, for the team to play again as it had before the lockout.

If there was a benefit to the lockout, it was that it gave me a chance to see what retirement would be like, and quite frankly, it wasn't that bad. I actually enjoyed the months away from the game, and loved spending time with my kids that I wouldn't have had otherwise, and which I began to miss once the league started up again. I skied with my children in Montreal, and enjoyed the chance to be a real hockey dad. I took a winter vacation in Florida, which I hadn't done since I was a boy going with my family to spring training with the Montreal Expos, the team that employed my father as its official photographer for 29 years. I learned to ride a motorcycle, and began to cook more.

—∿∿—

For years, I have definitely enjoyed living the life of a player, but the eventual end to my career isn't as threatening to me now as it was when I was 25, and that's partly because of the experience of the lockout. I feel more confident now that when I retire, I'll figure something out, and with the friends and family I have, I'll be all right. I feel sure I'll be able to live some day with not being a hockey player. I lost a great deal of money when the

2004–05 season was erased, and I lost an important year off my career. But I don't feel bitter. Larionov once told me that going to Switzerland for a season and then going back to the NHL added a few years to his career. Perhaps taking a year off from the grind of the NHL will give me an extra season or two at the end of my career at a higher level of play. Having experienced two lockouts, I can only hope I won't see another.

The Toughest Shooters

(and how many times they beat me)

WAYNE GRETZKY

23 games, 7 goals*

At the 1998 Olympics, the coaches asked me before the playoff game against the Czechs who I thought would be good on shootouts. I never mentioned Wayne, because I just assumed *he'd be one of our shooters. I remember being on the bench and not believing he hadn't been picked. He didn't have a great shot, but when it was time to score, he could get it off quickly. He was so deceptive, and the fact that he always had the threat of both shooting and passing made him tough.*

Source: Elias Sports Bureau. Statistics combine regular season and playoffs and are current as of conclusion of 2005–06 season.

chapter 9
Selling the Sizzle

IT WAS CALLED "THE FACE PAINTER," episode 109 of the incredibly successful television sitcom *Seinfeld*, an episode that aired for the first time on May 11, 1995.

Written by Larry David, who later starred in his own show, *Curb Your Enthusiasm*, the storyline revolved around one of the show's main characters, Elaine Benes, played by Julia Louis-Dreyfus, and her slack-jawed boyfriend David Puddy. While preparing to attend a Devils-Rangers playoff game, Puddy (played by Patrick Warburton) emerges from the bedroom wearing a red New Jersey road jersey with his face painted in Devils' colors.

The scene went like this:
Elaine: What the?
Puddy: So what do you think?
Elaine: What is that?
Puddy: I painted my face.
Elaine: You painted your face?
Puddy: Yeah.
Elaine: Why?
Puddy: You know, support the team.
Elaine: Well, you can't walk around like that.
Puddy: Why not?
Elaine: Because. . . it's insane?

Puddy: Hey, you gotta let them know you're out there; this is the playoffs.

At that point, there's a knock at the door and Puddy answers it, revealing Jerry (Jerry Seinfeld) and Kramer (Michael Richards). Kramer does his usual double-take, and the story continues from there. But the other item of interest, at least to me, was that when Puddy answers the door, on the back of the Devils jersey he is wearing, in white lettering and numerals, is my surname across the shoulders and my familiar No. 30. Nobody ever asked my permission, although the league did give its blessing when approached by the producers of the show; the first time I ever saw it was on the video board at the Meadowlands when it became popular to show it at our home games.

Not surprisingly, it blew me away. The Rangers, of course, had won their first Stanley Cup in 54 years the previous spring, after which *Sports Illustrated* published a cover questioning whether the NHL had supplanted the NBA as the hottest pro sport on the North American landscape. Having an NHL sweater featured on one of the most famous episodes of one of the best-loved American sitcoms of all time a year later was evidence, to some degree, of the potential for growth that was available to the NHL at that time, despite the fact the first four months of the 1994–95 season had been wrecked by the first lockout in league history. A month after "The Face Painter" initially aired, the Devils won our first Stanley Cup in dramatic fashion, sweeping the Detroit Red Wings in the final.

It wasn't as if the NHL had already reached a new plateau, but the possibilities seemed endless. It killed me to see the Rangers win the Cup in '94, but it seemed as though it would do great things for our sport. The NFL was king, but the NBA was losing some of its most marketable players in Larry Bird and Magic Johnson, while baseball was having terrible labor problems and had canceled the 1994 World Series in a dispute with its players' union. The NHL at least seemed to be in the game, and the *Seinfeld* episode seemed to give the impression that the sport might have growth potential beyond its hard-core Canadian market and in traditional non-sports settings. Looking back, it's funny that it didn't seem such a big deal back then, that neither I nor the Devils nor the NHL seemed to grasp the potential that was demonstrated by our inclusion in *Seinfeld*. I guess I thought it wasn't me in the show, just my jersey. The Devils showed it regularly as a comedy bit at home games, but not as a vehicle to sell tickets and merchandise.

Fast forward to October 2006. After the second lockout in league history had wiped out the entire 2004–05 season and forced the cancelation of the Stanley Cup playoffs, the NHL worked with an outside firm to create a new ad campaign designed to energize the business—that is, to bring fans back to the sport. Entitled "My NHL," the first installment began with a quotation from ancient Chinese military strategist Sun Tzu and his book, *The Art of War*, and then flashed to an unidentifiable hockey player sitting shirtless in his pants and skates as a woman wearing a bra and some sort of negligée tells him, "It's time." The theme was that of a samurai warrior going out to battle, and in later action episodes, actors wearing generic red and black jerseys were shown in various sequences designed to illustrate the intensity and passion of the sport. The fact that neither team was wearing white, of course, illustrated a lack of hockey knowledge, since in any game one of the teams would be home and one away, so both would not be in their home jerseys. Each commercial ended with a shot of an anonymous young child, followed by the inscription, "My NHL."

To me, it was a very strange way to promote our sport, which has so many good personalities and elite players. Perhaps it was because we had just come out of a protracted labor war with the owners, but it seemed the league was intentionally avoiding the stars and well-known veterans and instead promoting the league ahead of teams and players. Given that the lockout had produced an agreement that was supposed to result in a new "partnership" between the NHL and the players' union, it was a curious way to start the partnership. The NHL still wasn't focused on what I believed was the untapped strength of the league, its individual players.

That's how far we had come—or hadn't—since the days of "The Face Painter." Eleven years later, not only had the league and the players' association failed to work together and avoid a destructive labor mess, but the essence of the game and the players who play it were still being obscured behind a strange ad campaign. With all the well-known, talented players in the league that were possibly available to demonstrate the new "partnership" between the league and its players, the NHL had instead chosen to use unknown actors. No Jeremy Roenick or Jaromir Jagr or Joe Thornton. Nameless actors. Could you imagine the NBA doing something like this, or the NFL?

The NHL was a bigger business than it had been in 1995. Teams had been added in Columbus, Saint Paul, Minnesota, Atlanta and Nashville, league merchandising sales had increased and television revenues had temporarily increased before crashing during the lockout with the decision by ESPN not to continue as one of the league's broadcast partners. NHLers had participated twice in the Winter Olympics, first in 1998 in Nagano, and again in 2002 at the Salt Lake City Games. The game itself, however, had come under heavy criticism for a low-scoring, unexciting brand of hockey, with much of the criticism pointing back to the Devils' Stanley Cup win in 1995 as the turning point.

What had not changed materially was the inability of the league to use its players to market and sell the sport. The *Seinfeld* episode of May 1995 now seemed emblematic of the unrealized potential for players and the league that had gone untapped over the years.

By the time we were lining up to play the Rangers in the play-offs again in April 2006, however, it seemed as though the league had started to understand this better, maybe because the "My NHL" ads weren't a hit. New commercials, based on the theme "My Stanley Cup," were produced. They were built around similar themes, but this time they featured real NHL players, not actors, players such as Brendan Shanahan, Henrik Lundqvist and Scott Niedermayer, with voiceovers by actors Dennis Leary, Howie Mandel and Kiefer Sutherland (all well-known hockey fans), as well as champion cyclist Lance Armstrong. They showed Rod Brind'Amour breaking a stick over his knee, and Mike Grier of the Sabres with flames seemingly coming out of his outstretched hand. For the Devils version, they shot me, Brian Gionta and Scott Gomez. Finally, it seemed to me, a decision had been made to sell the game by selling the players. Real players. During the 2006 Stanley Cup final, commissioner Gary Bettman said that approach is the wave of the future. "We're going to continue to market the players," he said.

The new commercials came on the heels of what had been a much improved season as far as letting players showcase their talents, particularly the goal scorers. With new regulations on goalie equipment and a crackdown on certain types of penalties designed to allow players more offensive freedom, regular-season scoring was up more than a goal per game as compared to the last season before the lockout. Seven players had 100 points or more, and five forwards scored 50 goals or more. By comparison,

Martin St. Louis had led the NHL in scoring in the 2003–04 season—the last season before the lockout—with 94 points, and three players had tied for the league lead in goals with 41. For goaltenders, of course, it was a lot tougher, but at least we were all in the same boat. We had to accept the changes, even though they made the game a lot tougher physically for goalies. The game itself had returned to the style of hockey that was very similar to the NHL when the Rangers had won the Cup in '94. I didn't like the 5–1 and 6–1 scores, but a 3–0 lead sure didn't mean what it used to, and that kind of unpredictability made the fans want to watch longer. The playoffs that followed were the most exciting in years, concluding with a thrilling, seven-game Stanley Cup final between two surprise finalists, Carolina and Edmonton.

Why had the league's dominant style of play slowed down and become so defensive after the promise of that '94 championship by the Rangers? A lot of people blamed the Devils and our close-checking style, but to me, it had a lot to do with the economics of the game. After '95, it seemed to become a league in which only three or four teams—the Devils, Detroit, Dallas and Colorado—really dictated their futures. The majority of teams found themselves unable to afford top-drawer talent, particularly with expansion pushing the league up to 30 teams and the costs of individual players increasing dramatically, and many of those teams decided the only way to compete effectively was to keep their payrolls as low as possible and then play a very defensive style. The league, which was so conscious of trying to sell its product, was reluctant to make changes that would have suggested the league's style of play was boring and in need of change.

The new economic system that emerged from the 2005 collective agreement significantly changed the business. Teams had to abide by a league-enforced salary cap rather than simply spending whatever amount of money they chose. That restrained the few wealthy teams and made them get rid of players they couldn't afford to keep under the new cap rules, and in so doing gave the majority of clubs better access to personnel that would allow them to play a different way. Perhaps the best example was Anaheim, which was able to sign Scott Niedermayer away from the Devils and become a totally different type of team than the Ducks had been before. The Oilers were able to trade for Chris Pronger and Mike Peca, then added flashy winger Sergei Samsonov during the season. The Hurricanes made deals to acquire Doug Weight and Mark Recchi, proven veterans with strong offensive résumés.

The institution of the shootout for the first time in league history, meanwhile, added a stylish new showcase for talented offensive players. Early in the season, Sidney Crosby scored a gorgeous shootout goal for Pittsburgh against Montreal goalie José Théodore, a moment that hit the highlight reels everywhere. A little-known player such as Jussi Jokinen of Dallas, meanwhile, was able to become a star solely for his talent at scoring in the shootout. Fans in all 30 arenas stayed to the end in anticipation of the shootout, and usually stayed on their feet during the breakaway competition.

The league also welcomed two years' worth of rookies, brand new faces in new cities that added an element of variety as the game opened up. There were Crosby and Alexander Ovechkin, who waged a lively battle for rookie-of-the-year honors. (They were eventually captured by Ovechkin.) There was also shifty Marek Svatos in Colorado, rock-ribbed Dion Phaneuf in Calgary, Mike Richards and Jeff Carter in Philadelphia, Alexander Steen in Toronto and goalie Henrik Lundqvist in New York. We'll probably never see another crop of rookies like that again, mostly because they were the combined product of two drafts, the 2004 version that hadn't previously seen the light of professional competition because of the lockout, and those from the 2005 proceedings. Many of these players are the type of athletes who will be easy to market, or, as in the case of Crosby, will be able to market themselves.

The result of all these changes—a more offensive style, more teams trying to score goals, the shootout, a crew of flashy rookies—was a changed focus for the NHL and a shift into a new gear. Instead of an intense, low-scoring league, it was suddenly a more open, exciting NHL that had finally started to capitalize on its greatest strength, the players.

—⚹—

This, however, is where it gets more complicated as the league—and the players' union—tries to figure out ways to sell the game more effectively and increase revenues through television and other sources in the coming years. The marketing of individuals is important, and I've certainly benefited through some endorsement deals. I've long had an equipment deal with CCM for my goaltending equipment, and in spring 2006 I signed an exclusive marketing deal with Steiner Sports, a New York-based company, that could pay me more than six-figures over five years. Instead of going to autograph shows and agreeing to sign a certain number of autographs, this allows me to work out of my home with one company that can distribute my autographed products around the world and, hopefully, increase the value of those products.

These kinds of deals are, unfortunately, very rare for NHL players, though there are notable exceptions. Wayne Gretzky, even in retirement, has an agreement with Ford. Crosby signed lucrative deals with Reebok and Gatorade before he played even one game with the Penguins. But in general the opportunities for NHL players on an individual basis are still very limited. As well, for years players have signed a group licensing authorization agreement with the union that gives the NHLPA the exclusive right to use the names and images of any member for its retail and sponsorship licensing programs involving more than two players. The idea was that revenues from these programs would go into a strike/lockout fund that could be accessed by players during work stoppages, as was the case in the 2004–05 season. Traditionally, this agreement has been signed by players at annual meetings, usually without a great deal of consideration. It's been almost like an attendance form.

The open question, however, is whether it's fair that each and every player should have to abide by this agreement, and whether players should all share equally in the proceeds. I know, for example, that for years Brodeur jerseys were among the best sellers in the NHL, but I have never directly received any money from those sales. It goes into a large pot, and certainly I received money during the lockout from this fund. The system basically has the marquee players subsidize the rest of the union membership. As well, there has been very little hard information made available to players on where the dollars are going. We're currently on a multi-year agreement with the union, but when the next opportunity comes along to sign that form, I don't think I will, at least not until I can understand the benefits a lot better. With labor peace for the next six years, I'd really like to know where the monies from these programs are going.

The NHL, meanwhile, has always been very restrictive in terms of advertising on uniforms and equipment. My deal with CCM is a straight money deal for me to wear their equipment when I play. It's difficult for them, for example, to promote a Brodeur line of equipment because they wouldn't be allowed to put a unique logo on the equipment I wear in a game to push the line because of the league's restrictions. Once, we were playing a game in Atlanta and Ray Ferraro, who was playing for the Thrashers, complained about a small, egg-shaped reflective Heaton logo on top of my pads. Shortly after, the NHL forced me to put a sticker over the logo. Having played at different times in Europe where advertising regulations for teams and players are much less strict, I can see how limited the opportunities are in North America and, specifically, the NHL. So, when you add up the natural limitations of a sport still fighting for a wider North American profile, years of failing to grasp the possible marketing potential of individual players, the union's group licensing agreement and the league's traditional reluctance to expand advertising on player uniforms and equipment, it's not hard to understand that NHL players aren't exactly ideally positioned to aggressively maximize their earning potential off the ice.

A unique concept that really intrigued me coming out of the lockout was The Goaltenders Club. The idea was that it would help market goalies for commercial and charitable purposes, and also give goalies a unified voice in terms of improving the game, including rules. I was one of the organizers, along with Marty Turco of the Dallas Stars, Ed Belfour of the Toronto Maple Leafs, Dominik Hasek of the Ottawa Senators and José Théodore of the Canadiens, as well as Brad Robins, a Toronto-based marketing expert. A letter was drafted from that group of five veteran goalies to other NHL goalies. The letter stated The Goaltenders Club was to be "a method to raise awareness for goalies and create a separate identity concentrating on improving the sport and increasing our charitable giving." The letter also proposed establishing a permanent presence for goalies on all NHL committees, developing marketing opportunities specific to goalies, pushing for innovative broadcasting technology involving goalies and establishing a consensus among goalies on key union issues. It also urged all goaltenders not to sign any new NHLPA licensing agreements.

Turco and I were the most involved, and there were many good ideas tossed around, including selling advertising specifically on goalies' jerseys for commercial and charitable purposes. Given that goalies are seen more than any other player position during televised hockey, we thought the concept would have a lot of appeal for advertisers. The letter, however, was never circulated among all NHL goalies. Instead, the concept was put on the backburner as the NHL came back to life during the 2005–06 season, and it's unclear whether it ever will come to fruition.

To make it happen, The Goaltenders Club would need the support of the league and the union, rather than being a rebel outfit, and it's hard to see how that would happen anytime soon. The NHL, despite all it says about partnership, doesn't seem interested in that kind of input, and the union has been so busy fighting various internal battles that it has been difficult to forecast what direction it will take in the future on new initiatives such as The Goaltenders Club. After the lockout, with the leadership of Ted Saskin immediately under fire, new ideas were often received as challenges, rather than as worthy of serious consideration. I really believe The Goaltenders Club is still an idea that could help build the game, but there appear to be too many obstacles at this point, and netminders might end up isolating themselves.

Focusing solely on individuals, meanwhile, isn't necessarily the right way to go. Hockey players are different from athletes in other sports, and the things that might best promote the sport might not translate into everybody being on Letterman or Jon Stewart. Hockey players are brought up not to focus on being individuals. From the time we are young, we are told that the crest on the front of the jersey is more important than the lettering on the back. It sounds corny, but hockey people believe in that philosophy. I believe the objective should be to enhance the profile of all NHL players, and everyone will benefit.

For starters, I think we need to focus on establishing a presence with a major national charitable organization in the United States and Canada. Hockey players are, to my mind, special people with big hearts for charity and community works. But that fact is not widely recognized. Even during the lockout, when many people believed we were scumbags, players were out raising considerable dollars for charitable organizations, not just sitting at home sulking or counting their millions. Linking NHL players with a major charity could profile the unique nature of hockey players and, in so doing, provide energy to make the game bigger.

People are sensitive to the way in which athletes deal with important issues. Look at what golfer Phil Mickelson did for the 2006 Zurich Classic of New Orleans, the first pro sporting event in the city after Hurricane Katrina struck and caused widespread damage in 2005. Mickelson arrived in the Big Easy two weeks after winning the 2006 Masters and created a lot of goodwill for his sport when he promised to donate his earnings for the week to hurricane relief organizations. For golf, that had an enormous impact, and shows athletes connected to communities in general, not just to their local concerns. It fits the hockey model and the way players have grown up to understand the sport. Once players are seen as the special people they are, they will become more attractive to fans and to corporations, who will grow to believe they want to be associated and to do business with these athletes.

In March 2006, all NHL team presidents gathered in New York to discuss the marketing aspect of the sport. An idea that came out of those meetings was that, starting with the 2006–07 season, one player from each team will be designated as a business representative for that club to work in conjunction with the union and the league on all revenue-generating initiatives. In theory, NHL players will have direct input into how the game is marketed and whose names and faces are attached to future campaigns. We'll see how that works out, but my early sense is that the union seems more prepared than ever to work with the NHL, not against it, and is a lot more oriented towards marketing of players. A major marketing meeting involving NHL executives, team officials and players that I attended was held in Montreal in July 2006. It all seemed like progress to me.

—⁓—

It may seem strange that a member of the New Jersey Devils has such a strong interest in developing the business side of the game. Let's face it, the Devils have not been one of the league's most commercially successful teams, despite winning Stanley Cups in 1995, 2000 and 2003. The club has never been at or near the top of the NHL in average attendance, and it was noteworthy that in the second round of the 2006 playoffs, our first home game against Carolina wasn't sold out. From the outside, New Jersey isn't viewed as a glamorous place to play, and our arena, the Continental Airlines Arena, which is part of the Meadowlands Sports Complex, isn't a state-of-the-art facility that draws fans just to be in the building. It's a plain, box-like arena that sits alongside Highway 3 in northern Jersey, the same road that would take you through the Lincoln Tunnel and into Manhattan if you traveled east.

During the 2005–06 season, the arena seemed even less inviting. It was surrounded by fences, cranes and construction equipment as the site was being redeveloped in anticipation of the Devils' move south to a new building in Newark in fall 2007. The other major tenant, the NBA New Jersey Nets, were planning to move to Brooklyn. Inside the Continental Airlines Arena, the building is unremarkable, blue with beige trim, with faded lavender and blue seats and a high black roof with 13 Devils banners, all white with black and red lettering. At the other end are all the banners and retired numbers of the Nets. When the Devils officially retired the numbers of Ken Daneyko and Scott Stevens during the 2005–06 season, those were the first banners raised to recognize individual achievements. Behind the goal I defend twice every night—the first period and the third—is a tribute to

Bruce Springsteen and the E Street Band for their 15 consecutive soldout shows in 1999. It's a building that is our home, but not exclusively our home.

Since the club moved east from Denver to East Rutherford a quarter century ago, it has struggled to survive and thrive in the shadow of the big-city Rangers. As long as Lou Lamoriello has been in charge, the focus has been almost exclusively on the development and maintenance of a world-class team. The Devils are different than most NHL teams because we're not associated with a specific city. Instead, we appeal to a large number of suburban and urban communities. Central Jersey, for example, is big-time Devils territory, but if you go too far south, you start getting large numbers of Flyer fans. The farther north you go, the more Ranger fans you see. You can almost calculate the percentage of Devils fans by the exit numbers on the New Jersey Turnpike. The people that are Devils fans and season ticketholders are die-hards, and the scene outside the arena before playoff games is unique, with tailgate parties and street hockey and fans wearing Devils jerseys throwing footballs. They're good fans, but the problem is we have only about 14,000 of them.

Still, if this wasn't a successful franchise, I believe it would have moved long ago. It's not like the team operates in a cave. Our home games are broadcast on the Fox Sports Network New York, sponsored by advertisers such as Mercedes, Panasonic and Dell and feature Hall of Fame play-by-play man Mike Emrick, along with analyst Glenn (Chico) Resch, a former Devil, and Stan Fischler, one of the best-known American hockey journalists. Inside the arena, the boards and ice are covered with ads from companies such as Sharp, Geico, Bud Lite, Gulf, Verizon and Prudential. These are major companies, and they want to do business with the Devils. This is evidence that the Devils have tangible value and appeal in New Jersey, outside of the current numbers through the turnstiles, because there have been too many nights when I have looked out and seen only 8,000 or 9,000 people in the building.

When we go on the road to cities such as Montreal, Toronto and Philadelphia, I often wonder why players in those cities, with such intense fan support, can't always get up for games. Playing for the Devils, it's harder. You have to learn to get yourself ready and not rely on getting adrenaline from the fans. I don't know if it would get old to play for a madhouse every day. I've never lived it, so I just don't know.

Any celebrity status we get playing for the Devils is solely related to the success of the team. In other words, you don't get famous by being a Devil. You get recognized for being part of a winning Devils team. I have met U.S. presidents twice, Bill Clinton in 1995 and George Bush in 2003, both times after the Devils won the Cup. (Unexpectedly, Clinton was the one who was distant and businesslike, while Bush was so welcoming he not only hosted our team in the Rose Garden, he invited us and our families into the Oval Office for an unscheduled tour.) As a team, we were on *Late Night with David Letterman*, although Scott Stevens was the only player interviewed. That same night, we listened to a concert with Bon Jovi on the roof of the building in which the Letterman show is taped and later joined the band for a picture. We've been on *Regis and Kathie Lee*, and were recognized by Bruce Springsteen during his concert at Madison Square Garden because his drummer, Max Weinberg, was a big Devils fan. All these bits of special treatment were enjoyable, but all were related to the team, not because any individual was particularly famous or even notorious. As a Devil, you're just not as likely to be recognized away from the arena as you would if you played for the Flyers or the Maple Leafs. To some of us, that is one of the many benefits to playing in New Jersey.

That the Devils aren't widely seen as a successful franchise isn't surprising. Outsiders see only the empty seats on television and believe most of the players would rather play in larger markets—New York, Chicago, Los Angeles—where the attention and celebrity status might be greater. That's just not true, certainly not for me. For example, would I want to play in Montreal, my home town? No, I wouldn't. In Jersey, I don't mind being the nice guy and available to everybody, but if I had to play in Montreal, I would have to change my ways of dealing with people. The demands of family, friends and fans would just be too great. I would need to concentrate more on myself instead of trying to please everybody. Now, it's easy to accommodate others because I don't visit Montreal very often, and so when I do I'm prepared for the demands of friends and family, as well as fans and media. But if that was expected of me all season long, I don't think I could manage it without it becoming a distraction for me. If I were a member of the Canadiens, I think people there would see a different me, one they wouldn't enjoy as much. Playing for the Devils, by contrast, gives me a lot of freedom and privacy.

Another benefit is the travel schedule or, more accurately, the lack of travel. Understand this: 12 of our 41 road games are in Manhattan, Long Island and Philadelphia, and for most of those we drive rather than fly, and are back in our beds by shortly after midnight. In fact, the worst element to being a Devil is the commute from home to the arena, 30 minutes to an hour for most of the players, without the option of taking a train or subway. Shortening the drive was one of the major reasons our family moved from Morristown to Llewellyn Park in West Orange after the 2005–06 season. Otherwise, the neighborhoods available for the players to live in are terrific, and the schools are excellent. The restaurants, shopping and theater of New York City, of course, are just a short drive away, another one of the benefits. When family and friends visit, that's where they want to go.

So would I want to play anywhere else? Boston would be a great city to play in, I think, and Philadelphia has great fans. That would be an experience. Out west, the only place I would want to go would be Dallas. I have memories of it being a great place to celebrate after we won the Cup there in 2000, and for whatever reason, I just have a warm feeling for the state of Texas.

But then you bring in the most important factor about being a Devil. The organization is totally committed to winning championships. If the Devils haven't sold the sizzle particularly well, we have always delivered the meat. If playing out of East Rutherford hasn't made me or other members of the team into enormous celebrities and hasn't allowed us to rake in the endorsements, we have all benefited financially from the team's extraordinary success, starting with the first Cup in 1995. There have been hundreds of thousands of dollars available to Devils players in playoff and team bonuses. I've enjoyed all of those, plus I have won the Vezina Trophy twice and been nominated as a finalist multiple times, including in 2006. To have those financial windfalls available to a goaltender requires an organization committed to playing defensive hockey and winning championships. Playing for the Devils has earned me money, and it has also allowed me to be part of Cup-winning teams, experiencing the pride and fulfillment that brings. With this team, I have the opportunity to take a run at some of the greatest goaltending records in NHL history, a wonderful feeling for any athlete. Playing in New Jersey and gaining the personal success I have through the team's success has also positioned me to be invited to play for my country on many occasions, something that has added to my life as a pro.

Here's my point. When you add it all up, New Jersey is just about the perfect place to play, except for the attendance. That's why, starting with the 2006–07 season, I committed to playing six more seasons with the Devils. It's not as glamorous as being a New York Yankee or a Los Angeles Laker, or even a member of the Montreal Canadiens. But the upside is still there, and with a multi-year contract in place, my business focus is now on trying to develop long-term relationships with sponsors and advertisers to sell my personal "brand" and enhance the profile of the Devils. I want to be viewed as an athlete who stands for quality, integrity, honesty and excellence, and hopefully that will appeal to companies to help me develop endorsement income for myself and my family and allow me to help raise money for charitable causes I support, like children's hospitals and seeing-eye dogs for the blind. This can all happen, I believe, while playing for the Devils.

—⁓⁓—

It could be that the lessons of the lockout have positioned the NHL to take a more aggressive, productive approach to selling the sport, focusing more on our great game and terrific individual players. The union will, I hope, eventually get its act together again, and start mapping out a clear strategy for the future. Between them, the league and union need to enhance all revenue streams, particularly television in the United States and marketing and merchandising possibilities in Europe. At the Turin Olympics, it was remarkable to see what a limited presence the NHL had despite the participation of the league's top players. The national charity strategy I've talked about, finally, would definitely enhance the stature of NHLers, particularly those outside the major markets.

For the Devils, meanwhile, I believe the big payoff is coming, starting with the new arena that we'll move into in fall 2007. It's been a challenge living in the shadow of the Rangers since the early 1980s. But, really, the Devils only started attracting hard-core supporters when we started winning in 1994 and became an attractive club to follow. Since we're not attached to a city, we have to make the people want to come to us, and it's not like we're in the middle of the country by ourselves. The Devils exist in one of the world's largest entertainment markets, and we compete for coverage and attention on a daily basis with the Rangers, Islanders, Knicks, Yankees, Mets, Giants and Jets. My theory is that when we started attracting our own community of fans in '94, those adults had children, and those children are now in college or just beginning their working lives. In another five or six years, they'll be able to afford to be Devils fans with their kids, and it will happen in a spectacular new arena.

Selling the Devils can't happen on its own. It has to happen at the same time as the NHL and the union do a better job of selling the sport both on and off the ice. If both happen together, maybe another *Seinfeld* moment will come along some day, and this time we'll be ready.

The Toughest Shooters

(and how many times they beat me)

PAVEL BURE

20 games, 6 goals*

I didn't face him often during those years he was in the Western Conference with Vancouver, but I knew he was a pure goal-scorer. He was there to score, and he made that obvious to everybody on both teams. Sometimes it seemed that was all he was interested in. He was explosive on his skates and he had a dangerous shot. He always shot high, and you'd hear his teammates complain because the puck would be going at their heads. If you let him play, he could do a lot of damage.

---

*Source: Elias Sports Bureau. Statistics combine regular season and playoffs and are current as of conclusion of 2005–06 season.

chapter 10
Rebound

THE NEW JERSEY DEVILS had started the 2005–06 regular season as a team locked in turmoil, stung by the resignation of a respected head coach in the third month of the campaign and seemingly lost in the vastly altered economic and competitive environment of the "new" NHL.

We ended it as the hottest team in the sport.

Statistically, it was one of the most extraordinary turnaround seasons in NHL history. The climax came in my hometown, Montreal, on the last day of the season, when we trailed the Canadiens 3–1 with less than nine minutes to play in the third and roared back to win in the final minutes of play. It was our 11th straight victory, an NHL record for any team to close out a season. The triumph clinched the Atlantic Division title for the Devils, and by coming back to win the division after being 19 points out of first place on January 6, we set another record.

It was a fabulous conclusion to a season that had started out so badly.

Three weeks earlier, after all, we hadn't even clinched a playoff berth. That didn't happen until April 11 in Carolina, when we won our eighth straight game, a thrilling 4–3 overtime victory that held a lot of symbolism for our team because on December 17 we had lost to the Hurricanes in Larry Robinson's last game before quitting as head coach. At that time, despite undeniable talent and great tradition, we had no sense of collective energy or direction. But between December 17 and April 11, we had fixed many of our problems, and the win that clinched our playoff berth was evidence of that.

But we didn't stop there. We kept winning, and at the same time, the New York Rangers, who had been jostling for first place with the Philadelphia Flyers at the top of the Atlantic Division all season, started doing a little speed wobble.

"If the Rangers don't take care of business, we can still catch them," said Lou Lamoriello, who had added the coaching job to his general manager's duties when Robinson stepped down.

Sure enough, with five days to go in the regular season, we beat the Flyers at home to pull closer to the Rangers, and a second victory over Philly at the Meadowlands three days later sent us into Montreal on the last night of the season riding a 10-game winning streak with a chance to finish first in our division. It was an incredible scenario to contemplate, given the misery we had endured months earlier. For it to happen, we needed to beat the Habs, and the Rangers needed to lose at home to Ottawa. Even a Flyer victory over the Islanders couldn't stop us from claiming the division title because we would have more wins on the season.

But as the third period relentlessly moved along in Montreal that night, it looked as though Philadelphia was going to finish first. The Flyers had defeated the Islanders easily that night, while the Rangers had been beaten soundly at Madison Square Garden by Ottawa, 5–1. We'd fallen behind 3–0 to the Habs, but Brian Gionta had scored late in the second period to give us life, a goal that was his 47th of the season and broke Pat Verbeek's team record.

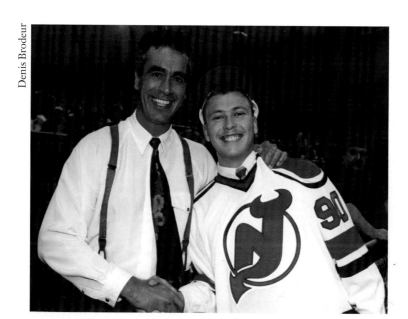

All smiles on NHL draft day in June 1990 with agent Gilles Lupien. Later, the two would split and Martin would choose to negotiate his own contracts.

March 26, 1992. Martin's first NHL game, wearing No. 29, with St. Hyacinthe mask and pads. The Devils won 4–2. No. 49 for the Bruins is Joe Juneau, the first NHLer to score on Martin. No. 3 for New Jersey is Ken Daneyko, who played 1,458 games for the Devils—the only team he ever played for—before retiring in 2003.

Amazingly, this puck stayed out in the 1995 Stanley Cup final against Kris Draper and the Detroit Red Wings. The Devils won their first Cup in four straight games.

Devils players celebrate the 2000 Stanley Cup victory with rock band Bon Jovi when they were all on the *David Letterman Show* together, taken on the roof of the building after the show. Martin is second from the right in the back row.

Celebrating Canada's victory at the 2004 World Cup of Hockey along with Team Canada Executive Director Wayne Gretzky and Captain Mario Lemieux.

Playing the puck became a Brodeur trademark. By October 2005, however, goaltenders were prohibited from venturing into the corners, where Martin made this slick play.

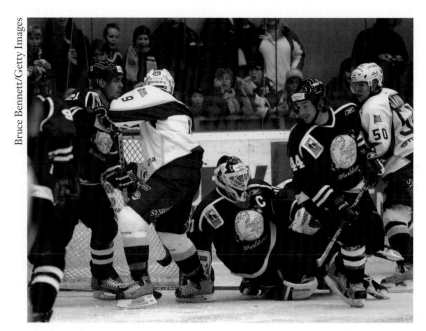

Overseas with the Primus Worldstars Tour during the 2004–05 NHL lockout. No NHL goalie had worn the C since Bill Durnan in 1948, but here Martin, a true team leader, gets the honor.

Worldstars' Assistant Coach, Marc Bergevin, was more cut-up than taskmaster. He kept things loose by doing something crazy before every game. Here, clowning in a toga, he delivers a pre-game speech.

Ancient hockey rivals Canada and Russia meet in a pivotal quarter-final game at the 2006 Olympics in Turin.

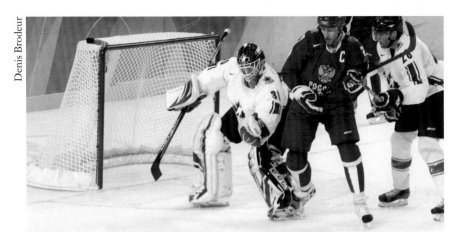

Crowded in the crease by Alexei Kovalev, with Robyn Regehr next to him.

Kick save on Maxim Sushinsky.

Washington Capitals star Alexander Ovechkin scoring the winning goal on Brodeur in a 2–0 Russian victory.

Gen and the boys — from left William, Jeremy, and Anthony — in the crowd at the Turin Olympics.

The ultimate prize. Hoisting the Stanley Cup for the third time, at his cottage in St. Adolphe d'Howard in the summer of 2003.

Mireille Brodeur's artistic impression of her son's cottage retreat at St. Adolphe d'Howard, Quebec. The painting, done during the winter of 2005, hangs in the main house on the property.

April 8, 2006, New Jersey Devils at Montreal Canadiens. Even after 13 seasons in the NHL, it's still special for Martin to play in his hometown before family and friends. Notice the classic Brodeur technique with one knee down, unusual in an era dominated by the butterfly style.

In the third, we killed off a tripping penalty to Jamie Langen-brunner, and then Montreal center Radek Bonk was assessed a hooking penalty, a call that had become very common in the new NHL. With 30 of my family members and friends in the audience, including my father, my brothers Claude and Denis, and my sister Line, Gionta scored again at 11:29 to cut Montreal's lead to 3–2. Suddenly, the momentum had turned, and the energy that had helped us put together victory after victory in the final days of the season began to build again.

Just over three minutes later, Patrik Elias scored to tie the game, and with 2:23 left in regulation, Langenbrunner completed our terrific comeback by putting the winner past Cristobal Huet in the Montreal net, giving us the 4–3 victory and the division title. My teammates and I erupted in a wild celebration, surprisingly emotional considering that many of the players had won one or more Stanley Cups as members of the Devils. But this was special because of all the obstacles that had been overcome. Gionta had his record, and his goals had been very important to us in our turnaround season. "It was fantastic to do it when it was so meaningful, and never trying to force it," said Lamoriello.

Even I had reached a personal milestone, as the victory was my 43rd of the season, and that ended up putting me past Mikka Kiprusoff of the Flames for the most victories by any goalie in the league. I take a lot of pride in winning, and after a season in which many people had said I hadn't played that well, it was very special. With eight of the wins coming through shootouts, the number was somewhat inflated. In other years, after all, those would have been ties, not wins. But I was grateful all the same, given the sense around the league that the season hadn't been my best. As well, it was the 10th straight year I'd had at least 30 wins, an NHL record that only Patrick Roy is close to, with eight seasons.

As we rode on the bus to Montreal's Pierre Trudeau Airport after beating the Habs, we just sat looking at each other. "Unbelievable," said John Madden, shaking his head. "Unbelievable," said Langenbrunner, then Scott Gomez. Then me.

—ᴡᴡ—

NHL seasons are so long, with so many twists and turns, that it's difficult to pinpoint one game as pivotal. In our case, however, the 2005–06 season had seemed to change from uncertain to promising on January 9 against Philadelphia at home. The Flyers were first in the conference going into that game, but we won 3–0, held them to 22 shots and picked up our fourth straight win, all of which had occurred with Elias back in the lineup after missing the first half of the season.

After the game, Gomez sat in his stall happily chirping to teammates and reporters. He had scored once and assisted on a goal, giving him 16 points in seven games, and he seemed more relaxed now that the team wasn't bugging him about his weight every day. It was a happy, relaxed night in the dressing room, and a busy night in my stall, still located where it has been for years, a corner location off by itself near the entrance to the showers. After weeks of dealing with "what's wrong?" questions, this night the media inquiries were positive and full of praise. First came one group of reporters, mostly TV and radio people, and then four or five minutes later a second wave arrived, mostly newspaper reporters. After the crowd cleared, *New York Post* columnist Larry Brooks stopped by to ask about the possibility of a new coach to replace Lamoriello, who at that point was still telling the hockey world he was there only on an interim basis and was looking for a full-time replacement. Rumors were still in the air that Brent Sutter or Paul Maurice might be coming in to take over. Veteran beat reporter Mark Everson, one of the writers I've known for years, made a wisecrack as he headed off to write his story.

Afterwards, I showered and put on a gray suit and red tie, walked down the same corridor I've walked for years and met Geneviève in the usual meeting area for family and friends. There has never been the kind of post-game craziness after Devils games that you might find in Toronto or Montreal, partly because the arena isn't located in a downtown area, and partly because it's the nature of playing a sport that isn't the No. 1 attraction in the larger New York marketplace. As we rode the escalator up one level and walked through the ticket window area, a couple of lingering fans shouted encouraging words, and then Gen and I walked out into the cool, clear night. The engine of my new sportscar roared and the satellite radio boomed to life as I headed home down Highway 78, then Highway 24 and finally into quiet Morristown, about half an hour after leaving the arena.

That night, after 43 games, it seemed that our team had finally taken definite shape. There was, of course, me and backup Scott Clemmensen in net. I'd played with many backups over the years, and the only time I'd felt a real challenge was when Mike Dunham had been pushing me for two years, from 1996 to 1998. Clemmensen was from Des Moines, Iowa, and had finally cracked our team as the full-time backup at the age of 28. He was a big kid, 6-foot-3 and about 200 pounds, and he had played college hockey at Boston College as a teammate of Gionta's. He'd moved ahead of Ari Ahonen in the organizational depth chart despite the fact Ahonen, a Finnish prospect, was a higher draft pick. Coming out of the lockout, there was the possibility that Jean-Sébastien Aubin (who used the same financial advisor as I did in Montreal) would join our team as a backup. Instead, Clemmensen was signed to the Devils. Aubin signed with the Leafs and, after spending most of the season in the minors behind Ed Belfour and Mikael Tellqvist, emerged late in the season to put together an impressive winning streak as the Leafs desperately tried to reach the playoffs.

Clemmensen had done a solid job when I had gone down with a knee injury in the fall, winning two and losing two in regulation, and losing two more in overtime. I'm sure he would have liked to play more, but I like to play a lot myself. After Clemmensen had played and lost in Pittsburgh on December 29, I started 43 of the final 44 games of the season. I was pulled twice, and he got one final start, March 24 at home against Boston. Still, we worked closely together, and he was a nice kid. We both spent as much time as possible with our goalie coach, Jacques Caron, although with the schedule compressed because of the Olympics, there wasn't much time in between games to do that kind of work.

The goaltending had been set from the opening day of the season, but the defense was weeks in taking form. After Scott Niedermayer chose to go to the Mighty Ducks in free agency during the summer, Lamoriello had signed Vladimir Malakhov and Dan McGillis to expensive free agent contracts with the idea that both would be important defensemen for us, but neither had worked out. Malakhov retired in mid-December and McGillis was sent to the minors soon after. From there, we had to pick up the pieces. Our key veterans were Brian Rafalski, the second-highest-paid player on the team at $4 million per season, and Colin White, a holdover from our championship teams. Rafalski, who was from Dearborn, Michigan, and had been a star at the University of Wisconsin, was never drafted and had spent four years in Sweden and Finland before being signed by the Devils. He had been a teammate of mine for six years, but we'd never been particularly close. Like Malakhov and McGillis, he had been

re-signed by the Devils after Niedermayer left. He was our best
offensive defenseman, but he was being forced to play the minutes that Niedermayer had always played, a tough adjustment.

White, a big, strong defenseman from New Glasgow, Nova
Scotia, was left to fill the physical presence of Ken Daneyko and
Scott Stevens, but he had to do it in the new environment in
which NHL rearguards couldn't be as punishing and physical as
they once could. A good athlete and a good skater for a big man,
his challenge had always been controlling his emotions, which
sometimes got in the way of doing his job. Many times, I'd seen
him make a mistake, and then, while still thinking about that
mistake, take a penalty on the next shift. He and Ralfaski didn't
work really well together, and instead White gradually became
part of a tandem with Paul Martin. Together they were the defense pair we used to shut down enemy players such as Jaromir
Jagr, for instance, when we played the Rangers. Martin, 24, was
a quiet, rangy and talented player from Minnesota, more of a
finesse player than a physical one. Many people would meet him
and be shocked he was an athlete, but in reality he'd been a star
in a number of sports growing up and could have played any one
of them professionally. It was only his second NHL season, but it
became evident to me that he was a player that could eventually
become almost as good as Niedermayer once he mastered all the
elements of his game.

After Rafalski, White and Martin, the rest of the defense was
made up by various combinations of Richard Matvichuk, Tommy (The Stalker) Albelin, David Hale, Sean Brown and, later in
the season, Ken Klee and Brad Lukowich. Matvichuk was an old
school player born in Edmonton who had learned his craft with
the Dallas Stars and loved to dive and block shots, the kind of
thing we didn't do a lot in Jersey. He was an honest player who
did everything as though it was still 1990. It took a while to get

used to his style, and for him to adapt to the Devils' style of play, but he was a gutsy, hardnosed player who could play through pain. As the season wore on, he suffered from a herniated disk in his back, and at one point missed 14 games. When he came back, his left foot was still numb most of the time, but he played anyway.

Albelin had been signed in December and played the same game he always had, a contain-type approach that was anything but flashy. He was Swedish and had first broken into the NHL with Quebec in 1987, five years before my first NHL game. Hale, a star at the University of Dakota, had been called up from the minors when McGillis was sent down. He and Martin had both made their NHL debuts in the same game on October 8, 2003, but Martin had progressed more quickly. Brown was a big, strong veteran who had started his career in Edmonton and played for the Bruins as well before joining our team after we won the Stanley Cup in 2003 and Daneyko had retired.

While we had experience, our defense was the least consistent part of our team, and before the March 9 trade deadline Lamoriello tried to solidify things by trading Brown to Vancouver and bringing in two more veterans, Klee from Toronto and Lukowich from the Islanders. Lukowich, an easygoing player from Cranbrook, B.C., who loved to put on headphones and play air guitar, or even air drums, struggled initially but gradually formed a good pairing with Rafalski. With White–Martin and Rafalski–Lukowich, our two top pairs were set by late March, with Matvichuk playing when he was healthy alongside one of Albelin, Klee or Hale. It had literally taken us the entire season to put together a blueline corps after losing Niedermayer, Stevens and Daneyko, the cornerstones of our defense for more than a decade. No other team in the league had enjoyed that kind of stability. We had always known there would have to be a changeover at some point, but playing behind an uncertain defense for long stretches, as I had to do for much of the 2005–06 season, was something I just hadn't been used to.

Along with Malakhov and McMillis, winger Alexander Mogilny had been an expensive free agent acquisition the previous summer who hadn't panned out. He was sent to the minors on January 3, and afterwards it clearly became a team that revolved offensively around Gomez, Gionta and Elias. In fact, the three played as a forward line until late March when Elias was shifted to another unit, giving us a second scoring line. Gomez and Gionta were small, speedy and very talented forwards, and during the 2005–06 season they established themselves as bona fide first line players.

Gomez, born in Alaska and a folk hero there for going back north to play for an ECHL team in Anchorage during the lockout, had been a Devil since 1999. Coming out of the lockout, he had never scored 20 goals in a season. But smaller players were having more success in the post-lockout NHL, with hooking and interference no longer allowed as much, and the offensive game becoming more about skill than physical strength or courage, and Gomez was able to use his speed and skill to put up the best numbers of his career. He was a fiery player and a trash talker, whether the words were directed at the other team or our own players. When a power play didn't work that well, I could hear him swearing at Rafalski on the ice, demanding to get the puck in better position in order to create a better attack. More chunky than lean, he has always surprised other teams with his speed. Blessed with an ability to always play with his head up, even at top speed, he took the suggestion of assistant coach Jacques Laperrière to focus on improving his shot by being more accurate, and as the season wore on he became more and more confident he could beat goaltenders with his shot, not just by being clever or shifty. By the end of the season he had 33 goals after previously never having scored more than 19 in a single year.

Gionta, from Rochester, New York, had been drafted in the same year as Gomez, 1998, but it had taken him four years longer to crack the Jersey lineup on a full-time basis. Only 5-foot-7, he had blazing speed and no fear. In the 2003 playoffs, he went toe-to-toe on numerous occasions with Ottawa's 6-foot-9 defenseman Zdeno Chara, behaving like he was seven feet tall himself. He had never used his size as an excuse. Like Gomez, under the new rules he had a breakthrough season. When we had our Gold Circle luncheon with our season ticketholders on April 6, he was voted the team's MVP, and he deserved it. All season, he hadn't gone longer than four games without scoring a goal, and during those last 11 straight wins, he scored nine goals to finish the year with 47. It had become clear that not too many players in the league could skate with him, and that to stop him you had to risk taking a penalty.

Other teams had always viewed the Devils as a team that played a deliberate game focusing on the neutral zone trap. But with Gomez and Gionta flourishing under the NHL's new commitment to calling fouls for hooking, holding and interference, we were one of the teams that went into the '06 playoffs praying that the officials would keep using their whistles.

Elias, meanwhile, had also been drafted by the Devils, but he had been part of the organization since 1994, a regular since the 1997–98 season and a key part of our Cup-winning teams in 2000 and 2003. Still, with veterans like Stevens, Daneyko, Niedermayer, Mogilny, Gomez, Bobby Holik, John Madden, Petr Sykora and Jason Arnott prominent on those teams, Elias had always been slightly in the background despite his great talent and the fact that, going into the 2006 playoffs, he had already played 102 playoff games, all with the Devils.

During the NHL lockout he had returned, like many of his countrymen, to the Czech Republic to play in its elite league. He skated for Znojemsti Excalibur Orli for part of the season, but then decided to join Sykora in Russia to play for Magnitogorsk Metallurg. After a game in Moscow in late February, he developed flu-like symptoms, and eventually it was determined he had contracted hepatitis A. He spent almost a month in hospital in the Czech Republic and lost 30 pounds. He missed all of training camp and didn't practice until December 19—the same day Robinson stepped down. When Elias was finally ready to play, we immediately started to win, reeling off nine straight. He suffered a rib injury at the Turin Olympics and missed some more games, but as we got hot again in late March and early April, he was a key contributor, giving us a second scoring line behind Gomez and Gionta and playing the point on our power play, which had been miserable before Christmas.

The most underrated part of Elias' game had always been his competitiveness and his willingness, as an offensive player, to play a role in a defensive system. Not every player can embrace that. For certain types of players, it's a big sacrifice to play for the Devils. He was as good as any player in the league at handling the puck and creating plays, but he also had an element of grit to his game and a determination not to take any crap from anybody out there. Years earlier, he had played on the exciting and productive "A Line" with Arnott and Sykora, and by 2006, I felt his commitment to the team was the reason he was still a Devil.

Arnott and Sykora were both eventually traded, and four years after he was traded to Anaheim, Sykora was still mystified as to why he had been dealt. There are always many reasons, but I believe he was traded after the 2002 playoffs because he wouldn't play through a foot injury. He'd been hit by a Scott Stevens shot with about 10 weeks left in the season, and it had left him limping and sore for a long time. We were scheduled to play back-to-back games in a first-round series against Carolina for games 4 and 5, and before the first game he told me he was ready to play but wouldn't be able to go in the next game. "I won't feel good, I'm sure," he said. Sure enough, with the series tied 2–2, he walked by me in the hall in his suit about 15 minutes before we were supposed to go on the ice in Raleigh for Game 5. "What are you doing?" I said. "I can't play," he replied. We lost that game in overtime, and then dropped a 1–0 decision at home three days later to lose the series in six games after making it all the way to the Stanley Cup final the previous two springs. About two months later, Sykora was traded to the Mighty Ducks.

The Sykora deal brought Jeff Friesen to the Devils. In his first year, Friesen scored a huge goal in Game 7 against Ottawa to help us win the Eastern Conference final. We then moved on to beat the Ducks and Sykora for the Cup. While his Czech countryman Sykora was dealt away, Elias was kept for a reason. Lamoriello, I think, saw something special in him that he didn't see in some other players.

We had tried various youngsters at forward during the season, kids like Alexander Suglobov, Barry Tallackson, Jason Ryznar and Tomas Pihlman, but none seemed to be the answer. Suglobov was eventually traded to the Maple Leafs for Klee, and as the season progressed we relied more and more on our usual collection of grinders and bangers. For years, our best checkers had been Mad Dog Madden, a center, and winger Jay Pandolfo, and as we started winning more games over the course of the season, they began to settle into their familiar roles. Earlier in the year, when Elias wasn't playing, Madden had been forced to play more offensively, which took him out of his usual role of being a pest all over the ice and checking the other team's best players. For years, he had been a key leader for us, particularly when he committed himself to playing against the best forwards on the opposition. He took a lot of pride in that, and was always disciplined, rarely taking penalties despite having the job of playing against the best.

Blazing fast but not elegant, Madden had joined the Devils as a rookie in the 1999–2000 season after playing at the University of Michigan. As a player, he knows how to focus on another player and get under his skin, and when he was in the lineup and playing well, everybody on the team was more at ease and could comfortably do their jobs. Maybe he and I shared that trait as hockey players.

Madden had grown up in a tough housing project in northeast Toronto, a place where he would see men in ski masks selling drugs 50 feet from his front door. He had grown up poor, and as Ken Dryden wrote about Guy Lafleur in *The Game,* "Where is the romance in beginning life poor, except if you didn't?" Madden's life as a boy had been very different from my own. He needed the generosity of others to help him play hockey and find opportunity. For me, there was always my father, my mother, my sisters and my brothers, my friends and my street, still recognizable today as the arena of all my childhood games. My life was different than Madden's, yet we became friends; he was one of my closest friends on the team after Daneyko retired.

His linemate was usually Pandolfo, a totally different character. Massachusetts-born, Pandolfo was like me, Gomez, Gionta, Elias, Madden, White and Rafalski—he'd never played for any NHL organization other than the Devils. In my time in the league, only the Detroit Red Wings were able to create that kind of continuity. It was almost like the old Montreal Canadiens teams of the 1970s, teams photographed by my father as they won four Stanley Cups. Pandolfo had played with the Boston University Terriers and joined the Devils for the 1996–97 season, after we missed the playoffs in '96 for the first and only time in my New Jersey career. He was a company guy, just like me, a player who was liked by all his teammates and did everything he was asked to do. He was always in great shape, would sacrifice his body for the team and stick up for his teammates. He carved out a role in the NHL by being a terrific checker, always in the right position and a player who understood the approach that Devils teams wanted to take.

At the Gold Circle gathering, Pandolfo was voted by his teammates as the most unsung player, and the "player's player." He was such a Boston Red Sox fan that he concluded his acceptance speech by saying quickly, "Go Red Sox."

During the season, it became obvious to me that the team played much better when it had a key player on the other team to check. As a team, if we didn't have a focus, a mission, more often than not we stunk. When Pandolfo and Madden shared that mission, it was difficult for an opponent to detect where one player began and the other ended. Turn left, there's the business-like Pandolfo. Turn right, there's the snarling Madden. As a team, we don't chase, we steer opposition players into areas that will compromise their interests and accommodate ours. We wait, we pounce. Nobody personifies that more than Madden and Pandolfo.

Sergei Brylin was another lifelong Devil, a Russian drafted in '92 and a teammate of mine longer than any other Jersey player. He always shifted between left wing and center, a resourceful player who never hurt you and could sometimes help. When rookie Zach Parise replaced Elias on the top line with Gomez and Gionta in March 2006, it was Brylin who moved into the middle with Elias on his left and Langenbrunner on his right. There was nothing extraordinary about Brylin, but his grit and experience were always useful. I had known him a long time, but I didn't really know him.

Langenbrunner was an American who hadn't gone the college route, but instead he had gone north to the Ontario Hockey League to play for the Peterborough Petes and was then drafted by the Dallas Stars organization. He had won the '99 Stanley Cup with the Stars, and played for them when we beat Dallas in the 2000 Stanley Cup final. Two years later, he was traded to us along with Joe Nieuwendyk for Arnott and Randy McKay, an unusually substantial deal between two of the NHL's better teams.

Langenbrunner was a very talented player with a cannon of a shot. He could get blistering hot, as he did with us in the '03 playoffs when he scored 11 goals in 24 games. It was his goal in the final game of the season, against the Canadiens in Montreal, that had won the 2005–06 Atlantic Division title for us. He was very streaky, however, and there were times it seemed the weather outside had to be just perfect for him to get even a shot on goal. Still, he was one of our better two-way players, he could kill penalties and play the power play, and by the '06 playoffs it was as though he'd always been a Devil.

The rest of the team fit the roles we needed. Grant Marshall could hit and fight. Parise, the son of former NHLer Jean-Paul Parise, was a really serious kid and a speedy, energetic player who was skillful enough to play with Gomez and Gionta. Viktor Kozlov was enormously skilled, particularly for a big man, and he was our best forward on shootouts. But as the season wore on, he found himself frequently scratched. Cam Janssen was a rugged and willing rookie from St. Louis, Missouri, who displaced Darren Langdon as the team's tough guy, just as, earlier in the season, Langdon had taken Krzysztof Oliwa's job. As the season progressed, Janssen joined with former Buffalo first-round pick Erik Rasmussen and winger Jason Wiemer, acquired from Calgary at the trade deadline, to give us a rambunctious fourth line. It was a group vaguely reminiscent of the "Crash Line" of Holik,

McKay and Mike Peluso that had been a big part of our first Stanley Cup victory in 1995.

The Devils had become a team dominated by American-born players, and I often jokingly told my teammates that we had too many Americans. I was the only French-Canadian, and one of my superstitions is that I have always believed we need at least one other to win it all. In '95, we had Claude Lemieux and Stéphane Richer, and Lemieux came back to help us win in 2000. In 2003, my fellow Quebecer was Pascal Rhéaume. Still, our team for the '06 playoffs was set, the distractions and problems seemed behind us, and the playoffs ahead were full of possibilities.

—ⱱⱱ—

Who deserved the credit for turning our season from disaster into success and promise? Every player did to some degree, of course, and the fact that our team had navigated successfully through so much muddy water made us dangerous, because we knew we could turn a defeat one night into victory the next, and then more after that. That type of confidence is invaluable to a team. The playoffs, after all, are about losing one night and bouncing right back to win the next game and regain control of the series.

Gomez had been just tremendous, and he and Gionta had been to us very much the same as Joe Thornton and Jonathan Cheechoo had been in the Western Conference to the San Jose Sharks. Thornton finished first in league scoring and Cheechoo won the Rocket Richard Trophy with 56 goals. Gomez and Gionta had, over the course of the season, given us that same lethal 1–2 punch, combining for 80 goals. When Elias was moved from their line to one with Brylin and Langenbrunner, it made us a tougher team to defend, and then when Elias, Gomez and Gionta were reunited on the power play, they enjoyed being able to pass to each other again.

Lamoriello, of course, deserved a great deal of credit. Under Robinson, we had won only 14 of our first 32 games. After the coaching change, we registered a 32–14–4 record the rest of the season, including winning streaks of nine and 11 games. He had made our players accountable, and whenever we started struggling again, he would always get back to basics, get back to what the Devils were supposed to be. Under Lamoriello, everybody rallied together. We had an endless series of team meals that drove me crazy and made everybody complain, but they worked. They helped make us more of a team. Lamoriello had done the coaching, made the tough decisions on Malakhov, McGillis and Mogilny, and then made a couple of moves at the trade deadline to help us, particularly picking up Lukowich, who got better and better the more he played with us.

I felt like my contribution had been just doing what I'd always done. I had seen myself as a "fixture" for years, and people around the team and in hockey just expected me to play the way I always had. If there was a difference, it was that since we hadn't named a captain to replace Scott Stevens, I had assumed much of that leadership role. Under NHL rules, goalies can no longer be captains. In league history, only three goalies had worn the "C," and Bill Durnan of Montreal, an ambidextrous goalie who wore special gloves so he could catch with either hand, had been the last one, back in the 1947–48 season. But even without the special designation on my Devils jersey, I felt like a captain. During the Worldstars tour of Europe during the lockout I had worn the "C," and I enjoyed that feeling of being a leader.

It may have been, however, that a couple of special evenings helped the process of restoring a winning atmosphere to our hockey club, reinforcing all that the franchise had accomplished and still had the potential to achieve, while also turning the page from one set of talented, dedicated players to a new generation.

On the night of February 3, the Devils held a ceremony hon-
oring Stevens, raising his No. 4 jersey to the rafters and featuring
his number all over the arena. He had played 22 seasons in the
NHL, but the 13 in New Jersey had been his most successful,
and he was the captain of our three Stanley Cup teams. He was
an all-star, and an icon in the game for his ferocious leadership
and trademark bodychecks. He was the pride and joy of New
Jersey fans, because he meant there was a Devil who had made
it big not just in the Meadowlands, but in the game. That night,
they showed all of his highlight hits, one after another. For my
money, the most memorable was the one on Slava Kozlov of the
Detroit Red Wings in the 1995 Stanley Cup final, a crushing hit.
With Kozlov lying on the ice, Stevens skated past the Detroit
bench, pointed and mouthed the words, "You're next." He could
be extraordinarily intimidating. Just as we came to hate Darius
Kasparaitis as much as the Rangers loved him, we understood
why other teams complained about Stevens and his big hits. He
always played against the best players on the other team, and he
made opposition players pay the price in front of the net, which
made my job much easier over the years.

We won the game 3–0 over Carolina on Scott Stevens Night,
my 80th career regular season shutout. Combined with the playoffs, it game me 100 for my career, third in NHL history behind
Terry Sawchuk (115) and George Hainsworth (102). It was my
fifth shutout in five weeks after I'd gone the first three months of
the season without any, and a fitting tribute to Stevens, who had
celebrated so many other shutouts with me over the years.

An incident after the game wasn't nearly as pleasant. We were
set to fly out of Newark on our regular charter flight for a game
in Toronto against the Leafs the next night. I was facing the back,
so I didn't see much as we hurtled down the runway. The plane,
however, couldn't lift off, and just as we reached the point of no

return, the pilot slammed on the brakes. On charters, everybody is not necessarily buckled in their seats, as would be the case on commercial flights, so there were a few players bouncing out of their seats, and food and drinks went flying everywhere. For a second, we were terrified, unsure what the problem was, or if there was another plane coming that was going to hit our plane. For three or four seconds, I didn't know if we were going to get hit, or roll into a ditch. There had been times during my career when it had been too windy to land at various airports, and once in Boston there was a snowplow on the runway that prevented us from landing. This was different, and pretty scary. We didn't leave that night, and stayed at an airport hotel before leaving the next day. We were scheduled to return from Toronto the next night after the game, but again there was a problem when the plane didn't have enough fuel to make the trip on schedule. After we returned to Jersey, Lamoriello fired the charter company, and hired another.

Seven weeks later, on March 24, we had another night to honor a retired player, this time, my old friend Daneyko. Clemmensen played, so that gave me a chance to really sit back and enjoy the ceremony. It was a different type of evening, for while Stevens had been a player recognized around the league, "Dano" was a local hero, a player who had played every one of his NHL games for the Devils, including every playoff game in the club's history until he sat out in the first round of the 2003 playoffs. He'd been there the very first game I'd played for the Devils.

It was an emotional night. Stevens was a good guy and a great captain, but everybody had a warm or funny story to tell about the beloved Daneyko, things he had done and stories he had told. He was given a crystal trophy and almost dropped it, then gave a speech in which he thanked everyone from the players to the security guards to John McMullen, the former owner of the Devils, with whom he had been very close.

Daneyko and Stevens were the first two players honored in this way by the Devils, and the ceremonies were very important to the organization and to the fans. History had been made in the previous 15 years, and it was important to recognize that history. Even more important was the standard of excellence those two players had set for the future of the franchise. Retiring those numbers made a statement that only the truly special would be recognized by the team. Other teams did it differently. The same season, the Maple Leafs had held a night for Tie Domi when he had played his 1,000th game—Daneyko played 1,458— and the Buffalo Sabres had retired Pat LaFontaine's number even though he had played more seasons for the New York Islanders. The Devils wanted to be different. In fact, Lamoriello had made it clear during the season that there would be no ceremony to honor Gionta if and when he broke Verbeek's team record for goals. "This is a team game ... a lot of records are broken every night," he explained.

We won on the night Daneyko's No. 3 was retired, 4–2 over the Bruins, just as we had won on Stevens' special evening. Call it karma, call it tradition, but those evenings seemed important in a season in which the club had foundered for a time, then returned to being the Devils again.

—⚒—

Overall, it had been a season of great change in the NHL, and a surprisingly successful one for the league. For all the public-relations damage we worried had been done during the lockout, the fans came back strongly in many cities. Even in the traditional hockey center of Montreal, the Canadiens set a new NHL attendance record of 872,193 fans for 41 home dates. As the season drew to a conclusion, there was a positive vibe everywhere, which nobody would have predicted a year earlier. The new rule standards had worked to produce a better game, even though I worried that an important part of the game, competing for the puck in high-traffic areas, had been compromised. The tradeoff, however, was a game with improved flow, a quicker game with fewer delays and scrums. The challenge was going to be maintaining that level for the playoffs, something our team certainly wanted, given the way we had developed over the season.

There were surprise teams, none more so than Carolina. Before the season started, I didn't even know who their goalies were, but by the end the Hurricanes had finished second in the Eastern Conference. Three weeks before the end of the season, I'd voted for Jaromir Jagr in the Lester B. Pearson Trophy voting, the players' award for most valuable player during the regular season. But after watching the final weeks of the season, I would have changed that vote to Joe Thornton, who had been simply amazing down the stretch, particularly in two games against Vancouver in the final week of the regular season that the Sharks won to eliminate the Canucks from the playoffs. I hadn't really considered how hard it must have been for Thornton to be part of such a big trade, to go to a brand new situation and then dominate that much. The wingman he had left behind in Boston, Glen Murray, had struggled after Thornton had left. After averaging 37 goals a season with Thornton, Murray had fallen to 24. Thornton's new sniper, Cheechoo, had led the league in goals. That in itself was a measure of Thornton's value.

But by far the biggest story of the season had been the arrival of so much bright young talent, a group of talented new players that kids could really relate to after missing the entire 2004–05 NHL season. That influx of talent was desperately needed for another reason: The league had lost star players such as Stevens, Ron Francis, Al MacInnis and Mark Messier to retirement before the season began and Brett Hull during the season. The most amazing rookies were, without question, Alexander Ovechkin of Washington and Pittsburgh's Sidney Crosby. Both ended up with more than 100 points on the season, remarkable efforts for two rookies.

Ovechkin, of course, had scored that big goal against me in Turin at the Olympics, the winning goal for the Russians in a quarterfinal game that knocked Canada out of the medals. Crosby, meanwhile, was a player I faced on the opening night of the season, and then five other times as the year went on. We played Washington four times with me in goal, and in the combined 10 games in which I faced the two young snipers, they scored six goals on 30 shots, two by Ovechkin and four by Crosby. Crosby, two years younger than the Russian, also picked up three assists, while I had one other save on Ovechkin during a shootout in March.

Everywhere they went, those two players drew crowds and lots of media attention, exactly what the NHL needed as it tried to heal the wounds of the lockout. Crosby, because we played Pittsburgh more frequently, was a player I saw much more often and gained a greater appreciation for as the season wore on. He didn't score on me in the first two games we faced each other, but on the third occasion he scored two goals and assisted on another, all before I was pulled less than six minutes into the second period in a 6–3 loss on March 11. We blanked him the next game with a much better checking effort, and on April 2, we came from behind in the final minute and won 3–2 in Pittsburgh, the first time all year we'd scored after pulling the goalie. He had scored earlier in the game, and then, with the score 2–1 and less than three minutes to play, he had a clear breakaway. I thought he was going to go backhand and top shelf, the same move he'd used on Montreal's José Théodore earlier in the year to win a much publicized shootout, but instead he snapped a shot high to my glove. It hit the edge of my glove, and stayed out. During the next TV timeout, he skated by and said, "Did it hit your glove?" I said, "Sorry, buddy. It sure did." Elias scored with 20 seconds left in regulation to tie the game before—guess who?—Gionta won the game in OT.

Three days later, we beat the Penguins again, this time at home, and after the game Crosby and I chatted briefly, and I asked him for one of his sticks. The day before, I'd asked his agent, Pat Brisson, for a Crosby stick, and when I approached "The Kid" after the game he said he'd left one for me in the morning. He's a special player, and, well, this was the only rookie season he was going to have. I own a few other sticks from players such as Wayne Gretzky, Patrick Roy and Ray Bourque, so obviously I was already feeling like this youngster was going to have an outstanding career. I had given him my goal stick after the first game of the year, his first NHL game, and as we parted that night we shook hands and he said, "You're the best. Good luck in the playoffs."

When I compare the two super-rookies, Ovechkin and Crosby, I believe that at the end of the day Crosby will be the better player. He plays well defensively, and as a center rather than a winger he has much more responsibility. Crosby's vision of the ice is tremendous, his passing skills are extraordinary and his skating strength is impressive, all at 18 years of age. Ovechkin is more colorful, and people will always go to see him and watch him score goals. He is a special breed. There are not too many players his size who can do all the things he does. That said, I believe he is a player that can be contained to a certain extent with good, solid team defense.

For Crosby, the worst aspect of his game in his first season was his attitude, or at least his habit of complaining and whining when he felt the other team was fouling him or doing things that should be penalized. He should be happy that players are keying on him and being hard on him. It's a sign of respect. In his first season, he just whined too much during games, and I really felt it took away from his game some nights, if only because it expends energy to spend time doing that. When he had three points against us, he didn't say a word. But when we played him much tougher, he complained a lot, both to our players and to the referees. I don't think his teammates liked it much, and even in the last game we played them, he took a hooking penalty and then an unsportsmanlike penalty when he complained too much. His team was trailing 6–4, with more than seven minutes left in the game, and by taking four minutes' worth of penalties he sure wasn't helping his team win.

Ovechkin, on the other hand, seemed to be a liability when he didn't have the puck. He wants to be the show, and sometimes wants to make everything happen by himself. Both of these young stars, of course, will mature and get better. They're the future of the game, the players who will be drawing fans long after I've retired to my cottage in St. Adolphe d'Howard.

Thanks to Crosby and Ovechkin, an improved game, the Olympics and, of course, the spectacular end to our rebound season, it had been a year to remember, a year that seemed a distant and unrealistic dream 12 months earlier when the league and union had wrecked an entire season.

Ahead lay the second season, and the fourth Battle of the Hudson between the Devils and Rangers in the first round of the playoffs. Turmoil had evolved into success and, we hoped, another chance for the game's ultimate prize.

CAM NEELY

13 games, 6 goals*

I didn't see Cam all that much, unfortunately, because his career was cut short by injuries. I can't imagine the numbers he would have ended up with if he'd been healthy for more years. He shot pucks right through me. Once, he ripped the catching glove right out of my hand. He could read the game and was very good at establishing body position in front of the net. When I was young, new to the league and we were playing on a small rink like they had in Boston, he was an impressive player to watch.

---

*Source: *Elias Sports Bureau. Statistics combine regular season and playoffs and are current as of conclusion of 2005–06 season.*

chapter 11
Me and Lou

HAPPINESS, ON THE EVE of the 2006 Stanley Cup playoffs, was cruising around the roads and highways of New Jersey on a gleaming American IronHorse Texas Chopper.

Radical 42-degree rake frame, 111 cubic inch S & S Super Sidewinder Plus Engine and super-stretched Chopper fuel tank. Chrome custom V-handlebars. Phantom solo seat. Dark gray paint, with light gray flames. I saw it one day at Black Label Choppers in New Jersey and it was Geneviève, my girlfriend, who loved it at first sight.

"You've got to get this," she said.

So I did. It was my second, bought to go with my 2004 Harley Fat Boy, the first motorcycle I purchased after getting the itch to learn to ride the summer after we were prematurely eliminated in the 2004 playoffs. Pat Burns, who was still in cancer therapy at the time, went with me to buy it and followed me all the way home to make sure I arrived safely.

Without a season or post-season the following year due to the lockout, I had all kinds of time to pursue my new passion, including going to my first bike rally in Myrtle Beach. We stayed in a lousy hotel I'd rate as a quarter-star facility and just hung out, looking at other motorcycles. Nobody knew who I was, although one guy stopped to ask if those were three Stanley Cups painted on my Fat Boy's gas tank. I said yes, and he revved his bike and drove away.

Getting out on the Chopper was a chance to have a little freedom between the end of an eventful 2005–06 regular season and the '06 playoffs. By capturing the Atlantic Division title on the final day of the season with our 11th straight victory, and earning home ice advantage for a first-round playoff matchup with our archrivals, the New York Rangers, we automatically picked up three full days off before the series began on a Saturday afternoon for NBC network television. The first day I golfed and the second day after practice I hopped on the Chopper and went for a 40-mile cruise around Morristown with my buddy Mike Citarella, owner of a bar in West Orange called the Rock Bottom. With a shaved head and tattoos covering most of his body, he looked a lot more like a biker than I did. Actually, I do have five tattoos. My first, on my left hip, is of a goalie mask with the initials of my three sons. Then, on my right hip, I have a tattoo in the shape of my daughter's foot when she was an infant. Finally, I have three Chinese characters representing Winning, Dignity and Courage arranged vertically down the middle of my back, starting at my shoulders. The weather was gorgeous, and it was a great day to go for a nice, relaxing ride, just to clear my mind for the challenge ahead. It did, of course, cross my mind that it probably wasn't exactly what Lou Lamoriello, the only boss I've ever had in professional hockey, would have wanted me to be doing. I wasn't breaking any team rules or any clauses in my contract, and to be honest, I'm pretty safe on a bike. Under New Jersey state law you have to wear a helmet, and truthfully, it's an accident if I ever get above 60 miles per hour. Still, athletes make mistakes too, and I sure noticed in mid-June 2006 when the hero of the Super Bowl, Pittsburgh Steelers quarterback Ben Roethlisberger, suffered a broken jaw and busted nose when he fell off his bike in downtown Pittsburgh. There are always risks.

The bike was my release, and at the same time Gen and I were about to move into a new home in Llewellyn Park, a community in West Orange most famous for once being home to Thomas Edison. Riding motorcycles and buying homes in the middle of the playoffs were the kinds of things Lou always viewed as "distractions," his favorite word for anything and everything that might take away from the team's performance or an individual player's performance. For me, however, they were moments of escape, a chance to get away from the heavy pressure of hockey, particularly in the playoffs. Just as competing in the 2003 Stanley Cup playoffs had helped me escape the troubles of my personal life at the time, having a motorcycle to ride and the details of a new house to manage gave me room to breathe when the playoffs started.

That freedom, of course, didn't last long. On the night before Game 1 against the Rangers, we had to check into "jail." That's what we call the traditional Devils practice of staying in a hotel before all playoff games, even those at home. It had always been that way since I first became a Devil, and certainly the track record was there to suggest it was a formula that worked. Still, players love to complain about it. We stay at a five-star hotel, we don't have to pay for it, they feed you and take care of your every need, and still we've got to complain.

For the '06 playoffs, we were staying at the Renaissance Hotel, just west of the Continental Airlines Arena on Route 3. The anticipation was enormous for our first playoff meeting with the Rangers since 1997, when they had Wayne Gretzky and Mark Messier and beat us in five games. We had never beaten the Rangers in the "Battle of the Hudson" on three previous tries, just another reason to feel as though we were forever in their shadow despite the three Stanley Cups we had won.

As the series was about to start, my "playoff posse" gathered, a group of supporters that grows and shrinks with different people depending on the series and the year. My lawyer, Susan Ciallella, was a constant, along with my family and Montreal friends like Big Boy and Dancing Guy. Brad Robins, my pal in Toronto, wasn't coming and wasn't even communicating with me. He had stopped calling late in the season, once our win streak had started, and now that it had reached 11 games and counting, he didn't want to risk being blamed if we lost. His job was to stay at home in Toronto. Coyle Connolly was another member of my playoff posse. When we won the Cup in '95, I went on my first golf vacation in Florida. One night, I was sitting at the Baha Beach Club in Fort Lauderdale having a beer and I was approached by this guy who said he was a big Flyers fan. He offered his congratulations anyway, and went away in a few minutes. Then he came back and wondered if he could ask me one question, something about Eric Lindros. I said sure. Well, we ended up talking for a few hours that night, and over time we have become close friends. He's a dermatologist down on the Jersey Shore, and I'm the godfather of his first son. Strange, the friends you end up making in this business.

So there we were in jail, the posse was forming and there was only one other tradition to keep, and that was going out to a movie the night before every playoff game. It's relaxing, something to do to break the boredom of hanging around the hotel. Of course, if you get into a long playoff run, you can't be all that choosy after a while. In the '95 playoffs, I remember we were so desperate over the eight-week run we were seeing children's movies by the end.

Movies were even more important in these playoffs because it wasn't as if we could sit around and watch other teams play in the first round of the playoffs. ESPN and its sister network, ESPN2, were no longer carrying the NHL, which had struck a new deal with the Outdoor Life Network during the lockout to broadcast NHL games, along with some coverage by NBC late in the season and the playoffs. OLN, however, not only didn't carry as many games, it was often difficult to find cable companies that carried it. At the Renaissance they didn't have it, and the Devils had to pay for a special feed so we could get some NHL playoff games. So while my friends and family in Canada were getting multiple series and games on TSN and CBC, all I could watch on the opening night of the playoffs was one game, Edmonton at Detroit. For a player like me who loves to watch games, that's tough.

So the movies came in handy, and the '06 playoffs began with *The Sentinel*, starring Kiefer Sutherland, the star of my favorite TV show, *24*. I went with Tommy Albelin, Jay Pandolfo, Patrik Elias, Grant Marshall and Scott Gomez, and like the posse, this group would change as the playoffs moved along. After the movie, I watched a bit of the Oilers and Red Wings, not knowing then that it was going to be the start of a thrilling playoff ride that would take Edmonton all the way to the Stanley Cup final. Since it was an afternoon game the next day, I popped a sleeping pill, something I don't generally like to do except before a day game when there's no morning skate and I want to make sure I get a good sleep.

Game 1 was my 134th consecutive playoff start, just two fewer than Patrick Roy's record, with the difference being that all my starts had come for the Devils. Interestingly, the streak had begun 12 years earlier against the same Rangers. As per my usual routine, in the morning I watched selected clips of all seven games I had played against the Rangers that season on a DVD that had been prepared by our team staff. I was looking for clues in scoring chances, goals scored, number of times I touched the puck—any and all small indications of what might work well in this series. In general, my intention was to try to stay the same, behave just as I would during the regular season. I want to make my teammates feel comfortable, and my confidence needs to show.

Gamesmanship, of course, always plays a part in these match-ups, and that seemed to be the case on the eve of Game 1 when Ranger head coach Tom Renney said publicly that he could "see holes" in my game that he believed his team could exploit. Maybe that was a way for him to make his team feel more confident. One of the Ranger theories, expressed mostly through the Manhattan media, was that because they had scored crucial goals against me in the 1994 and 1997 playoffs on wraparounds, I was vulnerable to that type of goal-scoring attempt. In particular, the wraparound goal by Stéphane Matteau in double overtime on May 27, 1994, which had won Game 7 of the '94 Eastern Conference final, always came up. The Rangers moved on to win the Stanley Cup that year, their first in 54 years, and Matteau's goal had become a big part of Ranger history. No matter that I was a rookie that year. To some, at least for the purposes of playoff chatter, it was evidence of a problem I had never corrected, so 12 years later I knew it would be a discussion point again. The Ranger beat writers were all over me, and I told them I thought it was great they were using all their saliva on this issue. "I'd be disappointed if you didn't bring the Matteau goal up one more time," I said.

The scene for Game 1 was the same raucous, enthusiastic atmosphere that has always been the case when the Rangers and Devils meet, even for regular season play. We sold out the game with 19,040 fans, but that was mostly because of the Ranger factor. In fact, after we won in Montreal on the last night of the season to set up the series, Rangers fans had snapped up thousands of tickets in a matter of hours, and the best part for the Devils was that to get tickets for the first round they had to buy the second round as well. Playing the Rangers was always good for business in New Jersey.

The intense rivalry spilled over into the stands, where there were five or six fights during the game, but on the ice we dominated, winning 6–1 to extend our winning streak to 12 straight games. We scored five power play goals—incredible when you think back to how bad we were at extra strength earlier in the season—and Elias had six points. New York's star forward, Jaromir Jagr, left late in the game with an arm injury, and it was kind of strange as he seemed to make a real show of demonstrating to our bench how hurt he was before going to the dressing room. While he was playing, Pandolfo did a terrific job of shadowing him, and later in the game both Michal Rozsival and Marek Malik took turns at Pandolfo. It was as though out of frustration they were trying to hurt our players.

Before Game 2 two nights later, I went to see *Inside Man* starring Denzel Washington with Albelin, Pandolfo—and Elias, who insisted on wearing the same suit that he'd worn after his big performance in the opener. The movie was great, a 7 out of 10, and we would have had a bigger group but *The Sopranos* was on TV back at the jail. Believe me, when you live in New Jersey, that's a show that rings true. Lou gave us the team bus to take to the movies and had it wait for us until the movie was over.

In Game 2, we just kept rolling, winning 4–1 with Jagr sitting out for the Rangers. Mad Dog Madden had three goals, including two shorthanded, and when he scored his third, Devils fans littered the ice with hats in that time-honored hockey tradition. There were, however, thousands of Rangers fans in the building, and they weren't nearly as impressed. The team had given away plastic "thundersticks" to the fans before the game, and the Ranger fans had, naturally, decided not to take the popular noisemakers out of the package because they had a Devils logo on them. But when Devils fans started throwing hats on the ice to salute Madden, the Ranger fans started throwing the thunderstick packages, and soon the ice was a mess of hats and plastic and garbage with more than seven minutes still to play in the third period.

As I usually do when that kind of thing happens, I hid inside my net to avoid being hit by anything. My three sons were sitting with their friends in the seats right behind my net, and when I looked around I was shocked to see that they were joining in with the Rangers fans in trying to toss the thunderstick packages onto the ice. They had extras, as well, because they were sitting behind the tall netting that surrounds the rink, and many of the sticks being thrown by others were hitting the net and landing at their feet, giving them extra ammunition. (That netting has been recently installed in every NHL rink to protect fans from flying pucks, a necessary precaution that was taken after the death of a child in Columbus several years ago.)

When I saw the boys doing this, it really ticked me off. I skated out of my net and smashed my stick as hard as I could against the end glass, motioning for them to sit down. Jeremy left his seat a few minutes later and found Gen. "I think Daddy is really mad at me," he told her. After the game, I sat down with the boys and told them why I was so mad. I explained to them that by doing what they had done, they were basically acting like Rangers fans. "Daddy's working out there," I told them. "And when Daddy's working, he doesn't need to have to discipline his children." Just like any other father, I guess.

We were on a serious roll, one of the best I'd ever been on as an NHL player, and the Rangers weren't going to stop us. We saw an awful movie before Game 3, *American Dreamz* with Hugh Grant and Mandy Moore, but that didn't make a difference as we churned out a solid 3–0 victory to pull ahead in the series, three games to none. We were having great success in the playoffs, just as the NHL continued to have its referees call the same style of hockey that had been called during the regular season. It was a high-energy, high-speed game as opposed to the tight, clutch-and-grab playoff hockey that we'd seen for so many years, and we were handling it well.

The night before Game 4, we saw the movie *United 93* about the fateful flight of the hijacked plane that crashed short of its targeted destination on September 11, 2001. I'm not sure it was great preparation for the game, because it was the most intense movie I'd ever seen. The doomed flight had taken off from Newark airport, so it had special significance to people living in New Jersey. During the movie, you could have heard a pin drop. Only Pandolfo and Cam Janssen had been willing to come with me to see it.

We polished off the Rangers in four straight, winning 4–2 the next night. Finally, we had beaten New York in the playoffs, outscoring them in the series by a 17–4 count. The game was our 15th straight win and my 137th consecutive playoff start, which broke Roy's record. After Chris Terreri had played against Boston in the '94 playoffs, I had started every single post-season game in which the Devils had played. I take a lot of pride in my consistency and durability, and that's a record that shows a little bit of both. Roy was inducted into the Hockey Hall of Fame in 2006, so to top a record held by him was very meaningful. It made me feel so appreciative of the team, because unless an organization really believes in you, you don't get the opportunity to set a record like that.

The Rangers had been ahead of us in the standings all season until the final days, so the sweep was a shock. Lou was so happy with the result, it was hard to describe. You have to understand what it's like to be a Devil to understand what it means to beat the Rangers. We live with Ranger fans every day. My neighbors are Ranger fans, the guy who eats across from us at a restaurant is a Ranger fan, my kids' hockey coach is a Ranger fan. The person who handles my financial affairs in Manhattan is a Ranger fan. I'm sure if I didn't talk to my kids every day, they'd be Ranger fans. I hate the Rangers, and Lou hates them to death. To give him the satisfaction of that sweep felt as good as anything I'd ever been able to do for him.

—∽—

If you were to walk into Lou Lamoriello's office deep in the belly of the Continental Airlines Arena, you would be struck by the bank of large televisions on the far wall and the overall sense of neatness and order. It's a large and spacious office, but not particularly luxurious. It's an office for getting things done, and for getting things done Lou's way. In an age when most NHL general managers carry a Blackberry or personal messaging device of some kind, he still doesn't even use e-mail. In the office, there's no voicemail during working hours. He wants every phone call answered by a person, preferably after no more than two rings. On the wall behind his desk, there's a framed copy of a famous Vince Lombardi speech detailing the merits and importance of teamwork and discipline. If you know Lou, you know Lombardi is one of his heroes. And while they were different men from different times in the history of sport, I would imagine that being an important player in Lou's Devils operation would be similar in many respects to what it was like for men such as Bart Starr, Paul Hornung and Jerry Kramer to play for the Green Bay Packers during the incredibly successful Lombardi years.

To work for Lou is to understand that he is the boss and you are the employee. But at the same time, there comes to be a sense of partnership for those like me, Scott Stevens and Ken Daneyko who have played in his organization for a long time. For me in particular, there has long been the sense that while I work for Lou, we work together, and the benefits have been extraordinary for both of us. Since I was 18, he's the only general manager I have known. Likewise, he has never won a Stanley Cup without me in net. Somehow, despite being so different in so many ways, we clicked somewhere along the line. He's never been to my home, and I've never been to his. In fact, I really don't know where he lives. I would say we are friends, but that it is fundamentally a business relationship. So that makes it, I guess, a great friendship based on work. When I think about the six-year contractual commitment I made to the Devils in the winter of 2006, I really think that in many ways it was a commitment not to the hockey club, but to him. I want to play for the team he runs.

I wasn't there, but I can only imagine the difference Lou made when he walked in the door in April 1987 to take over as president and GM of the Devils. Until then, the Devils had struggled terribly for five years after moving north from Denver and been labeled a "Mickey Mouse organization" by the greatest player in the game, Wayne Gretzky. Lou, during his long run as men's hockey coach and athletic director at Providence University, was already very familiar with the Devils and their owner, John Mc-Mullen. Several members of the Providence team had been NHL draft picks, including Randy Velischek and Terreri, who had been drafted by the Devils. College players weren't allowed to have agents until their eligibility had expired, and in many of those cases Lou acted as the agent for players as they signed their first NHL contracts. He would get them a meeting with tax experts and accountants and show them the options available to them. He helped Ron Wilson, later the head coach of the Anaheim Mighty Ducks, Washington Capitals and San Jose Sharks, sign a contract with Toronto Maple Leaf GM Jim Gregory, and he helped Brian Burke, who would eventually become an NHL vice-president and GM of several clubs, work out a contract with Philadelphia GM Keith Allan to play in the Flyers system. So he knew people in the NHL, and he knew how the NHL worked. Most important, he had very strong ideas about how a champion could be built.

Born in Providence, Rhode Island, Lou began his sports career playing baseball at age six, but he was surrounded by hockey as a young boy. The Providence Reds, later the Rhode Island

Reds, were a colorful and successful American Hockey League team that played out of Providence, and his parents were avid fans and supporters of the team. Many future NHL players came through the Reds, and at one point when famed goalie Johnny Bower was playing briefly in Providence in the mid-1940s on his way to the NHL, his wife, Nancy, stayed at the Lamoriello house for two months.

Playing hockey at Providence College from 1961 to 1963, Lou would go to the Providence Auditorium between classes and take shots on future Ranger star Ed Giacomin, who as the backup goalie for the Reds didn't travel with the club on road trips in those days. Springfield, Massachusetts, meanwhile, was only an hour's drive away, and it was there that Hall of Famer Eddie Shore built a minor-league powerhouse as the owner, GM and coach of the Springfield Indians, a team that won three straight Calder Cups in the early 1960s. As he became increasingly interested in coaching, Lou would watch the Indians play the Reds in Providence, and then drive to Springfield just to see how Shore ran practices. Shore was seen by many as a hockey tyrant—twice, his players went on strike against him. One of those players was Jacques Caron, who eventually became my goaltending instructor with the Devils. Lou, however, saw Shore as a genius and an outstanding coach, particularly in emphasizing and teaching the fundamentals of the sport and developing big, mobile defensemen.

Like my father, Lou grew up steeped in both hockey and baseball, and captained both teams at Providence before moving on to become the freshman coach for both sports after graduating. He also headed north during one summer to play semi-pro baseball in Thetford Mines, Quebec, and for years afterwards he recruited Quebec-based players to come and play college hockey at Providence. Through those trips, he became familiar with the workings of the Montreal Canadiens, watched how they developed players and how decisions were made, all in pursuit of excellence and Stanley Cups. He saw, for example, how they fired Al MacNeil after he won the 1971 Stanley Cup because the organization simply felt it was the right thing to do.

As he developed a winning hockey program at Providence and ultimately oversaw 22 different team sports, he studied the lessons of great teams such as the Canadiens, Packers, Yankees and Celtics, the types of organizations he believed he could one day build. He identified with strong-willed men like Shore and Lombardi, sports architects who were uncompromising and disciplined, focused and dedicated to victory. He embraced the concept that a team was like an orchestra, and needed to have violinists and drummers and horn players, each with their roles and responsibilities, each understanding their limitations. He loved to tell a story about how Daneyko received the chance to play on the Devil power play at one point during the 1990s when Bruce Driver was injured, and he picked up a few points. When Driver returned, Daneyko was still hopeful of getting power play time, and he approached Lou when that wasn't happening. "Dano, you're a drummer," Lou told him. "If you want to play the violin, well, I'm going to have to find another team that needs a violinist."

McMullen initially approached Lou to coach the Devils in 1985, but Lou had bigger ideas and saw the need to have total control of an NHL operation, combining the hockey side with the business side. He stayed in Providence. Finally, in 1987, McMullen approached Lou and said he was sick of losing. He had a president from the Philadelphia system in Bob Butera, he'd had at one point a coach from the Islander system in Billy McMillan, and he'd had to pay the New York Rangers in indemnification fees for moving his franchise into the area. It was like the Devils were made up of bits and pieces borrowed from every other NHL team. McMullen had decided he wanted his own person, and he wanted to think outside the box. No NHL organization had ever given such responsibility to an American college administrator, but when McMullen hired Lou as president and general manager, the Devils changed forever.

In that first season, the Devils not only made the playoffs but pushed all the way to the Eastern Conference final against Boston before losing. That was the series of the famous Don Koharski–Jim Schoenfeld affair, and for a long time Lou was regarded as a rebel for having challenged the league. He felt, however, it was the right thing to do at the time, and that it would send an important message that the Devils were no longer the league's doormat.

McMullen turned out to be a terrific owner, and he and Lou built the same kind of warm, trusting business relationship that Lou and I would eventually form. As a sports owner, McMullen was colorful and outspoken. He was the one who famously said that "Nothing is more limited than being a limited partner of George Steinbrenner," in regard to the bombastic New York Yankees owner. During the NHL lockout of 1994–95, McMullen was the NHL governor who said, "To hell with the small market teams."

The team had previously contemplated moving from East Rutherford, New Jersey, to Hamilton, Ontario, because of a lack of fan interest, and by the time Lou arrived, it was still drawing only about 6,000 to 7,000 fans per game. By 1995, the team was still struggling to draw fans and make money, and during our run to the Cup that spring there loomed the distinct possibility that the team might move to Nashville. But McMullen and Lou always got along in a type of owner–GM relationship that rarely exists anymore because most teams are now owned by corporations rather than individuals. Eventually, through McMullen, Lou gained a piece of ownership in the team.

At the 1990 draft, there were three highly regarded goaltending prospects in Felix Potvin, Trevor Kidd and myself, as well as Mike Dunham, who shared the goaltending chores at the University of Maine with Garth Snow. The draft was in Vancouver, and Lou guessed that the Calgary Flames, in particular, would be under enormous pressure to take Kidd, a western Canadian boy who had played for the Brandon Wheat Kings juniors in Manitoba. Kidd was the highest rated of the goalies, but the Devils scouts liked me the most, particularly David Conte and Claude Carrier. Or so they later said. Regardless, the Flames traded up to get New Jersey's pick at 11th overall and did indeed draft Kidd. With the 20th pick, the Devils took me, and then with the 53rd pick they drafted Dunham as well. A partnership was born.

It was also, interestingly, the beginning of the Quebec influence on the Devils. Three years later, Lou made what he believes was the first major step towards moving from a team that could make the playoffs to a team that could win it all when he surprised the hockey world by hiring Jacques Lemaire as head coach. Lemaire had won eight Stanley Cups as a member of the Canadiens, the only NHL team he ever skated for in his Hall of Fame career. After two years coaching in Switzerland and a year coaching Longueuil in the Quebec junior league, he joined the Habs as an assistant coach, and then was head coach for two years. He resigned that position and became a member of the Montreal head office in 1985, with most people in the industry figuring he simply didn't have the stomach to be a head coach. Eight years later, however, he agreed to take over from Miracle on Ice hero Herb Brooks as coach of the Devils.

Lou figured the team needed a coach who had done it, had known the feeling of being part of a Stanley Cup-winning team.

Lemaire was that man. Soon after his hiring, Caron was brought on as the club's goaltending coach. By the following spring, I had become the team's starting goaltender and the Devils had made it to within an overtime goal of making the Stanley Cup final. A year after that, after sweeping the Detroit Red Wings in a stunning upset, we were champions. That's the impact Lemaire had.

Over the years, and over the course of winning two more Cups, Lou never asked for my opinion on a specific player he might be interested in acquiring, although he might have thrown out 10 names for my thoughts without letting me know which ones were of particular interest. He talked to me, but at the end of the day, he always made his own decisions. One thing never changed, and that was how he treated my family. Through two ownership changes and two league-wide lockouts, he was consistent with how he made me feel my family was important, particularly when I was going through marital troubles in 2003. Even during the bitter 2004–05 lockout, he didn't miss a single holiday. The Devils weren't playing and the NHL was shut down, but the kids still got presents from the Devils at Christmas, and my girlfriend, Geneviève, still received flowers on Valentine's Day.

He believed in running a first-class operation. When my teammates and I returned after the 2006 Olympic break, the final stages of a dressing room renovation had been completed, with new lighting, carpeting, wood trim and a gorgeous new wooden door with a silver Devils emblem on it. Even the showers had been replaced for the first time in all the years I'd been there. With the new arena in Newark officially on its way, there had been some suggestion that management wouldn't bother with expensive changes to the existing arena, but Lamoriello went ahead anyway, figuring the team came first and needed to be treated in a first-class fashion.

He always believed in putting the logo first, meaning the needs of the franchise and the team, and I found that philosophy appealing. When it came time to choose between the strong beliefs of my agent, Gilles Lupien, and Lou's notion of the team concept and playing the game for the right reasons, I chose Lou. I think he has always appreciated my independent way of thinking, and we've been able to develop a relationship built on total trust. He wanted to build not just a hockey team in New Jersey, but also a team with tradition modeled on great teams such as the Packers and the Canadiens. To a large extent, he's been able to do that, despite the challenges of running a team that really doesn't call any city its own. Seeing banners with the names of Scott Stevens and Ken Daneyko raised to the rafters of the Continental Airlines Arena partway through the 2005–06 season, to join the three Stanley Cup banners, was hard evidence of that. Maybe what Lou gave me was something to believe in more than just the money of pro sports, and it was a concept I embraced.

—⁂—

After sweeping the Rangers, we prepared for a second-round series with the Carolina Hurricanes, who had beaten Montreal after losing the first two games of that series on home ice. That team had been influential in our season, for it was after a game in Raleigh in December that Larry Robinson had stepped down as head coach. They were the team in town for Scott Stevens Night, and it was after beating them for our eighth straight win in April that we began to feel we could again take a serious run at the Cup. They'd finished with 112 points, second in the Eastern Conference, and we'd split four games during the regular season. We'd played them twice before in the playoffs, beating them in 2001 with Stevens delivering a series of knockout hits, including ones on Ron Francis and Shane Willis. Francis was literally left crawling off the ice, while Willis was never the same player again. The next year, however, they knocked us out in the first round. Just as the Devils had struggled to build a tradition and a fan base in New Jersey after moving from Denver, so too had Carolina worked hard to develop its team and business after moving south from Hartford in 1997.

In between the Ranger and Hurricane series, I found out I had been nominated by the Professional Hockey Writers' Association as a finalist for the Vezina Trophy, along with Calgary's Mikka Kiprusoff and Henrik Lundqvist of the Rangers. I'd won the Vezina twice and finished second twice, but given how difficult the season had been, it was very flattering. It spoke more about all I had accomplished in the NHL, not just that single season.

We had swept the Rangers and won 15 straight games, but after finishing with the New York series on April 29 we had to wait until May 6 to begin our series with Carolina, and that seemed to sap some of the momentum we had going. In the opener down in Raleigh, we were spanked 6–0, not a fun way to celebrate my 34th birthday. They had hot young stars in center Eric Staal and 22-year-old goalie Cam Ward, who had replaced Swiss Olympic hero Martin Gerber after the first two games against the Canadiens, and won the final four games. The result was almost as awful as *Silent Hill*, the horror flick we'd gone to see the night before as part of our usual playoff routine. The game seemed much faster and more physical than any of the games in the Ranger series. Colin White had barely played for us in the first round, and now his absence on our defense was really starting to show. The Hurricanes were diving and sprawling to block a lot of shots, which would drive me crazy as a goaltender but seemed to be working for them. They had a lot of puck possession time, and tore through our penalty-killing units to score five power play goals. After the game, Jason Diamos of the *New York Times* asked if it was my worst birthday ever. Thinking back to the events of three years earlier and the very public breakdown of my marriage, I replied, "Are you serious? It's hockey, man."

It was our first loss in 41 days. At a restaurant after the game, White and Richard Matvichuk did their best to lift my spirits by telling the waitress it was my birthday so she would sing a song to me. Very embarrassing.

Before Game 2 we saw *Mission Impossible III*, and soon it was clear that would become the theme of the series. We lost the game in the most disheartening way possible. Gomez seemed to have won it for us by scoring with 21 seconds left in the third period, a victory that would have tied the series as we headed back to New Jersey. But the game wasn't over. On the ensuing faceoff, Lou sent out Madden, Pandolfo, Gionta, Lukowich and Rafalski. Personally, I would have had Langenbrunner out there instead of Gionta, for experience and size, and Martin instead of Rafalski to give us a bigger body in front if the play came down to our end. A moment later, it did: Madden won the faceoff so cleanly he lifted the puck like a backwards slingshot deep into our zone, a terrible piece of luck. Carolina pulled Ward, a crazy scramble followed, and with three seconds left Staal banged the puck in to tie the game. We were stunned. Then, with just over three minutes gone in overtime, Carolina defenseman Niclas Wallin cut in from the right wing. As he lost control of the puck, it hit his left skate, then his right, and slid past me for the game winner to give the Hurricanes a 2–0 lead in the series.

We returned home to our first non-sellout crowd of the spring, always a bit disappointing but something we had become used to over the years. Before Game 3, we saw the movie *Stick It*, which turned out to be a movie for teenagers about gymnastics. There we were in the theater, four guys in suits, looking like perverts. It was a back-and-forth game, but Carolina won it on a goal late in the second period by Rod Brind'Amour. I received some criticism for a backhand goal I had allowed in the first period to Matt Cullen, and I appreciated Gomez coming to my defense afterwards. "I have two Stanley Cup rings because of this guy. He comes through," said Gomez.

The Hurricanes were up three games to none, and suddenly the series was about history. The Devils had never been swept in a playoff series, but only two teams in NHL history, the 1942 Toronto Maple Leafs and the 1975 New York Islanders, had ever fought back from a 3–0 deficit in a playoff series. On the day before Game 4, I told the media that I hadn't made enough difference-making saves, and that I was "planning on shutting them down."

"It's my personal thing. I need to do it. I'm not saying I'm going to do it, but I want to do it, that's for sure," I said. I didn't guarantee anything. I had always felt that guarantees before big games were meaningless, forgotten if they didn't pan out and blown up to mythical proportions when they did. But I really felt that it was important to step up to the plate as a leader, as a player who didn't wear the "C" but felt like a captain, and it was certainly important for the team to avoid being swept. Being easy to beat was not the tradition we had built.

Stevens appeared in the dressing room before Game 4. When you get to that point, it's all about trying to change things up, and he was trying to help. Gomez and White were both going with a new moustache-and-sideburns look. Gomez called it his Uncle Ernie look, the "mixture of a pizza guy and a taco stand owner." Matvichuk, still struggling with his disk problems, was taken out of the lineup, and Albelin went in. For one game, it all worked. We won 5–1, knocked Ward out of the game and created at least a scent of optimism that we could get hot again after our tremendous winning streak at the end of the season.

Me and Lou 273

That lasted less than 24 hours, however, as we lost 4–1 in Raleigh the next day and were eliminated from the post-season. We'd seen *Poseidon*, the remake of the 1972 film *The Poseidon Adventure* before Game 4, but because we were traveling overnight we hadn't had a chance to keep the tradition going for Game 5. Probably, however, that hadn't made the difference. Afterwards, I shook hands with Ward, and it made me think of being a rookie goalie myself going to the conference finals for the first time in 1994.

A season that had once held the promise of Olympic gold and another Stanley Cup ring had ended, sadly, without either. I believed we had the depth to challenge for the Cup, but we just couldn't pull it together. It was an opportunity missed, and the Hurricanes were simply half a step ahead of us for the entire series. Still, it had taken a special group to overcome the stuff we had dealt with during the season. We had learned to live with each other, and then some. A few days after the series ended, once the initial disappointment had worn off, we gathered as a team and went out in Manhattan for a season-ending party. After buying vacation packages for Stevens and Daneyko to commemorate their retirements, and giving end-of-season bonuses to the trainers and other staff, we still had $20,000 in the kitty to hold a party. All year long, we'd gathered money for the silliest of reasons—scoring a goal in your hometown, scoring a goal against a team you used to play for—and a night in New York, starting at a terrific Brazilian restaurant, gave us lots of ways to spend it.

—∞—

The season had started in the wake of the lockout with all kinds of questions. And, as with all seasons that end without a Cup, it ended with questions about the future of the team and the futures of individual players. For years, players such as Stevens, Niedermayer and I had accepted, either grudgingly or happily, contracts that some viewed as below market value, but that had helped keep our team together. Niedermayer had finally left the previous summer. There were no guarantees anymore that players would stay in Jersey for anything less than top dollar.

Under the new salary cap system, there's only so much that teams can pay to any single player, and only so much money out there. If players leave via free agency, we have to find another free agent. Every team will have that $4 million or $5 million to spend on key players, and it's a matter of finding a player to accept it. Offensive players will move around, and I believe the Devils have to put their money into defense. The immediate challenge was complicated, however, by some of the decisions made in the 2005–06 season. The salary cap was to rise to $44 million per team from $39 million, but the Devils would start out the '06–07 season with less to spend because, under the new collective bargaining rules, the combined salaries of the retired Vladimir Malakhov and the demoted Alexander Mogilny ($7 million) would count against the New Jersey payroll even though neither player was expected to play. That meant the Devils would effectively have $37 million to spend, not $44 million, certainly a competitive disadvantage.

My decision to rework my contract and earn $5.2 million rather than $6 million would help a little, and it came as an enormous relief when both Langenbrunner and Elias re-signed with the team after the season. Elias, in particular, looked to be on the move, but on his second day of free agency in July 2006 he signed a seven-year, $42-million contract that moved him to the top of our team's payroll, ahead of me. I'm okay with that. I want to win. We had seen the negative effect of losing Scott Niedermayer the previous summer, and while Elias could have been replaced eventually, keeping him improved the chances we would be able to start the 2006–07 season with a very competitive club. He not only has the talent we need, but the grit and determination as well.

Still, we need a new generation of Devils to keep emerging. Zach Parise enjoyed a good rookie season and could be a regular for years to come. The organization was excited about forward Travis Zajac from the University of North Dakota, and 2005 first rounder Niklas Bergfors—not quite Forsberg, but close in the spelling, I tell people—apparently has promise. The team signed Gionta's younger brother, Stephen, and he finished the season with the club's minor pro affiliate in Albany, New York.

Another source of uncertainty about the future was removed after the playoffs when the Devils hired former Montreal coach Claude Julien as our new head coach. Along with Jacques Lemaire, Pat Burns and Larry Robinson, Julien was the fourth former Canadiens player or coach to be hired to coach the Devils since 1993. Lou's admiration for the Habs never seems to die.

As always, I have great confidence in Lou, and know that coaching for five months has given him new insights into what the team needs. If we ever became average in this new NHL, it would kill him. It would kill me. I'm figuring he and I will be together for the next six years, at least, so I think our destinies are twinned. He gives me the opportunity to be who I am and to be the goalie I am. In return, I give him somebody he can count on.

In the '06 playoffs, it was interesting to see all the young goaltenders shining for their teams. Cam Ward and Buffalo's Ryan Miller had a terrific battle in the Eastern Conference final that went seven games, and netminders like Ilya Bryzgalov, Ray Emery and Vesa Toskala made their own statements for their teams. Most of them weren't even starters for their teams at the mid-point of the season, a sign of how fast a new generation of goaltenders is taking over the league. In the end, the Canes won the Stanley

Cup in seven games over the Oilers, and Ward captured the Conn Smythe Trophy as playoff MVP. When I played my first NHL game in March 1992, he had just turned eight years old.

Staying at the top will be a real challenge for me, but I'm planning to do just that. It was easier to get to No. 1 than it will be staying there, but I don't want to look back in 10 years and regret anything. I'll live it up and enjoy my time. I don't want to go through my career and not be noticed. I want to make an impact.

In the final analysis, I don't feel threatened by all these outstanding young goalies in the game today.

I feel challenged.

Epilog

THIS, QUITE CLEARLY, isn't the end of the story.

To write about Martin Brodeur, even after 15 years of NHL competition, is to observe a work in progress. He knows he's now closer to the conclusion of his brilliant career than to the beginning, but the 2006–07 season demonstrated vividly that there may yet be much to be unveiled. Even the context of his accomplishments remains a shifting landscape, and thus the process of evaluating the full Brodeur legacy is far from complete.

The '06–07 season proved to be eventful and fruitful for Brodeur, if not ultimately satisfying for Martin in his search for a fourth Stanley Cup title. The Devils, after knocking off Tampa Bay in the first round of the playoffs, fell in the second round to a determined Ottawa Senators club, and for the second consecutive season New Jersey could at least find solace in losing out to the team that proved to be the best in the Eastern Conference. Remarkably, given that he'd just finished a regular season in which he registered more victories (48) than any goaltender in history, both the Tampa and Ottawa series included surprising criticisms and questions of Brodeur. Was he tired after having played 78 of 82 regular season games? Was he allowing too many soft goals, thus indicating that enemy shooters had figured him out?

It was a lesson in the fickleness of both the game and its observers, a lesson Marty found frustrating and, at times, unfair. When he stoned the Tampa trio of Vincent Lecavalier, Martin St. Louis and Brad Richards, it didn't receive nearly as much attention as when Lecavalier scored on a tight angle shot. When Martin held the Senators to only 10 goals in the final four games of the series, it seemed less newsworthy than when he surrendered five goals in the opener of the best-of-seven set. Each win and loss seemed to be interpreted only as a reflection of Brodeur's play; to him, this made little sense, given that the Devils had always played a team game that relied more on shared contributions than the star system. When the team had won Stanley Cups, individual achievements had always been emphasized less than that of the group. In fact, this group approach was undoubtedly a key factor in June 2003 when the Devils beat Anaheim for the Stanley Cup in seven games but Ducks goalie Jean-Sébastien Giguère was named playoff MVP. Quite simply, no New Jersey player had risen above the rest of his teammates. Four years later, making it all about one player was uncomfortable for Brodeur.

It had been another year of change in the NHL, making it increasingly different since Brodeur made his debut in March 1992. Scoring went down in the 2006–07 season again, after a brief renaissance of offensive hockey the season before; not a particular concern to Martin but certainly one for the league, which again suffered terrible U.S. television ratings in the regular season and playoffs. Head shots were a controversial discussion point throughout the season, including following an incident in which Devils teammate Cam Janssen laid out Toronto defenseman Tomas Kaberle and was suspended. The players' union, with which Martin had experienced an uneven relationship at best over the years, fell into total disarray. A variety of accusations were lobbed at executive director Ted Saskin, including allegations that he had spied on the e-mail communications of his union's members. Ultimately, Saskin was forced out, leaving an enormous vacuum at the top of the union's leadership. The membership felt another body blow early in the post-season when New York Islanders defenseman Sean Hill became the first NHL player to be suspended for using banned performance-enhancing substances after the Islanders, with Hill in the lineup, made the post-season on the final day of the season in dramatic fashion by beating the Devils in a shootout, with Brodeur sitting on the bench in favor of backup Scott Clemmensen. Finally, at the end of the season Martin resigned his position on the prestigious NHL competition committee, feeling that his concerns and suggestions were being ignored. "I thought I would be able to make a difference, but I guess I was wrong," he said.

Anaheim hammered Ottawa in five games to win the NHL title, with former Jersey standout Scott Niedermayer winning playoff MVP honors. Niedermayer's decision to bolt the Devils via free agency had proved to be a pivotal decision for both the Devils and the Ducks, just as Brodeur had feared it would be. It was the first time the Cup had been won by a California-based club, and it came on the heels of victories by Tampa Bay in 2004 and Carolina in 2006. Clearly, the power base of the league had shifted from Canada, the northeastern United States and the old Original Six markets to places where the game is still a novelty and a niche sport in many ways. Expansion again became a hot topic, with Las Vegas and Kansas City cited as possibilities, and the 2006–07 season ended with the troubled Nashville Predators sold conditionally to Canadian billionaire Jim Balsillie, who planned to move the team to Hamilton, Ontario. The sale, however, hit roadblocks, forcing the Predators to go into the off-season uncertain of their future.

The Devils, meanwhile, had enjoyed breakthrough seasons from young players like Zach Parise and Travis Zajac, a 107-point season and another Atlantic Division title. That said, Claude Julien hadn't worked out as head coach and, with only three games left in the season, general manager Lou Lamoriello went behind the bench for a second straight year. After another season of mediocre attendance, moving to a new arena in downtown Newark for the

2007–08 season promised a new era for the team, and possibly new commercial prosperity.

For Martin, the 2006–07 season had, quite simply, been the best of his career, one in which he faced more shots—2,182—than he had ever faced in a single campaign as a Devil. He felt he had been able to contribute as a steadying influence on the Devils' younger players and was encouraged by the way in which those youngsters fit well into the team's style of play. Still, when he arrived in Toronto for the NHL awards in mid-June, flying up from Florida to join father Denis and brothers Claude and Denis Jr., there was a great deal of anticipation in both the Brodeur camp and the hockey world in general over whether this was to mark a passing of torch from one great French-Canadian goaltender to another. Roberto Luongo, who had grown up just blocks from the Brodeur clan in the Montreal suburbs, had been traded from the Florida Panthers to the Vancouver Canucks the previous summer and had gone on to enjoy a spectacular season, leading the Canucks back to the post-season. Some believed that Luongo, not Brodeur, deserved to be named the league's top goaltender and recipient of the prestigious Vezina Trophy, even though the older netminder had delivered superior statistics in almost every category, including 12 shutouts, a 2.18 goals-against average and a .922 save percentage. All the legendary records—Patrick Roy's career victories, Terry Sawchuk's career shutouts—were growing more and more within reach. By season's end, Marty was only 57 victories shy of Roy's NHL record 551 wins and only 11 shutouts behind Sawchuk's 103 career whitewashes, a hockey record long thought to be as unassailable as Joe DiMaggio's 56-game hitting streak.

Both Brodeur and Luongo were also up against Pittsburgh phenom Sidney Crosby for the Hart Trophy as the league's most valuable player, although both all but conceded that Crosby would get the nod, as he did. But the Vezina choice—made not by the Professional Hockey Writers' Association, like the Hart, but by the NHL's general managers—was far more dramatic. The tension was high at the gorgeous Elgin Theatre in downtown Toronto when the unusual, made-for-TV combination of female wrestler Trish Stratus and George Stroumboulopoulos, host of *The Hour* on the Canadian Broadcasting Corporation network, bantered back and forth in a light comedic routine while Brodeur and Luongo squirmed in their seats. For Brodeur, with his hair newly shorn "to the wood" and with a new tattoo (the Stanley Cup with an Olympic gold medal wrapped around it, and the entire picture engulfed in flames) hidden under the right sleeve of his tuxedo, it was a moment to hold his breath as he sat in the second row with his father and brothers.

"And the winner is," said Stroumboulopoulos finally, "Martin Brodeur." For the third time, the Vezina was the property of the boy from St. Leonard, and by the narrowest of margins. Sixteen GMs had voted for Brodeur with their first-place ballots and 14 with their second-place votes. For Luongo, the votes were reversed: 14 first-place votes, 16 second-place votes. The difference in the overall count was a mere six votes, with Calgary's Miikka Kiprusoff and Henrik Lundqvist of the New York Rangers far in the distance behind the two front-runners. Luongo, who backed up Brodeur at the 2005 world championships and 2006 Winter Olympics, would have to wait. His time was not yet at hand, and that of Brodeur clearly not over.

There was, to be sure, vindication for Brodeur in winning the Vezina in the wake of the frustrating playoffs. He'd felt during the Ottawa series that all he'd accomplished had been dismissed by some, as if he had something to prove all over again. As well, some in the Montreal media had fingered him as a conspirator behind Julien's dismissal, an accusation Martin vigorously denied. Anyone with an understanding of the Devils organization knows that only Lou Lamoriello makes those decisions, but still the suggestion that he had undermined Julien stung Brodeur. Those negative feelings, however, were washed away on awards night by a sense of personal triumph as he clasped the Vezina Trophy for a third time, and then by a sense of deep gratitude and emotion for his goaltending coach, Jacques Caron, who sat alongside Lamoriello a few feet away just to the right of the stage. Caron's wife, Marjorie, had passed away exactly two weeks earlier at the age of 69 after battling a variety of illnesses for several years, yet Caron had still made the trip to Toronto to be by his star student's side. "Jacques, this one's for you," said Brodeur, acknowledging the only NHL goalie coach he'd ever had.

Skipping the NHL post-awards party, Martin headed to a private dining room at the sumptuous Morton's Steakhouse in the Park Hyatt hotel with his family and friends, including teammate Jay Pandolfo, who had been a nominee for the Selke Trophy, and his family. What started quietly turned into a raucous celebration, with salty French barbs exchanged at one end of the table and laughter mixed with thick Massachusetts accents at the other. I sat in the middle of the long, rectangular table with my wife, Vicki, talking tennis with the Pandolfos and being noisily pressured by the Brodeur boys to reveal whether I'd voted for their brother in the Hart balloting, while Martin, having changed out of his formal wear into jeans and a green T-shirt, watched with delight. It was pure Martin, happily removed from the glamor of the NHL spotlight he's often in as a member of the Devils, sharing his success with his father right by his side. The cheeky decision to buy a second bulldog for the family during the season and name it "Vez" had proven to be somewhat prophetic, as Brodeur had enjoyed what he believed, despite the absence of a championship, was his finest NHL season so far.

The post-season began with big changes for the Devils. Center Scott Gomez, long one of Brodeur's favorite teammates, signed a free agent contract with Jersey's archrivals, the New York Rangers. Defenseman Brian Rafalski, a less costly loss, jumped to the Detroit Red Wings. Lamoriello responded by signing forward Dainius Zubrus as a free agent; two ex-Rangers, defenseman Karel Rachunek and backup goalie Kevin Weekes; and then another free agent, defenseman Vitali Vishnevski, once the fifth overall pick of the 1998 entry draft and a blueliner with a mean streak. The ability of teams to maintain roster stability, it seemed, had not been enhanced by the lockout and the new collective bargaining agreement that followed. The Devils, as had always been the case, declined to become involved in the high end of the free agent market, relying instead on the development of younger players and finding players to fit their team-oriented approach. Lamoriello then made his biggest splash in early July, persuading former NHL star Brent Sutter to leave his position as the general manager and head coach of the highly successful Red Deer Rebels junior club of Canada's Western Hockey League to take over the head coaching reins with the Devils. Sutter had not only been highly regarded as a NHL player for 17 seasons, particularly during his years with the Islanders, but in his junior coaching career he had twice led Canada to gold medals in the prestigious world junior hockey championships. While Gomez, Daniel Briere and Chris Drury had been viewed as the top free agents available, the truth was that Sutter, who few teams really even knew was available because of his ownership stake in the Red Deer club, was undoubtedly the off-season acquisition most likely to make a major impact on his new team. Just as Lamoriello had surprised the hockey world when he had hired Jacques Lemaire and Pat Burns to coach the Devils, he'd done it again with Sutter.

So much had changed, yet some things were the same. The Devils would go forward building around team play, quality coaching and the best goaltender in the world, trying again to use that combination to win another Cup. For Brodeur, a new chapter in his spectacular career beckons.

Damien Cox
July, 2007

Index